Parody and Counterimaging in the Apocalypse

Parody and Counterimaging in the Apocalypse

JOE E. LUNCEFORD

WIPF & STOCK · Eugene, Oregon

PARODY AND COUNTERIMAGING IN THE APOCALYPSE

Copyright © 2009 Joe E. Lunceford. All rights reserved. Except for brief quotations in critical publications or reviews, no part of this book may be reproduced in any manner without prior written permission from the publisher. Write: Permissions, Wipf and Stock Publishers, 199 W. 8th Ave., Suite 3, Eugene, OR 97401.

Wipf & Stock
An Imprint of Wipf and Stock Publishers
199 W. 8th Ave., Suite 3
Eugene, OR 97401
www.wipfandstock.com

ISBN 13: 978-1-60608-177-8

Manufactured in the U.S.A.

To the late Dr. Ray Frank Robbins: professor, mentor, role model, and cherished friend this book is affectionately dedicated. Ray was the first to introduce me to an interpretation of Revelation that did not require closing one's eyes to clear teachings of the non-apocalyptic writings of the Christian Testament. I accept full responsibility for the weaknesses of this book. Whatever strengths it has are due in large measure to what I learned in Ray's classroom.

Contents

Acknowledgments ix
Introduction xi

Part One: Counterimaging

1 Kings of the Earth 3

2 The Sword 16

3 Out of the Mouth 30

4 The Keys 39

5 The Mystery 47

6 The Crown 59

7 The Thrones 69

8 The Star 77

9 They Are Worthy 81

10 They Have No Rest Day and Night 84

11 Having Been Slain 89

12 The Lamb 98

13 A White Horse 102

14 From the East 106

15 I Heard the Number 109

16 The Smoke 114

17 The River 122

18 To Do Battle and to Conquer 129

19 The City 134

20 Rejoice! 153

21 A Great Sign 160

22 The Woman 167

23 The Diadems 176

24 Who Is Like . . . ? 182

25 Wrath and Passion 190

26 The Mountain 203

27 The Cup 210

28 In One Hour 213

29 One Purpose 219

30 The Supper 222

Part Two: Parody

31 Threefold Designations 227

32 The Holy Trinity and the Unholy Trinity 239

33 The Seal of God and the Mark of the Beast 252

Conclusion 262
Bibliography 277
Index of Ancient Sources 283

Acknowledgments

It would be impossible to acknowledge all the people who have influenced and encouraged me in the production of this work. I am indebted to my growing up in a Baptist tradition for teaching me the importance of reading the Bible for myself, even though that tradition and I have gone in different directions in recent years. I am indebted to such college, seminary, and graduate school professors as Joe M. Cooper, Rex Ray Pearce, Robert Soileau, Frank Stagg, J. Wash Watts, Tom Delaughter, J. Hardee "Judge" Kennedy, Ray Robbins, Ray Summers, Glen Hilburn, Jack Flanders—just to name a few. I am also greatly indebted to my late wife, Ora Lea McLeod Lunceford; and to my current wife, Rev. Stacey DeAnn Cruse. Both have encouraged, prodded, and sometimes pushed me to complete this project! Without their confidence that my work is worth publishing and their constant encouragement, this book would probably never have been written. I acknowledge my debt also to Diane Farley of Wipf & Stock Publishers, who first reviewed my work and deemed it worthy of publication. And last but not least, I acknowledge with thanks the guidance of my editor, Christian Amondson, in giving this work its final form.

Introduction

THE THESIS OF THIS study is that the author of Revelation consciously and deliberately cloaked much of his message in parody and counterimages. I define the latter as the use of a particular word or phrase at some points in the book within the realm of the operation of God and the forces of good, and using that same word or phrase at some other point(s) in the arena of the operation of Satan and the forces of evil. A slight variation of this pattern is simply the positive use of a word or phrase in some passages and the negative use of the same word or phrase in others. I define *parody* as the use of a term in the arena of evil that appears to imitate a similar term in the arena of good. A prime example in Revelation is the seal of God versus the mark of the beast. Though the terms are different, the mark of the beast appears to be a parody of the seal of God. If pressed I might plead guilty to a degree of arbitrariness in my definitions; however, I felt the need to make some distinction between cases in which the same word or phrase is used and those in which different terms with similar functions are employed.

Most commentators have noted the use of parody in Revelation, particularly in the cases of the unholy trinity of dragon, beast and false prophet versus the Holy Trinity; of the woman who gives birth to a male child (Rev 12) and of the bride of Christ versus the "great prostitute." In my research thus far, however, I have found very little attention given to the author's technique of counterimaging. Almost as an aside, Donald Coggan has said, "Antithesis, together with climax and parenthesis, is not the least effective of the principles, the stylistic devices, of which the Seer makes use."[1] As the context of Coggan's remark makes clear, the difference between antithesis and counterimaging is merely semantic. The most explicit comment I have found is that of Sleeper: "We have come to expect that any symbol in the Revelation will have its countersymbol, and that is

---

1. Coggan, *Five Makers,* 82.

true here (Rev 6:2) as well."[2] Though he makes this comment, he does not at any point attempt to pursue it systematically.

SOME ASSUMPTIONS

I should probably speak of *conscious* assumptions, as I am sure that many of my assumptions are of the unconscious variety. I am assuming a date of c. 95 C.E. as the date of the book's composition. As is well known, Irenaeus is the earliest authority for this date. Numerous scholars have challenged this dating, but it has proven to be remarkably resilient; it is the date accepted by most scholars at the present time. One recent commentator spends several pages discussing the possibility of dating the book in the reigns of Trajan, Domitian, Titus, or the so-called year of the four emperors; and ends up sitting squarely on the fence![3] Bell, on the other hand, is very precise in saying that Revelation was written between June 68 and January 69 C.E.[4] Many others, including Krodel, Summers, Robbins, McDowell, Barnard, and Beasley-Murray, basically accept the dating first advanced by Irenaeus.[5] I would leave open the possibility that some parts of the book may have been written earlier, as many have argued. Having said that, however, I am not convinced by any of the specific proposals that I have encountered as to what parts of the book may have been written earlier than 95 C.E.

This matter of dating leads naturally into the next assumption, namely that the Apocalypse is a unity. Again, no small number of scholars has challenged this point. The sophisticated textual surgery of R. H. Charles is perhaps the best-known attempt to divide the book and also to attribute parts of it to an editor who was "profoundly stupid and ignorant."[6] Charles's rearrangement of the text is primarily limited to brief passages that he claims have been dislocated by the editor's incompetence. Others have advocated a more thoroughgoing rearrangement. Oman has proposed the following: 1:9—3:22; 10:1—14:5, inserting 22:6–8a after

---

2. Sleeper, *Victorious Christ*, 60.
3. Court, *Revelation*, 97–103.
4. Bell, "Date of John's Apocalypse," 93–102.
5. Krodel, *Revelation*, 62; Summers, *Worthy Is the Lamb*, 85; Robbins, *Revelation*, 17–18; McDowell, *Meaning and Message*, 3–4; Barnard, "Clement of Rome," 258; Beasley-Murray, *Three Viewpoints*, 38.
6. Charles, *Critical and Exegetical Commentary*, 1:xvii.

10:10 and omitting 11:14–19; 15:5—16:16, omitting 16:15; 19:11–21, inserting 14:19b–20 after v. 16; 6:2–17, 16:17—19:9a; 21:9—22:17, omitting 22:6–9; 16:15, 19:9b–10, 22:1–10; 4:1—6:1; 7:1—9:21; 11:14–19, 14:6–11, 14:12—15:4, omitting 14:9b–20; 20:11—21:8.[7] A more recent work advocates transposing 8:6—14:5 with 1:1—8:5.[8] One serious objection to such textual rearrangements is that no two rearrangements of which I am aware bear any resemblance to each other. Garrow has said in one of the more recent works on Revelation, "This lack of consensus is in fact a sign of hope, since it suggests the possibility that it is our incompetence, rather than that of the author, (or editor, one might add), which is causing the problem."[9] Smalley is another scholar who has argued for the structural unity of the book.[10] Perhaps the strongest argument for the unity of the text, and the one that appears more and more frequently in recent works, is the way in which key terms tie together the various sections of the book. This literary characteristic will become more evident as this study progresses. Bauckham would seem to be on target with the following assessment: "The more Revelation is studied in detail, the more clear it becomes that it is not simply a literary unity, but actually one of the most unified works in the Christian Testament. The evidence discussed in this chapter should be sufficient to refute theories which divide the book into disparate sources. Theories of this kind have largely been discredited, but are still sometimes advanced: e.g., Kraft (1974); Ford (1975)."[11]

I am also assuming with Bauckham,[12] Beasley-Murray,[13] Garrow,[14] and others that Revelation partakes of three different genres: letter, prophecy, and apocalypse. Not only the letters to the seven churches in chapters 2–3, but the entire writing has most of the characteristics of the ancient epistolary genre. In fact, as Aune has shown rather conclusively, the letters to the churches actually have more in common with imperial edicts than with ancient letters.[15] These features include the sender's name in the

7. Oman, *Revelation*, 16–22.
8. Thiering, *Jesus of the Apocalypse*, 6.
9. Garrow, *Revelation*, 13.
10. Smalley, "John's Revelation," 565.
11. Bauckham, *Climax*, 1, n. 1.
12. Bauckham, *Theology*, 1–9.
13. Beasley-Murray, *Revelation*, 12–29.
14. Garrow, *Revelation*, 8.
15. Aune, "Form and Function," 183–94.

nominative case; the recipient(s)'s name in the dative case; the greeting *chairein*; and a stereotypical expression of greeting at the close.[16]

Outside chapters 2 and 3, the language of Revelation is on the whole clearly apocalyptic; and the opening phrase of the book prompts one to think of the book as an apocalypse. When speaking of the content of the book, however, the author clearly designates it as "the words of this prophecy" (Rev 1:3; 22:7, 10, 18–19). Further, the revealing angel speaks of himself as being "of your brothers the prophets" (Rev 22:9). Hence it appears that John is designated a prophet and that he considered what he had written to be prophecy.

The definition of the genre of apocalypse has proven to be notoriously difficult to delimit. A discussion of this difficulty would take us far beyond the scope of this study. For an excellent presentation of the difficulty the reader is referred to Adela Yarbro Collins's article, "Reading the Revelation in the Twentieth Century."[17]

My assumption regarding authorship is only a very general one. John the Apostle, John the Elder, John the Baptist, and John Mark have all had their advocates for authorship. I have chosen not to enter the debate on this issue. What I do affirm is that the author was of Jewish background; familiar with the land of Palestine in general and the city of Jerusalem in particular; and totally immersed in the Jewish Scriptures. While he probably was influenced by some of the deuterocanonical apocalypses, his primary source of imagery was the Jewish Scriptures—in particular the books of Daniel, Ezekiel, Joel, Isaiah, Zechariah 9–14, and Psalms. The reader is referred to Moyise for a graphic presentation of the source of John's allusions to the Jewish Scriptures.[18] Evidence of influence by extra-canonical writings is exceptionally difficult to prove due to the problem of dating these writings; if they are later than Revelation, they could have borrowed from it as easily as the author of Revelation could have borrowed from them.

Finally, I am assuming that the book was intended for public reading and that its first recipients would have heard rather than read the book. The macarism in 1:3 on the *one* who reads and the *ones* who hear would appear to indicate that the book was to be read to each of the congrega-

---

16. Ibid., 194, n.
17. Collins, "Reading the Book of Revelation," 229–42.
18. Moyise, *Old Testament in Revelation*, 16.

tions addressed. Further, each address to the seven churches closes with the injunction, "The one who has an ear, let her/him hear what the Spirit is saying to the churches."

For a more thoroughgoing argument for the orality of the Apocalypse, I refer the reader to David Barr's article, "The Apocalypse of John as Oral Enactment." That article concludes, "The orality of the Apocalypse is an essential element in its interpretation, for its oral presentation within the liturgy mediates the coming of Jesus to his congregation in salvation and judgment enabling them to carry on the divine service, that is, the realization of God's rule in their midst."[19]

Another supporter of the orality of the Apocalypse is John Court, who suggests the likelihood that ". . . not only the Revelation but all the New Testament books in their written form were related to oral performance in public."[20] If this assumption of orality be correct, the significance of this study is considerably heightened, in that varying the same symbolism between the realm of God and the realm of Satan would greatly assist listeners in grasping the essential message of the Apocalypse.

SOME INTERPRETATIVE PARAMETERS

While this study is not intended to be a complete interpretation of Revelation, it does lead into some part of each of the book's twenty-two chapters. Therefore I thought it appropriate to set forth some principles of interpretation by which I have been guided and which, in my opinion, must characterize any legitimate interpretation of the book. The first principle is to allow the book to speak in a meaningful way to its immediate recipients, located geographically in the area of ancient Asia Minor and chronologically in the second half of the first century of the Common Era. As Goldsworthy put it, "We must allow the author to use the literary conventions that exist for him in his time and culture, and to use them in the way that will suit his purpose."[21] This concession would appear to be axiomatic. Why bother to send a message to a specific group of people, the meaning of which lies not just years but millennia in the future? Yet the fact that many commentators have given the book such a futuristic

---

19. Barr, "Apocalypse of John," 243–56.
20. Court, *Revelation*, 89.
21. Goldsworthy, *Gospel in Revelation*, 15.

interpretation as to leave it meaningless to its first recipients is so well known as not to require demonstration.

At the opposite pole from the extreme futurists are the extreme preterists who lock up the book's meaning with the original recipients so completely as to leave it meaningless to anyone of a later time. In view of the obvious fact that the church canonized the book about three centuries after it was written, a legitimate interpretation must also allow the book to speak to succeeding generations of Christians. In my judgment these two principles are ironclad. I would suggest a third that, though less binding than these two, holds considerable significance. The principle is the question as to whether this interpretation of Revelation contradicts other New Testament writings that are not written in an apocalyptic style. I am not ruling out of court the possibility that one Christian Testament writer might contradict another at some points; but I think we should at least use considerable caution with any interpretation of Revelation that directly contradicts a straightforward teaching of Paul or words of Jesus which have a high claim to authenticity. As Goldsworthy expressed it, "In practical terms, we cannot allow a point of doctrine to be established on an apocalyptic vision against clear statements to the contrary in the epistolary material of the New Testament."[22]

Finally, I would suggest a principle set forth by Ray Summers: "In interpreting an ordinary prose writing, the language should be taken literally unless there is a compelling reason to do otherwise, whereas in interpreting an apocalyptic writing the language should be taken symbolically unless there is some compelling reason to do otherwise."[23]

I will now turn my attention to my main subject. I will be dealing first with the counterimages in Revelation, of which I have at this point found thirty examples. The approach will set out the terms in the immediate context in which they appear in Revelation, first as they are used in the arena of the forces of good; and then as they appear in the arena of the forces of evil (or first the positive, then the negative usage of the particular word or phrase). I have, however, deviated from this pattern at several points for reasons that I shall spell out later. Setting out the terms will be followed by an exegesis of the immediate contexts in which the terms appear. All translation of the text of the Christian Testament is my

---

22. Ibid., 16–17.
23. Summers, *Worthy Is the Lamb*, 48.

own unless otherwise indicated. The order of consideration of each term is governed by its earliest appearance in Revelation.

Before I begin the exegesis of the selected passages from Revelation, I would like to insert a caveat. I have not attempted much original argumentation in my exegesis. What I have attempted to do is to bring together and summarize the best of recent scholarship and apply it to the passages I have selected.

Part One
Counterimaging

1

Kings of the Earth

... and from Jesus Christ the faithful witness, the first-born from the dead (ones) and the ruler of the kings of the earth ...

(REV 1:5)

And the kings of the earth and the great ones and the military commanders and the wealthy ones and the strong ones; also every slave and free (person) hid themselves inside the caves and rocks of the mountains.

(REV 6:15)

And one of the seven angels who had been holding the seven bowls came and spoke with me saying, Come—I will show you the judgment of the great prostitute who is sitting upon many waters, with whom the kings of the earth committed fornication and those inhabiting the earth were intoxicated with the wine of her fornication.

(REV 17:2)

And the woman which you saw is the great city which reigns over the kings of the earth.

(REV 17:18)

... because she gave all the nations to drink from the wine of her fornication and the kings of the earth committed fornication with her and the merchants of the earth were made wealthy from the power of her sensuality.

(REV 18:3)

4   PARODY AND COUNTERIMAGING IN THE APOCALYPSE

And the kings of the earth who committed fornication and lived sensually with her will weep and mourn over her when they see the smoke of her burning.

(Rev 18:9)

And I saw the beast and the kings of the earth, and their soldiers, gathered together to do battle with the one sitting upon the horse and his soldiers.

(Rev 19:19)

And the city has no need of the sun or moon to shine in it because the glory of God enlightens it and the Lamb is its lamp; and the nations will walk about by means of its light, and the kings of the earth will bring their glory into it.

(Rev 21:24)

In this chapter I will deviate from the general pattern I established in the Introduction, because in this case there is not only a positive and negative usage of the term but also one that is possibly neutral. Moreover, it is possible in this instance to keep the passages in the order in which they appear in Revelation without any shift between the positive and negative usages of the phrase.

In Rev 1:5 we confront a threefold designation of Jesus as the faithful witness, firstborn from the dead, and ruler of the kings of the earth. Only two individuals are designated as faithful witnesses in Revelation: Jesus and Antipas (Rev 2:13). Both witnessed through giving their lives, anticipating the later-developed usage of *martys*, or "witness," as *martyr* in the contemporary sense. As Mounce has noted, "Throughout the Revelation the word is associated with the penalty of death which results from a firm and constant witness (cf. 2:13, 11:3, and 17:6)."[1] And while Aune may be correct in asserting that the exalted Jesus is the one who guarantees the truth of the revelation to John rather than the human Jesus,[2] I would respond that any absolute separation of the two may be true for such scholars as Bultmann but not for the Christian Testament. The exalted Jesus is the faithful witness *because* the historical Jesus witnessed to the point of giving his life.[3]

---

1. Mounce, *Revelation*, 70; cf. Aune, *Revelation 1–5*, 37.
2. Aune, *Revelation 1–5*, 37–38.
3. Cf. Boring, *Revelation*, 76.

As for the second designation, firstborn from the dead, Sweet points out that for Jews who believed in resurrection, the resurrection was a corporate event rather than individual resuscitation. Hence Jesus's resurrection would have been understood by his first followers—all Jews—as proleptic of the general resurrection.[4] This understanding is probably in accord with Paul's reference to Jesus as the "firstfruits" of resurrection (1 Cor 15:20, 23).

The third designation, ruler of the kings of the earth, will be the particular focus of this study. Krodel is not far wide of the mark in asserting that the basic issue of Revelation turns on the question of the identity of the true ruler of this world and the proper object of worship.[5] The title "ruler of the kings of the earth" was claimed by Roman emperors, but John is juxtaposing Jesus as the true ruler of the kings of the earth over against the false claims of Rome.[6] This title contains a rather obvious allusion to Ps 89:27 (LXX 88:28). The larger context of that psalm is an exposition of God's promise to establish the seed of David in perpetuity. The Seer used the words of this psalm to express the developing understanding of Jesus's identity.[7] John, along with early Christian tradition in general, understood Jesus to be the ultimate fulfillment of the promises made to David.

The root of the word *archōn*, translated "ruler" in this passage, may mean either "to rule" or "to begin."[8] Both "have preeminence over" and "source" lie within the range of usages of this word. While the former is probably intended here, we should not overlook the possibility that the Seer is presenting the exalted Jesus as the *source* of all human kingship. This usage would agree with the understanding of Paul (Rom 13:1–4) and the author of 1 Peter (1 Pet 2:13–14).

Crucial to this study is the determination as to whether "kings of the earth" is a positive or negative category. As Beale points out, and exposition of the following passages will confirm, the predominant use of the term in Revelation is negative. Beale is probably correct in claiming that this passage does not present Jesus as ruling over his redeemed people but

---

4. Sweet, *Revelation*, 685–86; cf. Boring, *Revelation*, 76.
5. Krodel, *Revelation*, 84.
6. Cf. Boring, *Revelation*, 76.
7. Cf. ibid.
8. Abbott-Smith, *Manual Greek Lexicon*, s.v. "*Archōn*"; cf. Louw and Nida, *Greek-English Lexicon*, 37:54, 67:65, 68:1.

over defeated enemies.[9] Beale bases this argument on the predominantly negative uses of the phrase noted earlier. I will later argue, however, that one exception to this rule is found in Revelation.

The next passage for consideration is Rev 6:15. The context is the opening of the sixth seal by the Lion or Lamb, i.e., the exalted Christ. This seal clearly depicts the judgment of God that seven classes of people attempt to evade. The number seven in apocalyptic literature conveys the idea of completeness or totality; hence the picture is that of *all* ungodly people attempting to escape the judgment of God.[10] As Sweet has pointed out, the reaction to the cataclysms following the opening of this seal are modeled upon Isa 2:12–19 and Hos 10:8.[11]

Scholars differ considerably in their interpretation of this passage. Garrow claims that not only this passage but also the entire series of seals and trumpets are not judgments but only warnings.[12] His arguments are not convincing, as they lean too heavily upon the notion of a literal scroll and the inability to read it until all the seals are broken.[13] Bauckham, somewhat surprisingly, has fallen into a similar trap of literalizing the scroll.[14] The majority of interpreters take the position that actual judgment is depicted, but they divide over the issue of present vs. future judgment. Krodel strongly affirms the judgment as "wholly future."[15] Others who claim that the judgment depicted is future include Beale, Boring, Maxwell, Aune, Chapman, Talbert, Roloff, Franzmann, Giblin, and C.A. Scott.[16] Those who argue that the judgment is already in progress or is past include Jeske, Sleeper, Rowland, Robbins, Summers, Corsini, A.T. Hanson, and Mulholland.[17] In my judgment Robbins has said it best: "This is just as

---

9. Beale, *Book of Revelation*, 191.
10. Cf. Robbins, *Life and Ministry*, 107.
11. Sweet, *Revelation*, 145.
12. Garrow, *Revelation*, 61–62.
13. Cf. Maxwell, *Revelation*, 58.
14. Bauckham, *Climax*, 249–50.
15. Krodel, *Revelation*, 179.

16. Beale, *Book of Revelation*, 399–400; Boring, *Revelation*, 126–27; Maxwell, *Revelation*, 58–59; Aune, *Revelation 6–16*, 421; Chapman, *Message of Revelation*, 53; Talbert, *Apocalypse*, 34; Roloff, *Revelation of John*, 92; Franzmann, *Revelation to John*, 63; Giblin, *Revelation*, 90; Scott, *Revelation*, 185.

17. Jeske, *Revelation for Today*, 71; Sleeper, *Victorious Christ*, 52; Rowland, *Revelation*, 81–85; Robbins, *Revelation*, 107; Summers, *Worthy Is the Lamb*, 145; Corsini, *Apocalypse*, 157; Hanson, *Wrath of the Lamb*, 169; Mulholland, *Revelation*, 179.

present as the preceding scene, and he is not just talking about the end of time. He is talking about the *end*; he is talking about the *past*; he is talking about the *present*; he is talking about *any time* (emphasis in original)."[18]

To return the reader's attention to the phrase "kings of the earth," these rulers are among the seven classes of people who attempt to hide from the wrath of God and the Lamb. Charles, however, has argued that mention of the Lamb here is an interpolation. He cites Vischer, Spitta, Weyland, Volter, and Weiss in support.[19] My research indicates that fewer and fewer modern interpreters are inclined to follow Charles at this point, but even if his position be accepted, it would not change the fact that the "kings of the earth" are clearly viewed negatively as unbelievers; and that is the significant point for our purposes.

As we move to the next passage (Rev 17:2), reference to the angel as one of those holding the seven bowls indicates that this passage is a further elaboration and particularization of the bowls judgments, as noted by Beale, Krodel, Sweet, and Boring.[20] The "great prostitute" is to be identified as Babylon/Rome. The reference to her as sitting upon many waters may be a double allusion. The first may be an allusion to the many canals that characterized historical Babylon, as suggested by Robbins, Boring, Wall, and Krodel.[21] The basis of this allusion in the Jewish Scriptures is in all likelihood Jer 51:13 (LXX 28:13). The second allusion may be grounded in the common usage in apocalyptic writings of "sea" as a metaphor for people in a chaotic state. "Many waters" would likely call to mind the sea for the first recipients of this writing. This usage would be appropriate to Babylon or Rome as John viewed it.

The kings of the earth are said to have committed fornication with the "great prostitute," and this metaphor gives insight into their character. Fornication and adultery in the Old Testament are most commonly metaphors for idolatry, in view of the fact that Yahweh was understood to be the "husband" of Israel.[22] As Aune points out, however, in a few passages of the Jewish Scriptures fornication is a metaphor for the commerce of a

---

18. Robbins, *Revelation*, 107.

19. Cited in Ford, *Revelation*, 112.

20. Beale, *Book of Revelation*, 847; Krodel, *Revelation*, 291; Sweet, *Revelation*, 250; Boring, *Revelation*, 178.

21. Robbins, *Revelation*, 195; Boring, *Revelation*, 180; Wall, *Revelation*, 205; Krodel, *Revelation*, 292.

22. See, for example, Jer 31:31–32; Isa 54:5; Hos 2:16, 3:1; and Ezek 23:1–49.

particular city. He goes on to suggest that a reasonable interpretation of this metaphor would be that John is denouncing the *political* alliances of Babylon/Rome.[23] We should probably also leave open the possibility of a literal dimension to the metaphor. A commonplace component of idol worship in the ancient world was sacred prostitution. Moreover, each trade association had its patron deity. Hence religion, politics, and commerce were so intertwined that the consideration of any one of these factors without the others is virtually impossible.[24]

In this passage the Seer continues to draw parallels between historical Babylon and Babylon /Rome. Jeremiah 51:7 portrays historical Babylon as a golden cup in the hands of the Lord who has intoxicated all the earth so that the nations go mad. The similarities to the present passage can scarcely be deemed accidental.[25]

The RSV and NRSV read the text of 17:2 as "by many waters" instead of "upon many waters." The latter is to be preferred.[26] The present text reads *epi hudatōn pollōn*, whereas the Septuagint of Jer 51:13 (28:13) reads *eph' hudasi pollois*, but any difference of meaning because of differences in case (genitive vs. locative) is unlikely. The Seer's use of Greek departs so much from standard usage as to cause R. H. Charles to formulate a specific Greek grammar for Revelation.[27] In the majority of cases the Seer uses *epi* with the genitive or accusative to express the idea of "upon." Of the 140 occurrences (by my count) of *epi* in the Revelation, only 15 times is it used with the locative. Of these 15 usages, five clearly mean "upon" (5:13, 7:10, 19:4, 14; and 21:5). In two instances, the translation "unto" would appear to be preferable (10:11, 22:16). In two others, *epi* seems to mean "over" or "beside" (18:20, 21:12). In 9:14 it appears to mean "beside" and in 12:17, "with."

To sum up the significance of this passage, the kings of the earth are depicted as committing fornication with the "great prostitute," Babylon/Rome. The "fornication" has commercial, religious, and political dimensions. Both the identification of the great prostitute and fornication with her identify the kings of the earth as a negative group within the general

---

23. Aune, *Revelation 17–22*, 930–31.
24. Cf. Beale, *Book of Revelation*, 850.
25. Cf. Mounce, *Revelation*, 308.
26. Conybeare and Stock, *Grammar of Septuagint Greek*, 357.
27. Charles, *Critical and Exegetical Commentary*, 1:cvii–clix.

classification of unbelievers. Beale suggests that the kings are not only the ones in political power in Rome itself but the local ruling classes throughout the empire who benefited from cooperation with Rome.[28]

Moving on to consider Rev 17:18, the woman is clearly the great prostitute discussed above. She is personified in John's day as Babylon/Rome, but should not be limited to this identification. As Beale aptly remarks, "She includes the entire evil economic-religious system of the world throughout history."[29] Here she is the one who rules over (*hē ēchousa basileian epi*) the kings of the earth. A comparison with the statement concerning Jesus in Rev 1:5 may be instructive: *ho archōn tōn basileōn tēs gēs*, "the ruler of the kings of the earth." John's readers or hearers were probably intended to see a contrast between the *archōn* of Jesus Christ and the *basileian* of the great prostitute over the kings of the earth. Only in 1:5 does John use any form of the *arch*-stem. As noted earlier, this stem has connotations of "source" as well as "sovereignty over." The great prostitute has sovereignty over the kings of the earth, at least on the human level, but the exalted Christ may be said to have the originating power of all human sovereignty.

In Rev 18:3 the kings of the earth are to be understood as in the two preceding passages. The great prostitute is the same as the one in 17:1. She is portrayed as one who gave all the nations to drink of the wine of her fornication, reading (with Mounce, Robbins, Beale, et al.[30]) *pepotiken*, "she has given to drink," instead of the variants *pepōken* ("she has fallen") or *pepōkasin* ("they have fallen"), which appear in some manuscripts of Revelation. Aune, on the other hand, supports the latter reading and renders the passage, "For all nations have collapsed because of the wine that is her immoral passion."[31] As noted earlier, the term *fornication* is not to be taken literally but metaphorically. In Mounce's words, "It is used here to denote the unclean and illicit relationships between the capital of the empire and all the nations of the earth."[32] Beale argues that the economic dimension of these relationships predominates here. In support he notes

---

28. Beale, *Book of Revelation*, 896.

29. Ibid., 888; cf. Robbins, *Revelation*, 195; Mounce, *Revelation*, 320; Maxwell, *Revelation*, 141; Jeske, *Revelation for Today*, 104; Boring, *Revelation*, 184; Rowland, *Revelation*, 129; Wall, *Revelation*, 211; Stagg, "Interpreting the Book of Revelation," 340.

30. Mounce, *Revelation*, 324; Robbins, *Revelation*, 204; Beale, *Book of Revelation*, 895.

31. Aune, *Revelation 17–22*, 987.

32. Mounce, *Revelation*, 324.

the probable allusion to Isa 23:27b and the oracle against Tyre. He further notes that in this passage the translators of the Septuagint changed the Masoretic (Hebrew) text from "She will play the harlot" to "She will be an *emporion* ("market")" for all the kingdoms of the earth.[33] Beale's argument is admittedly a strong one, but I would again counsel caution in separating economic activity from politics and religion in the first-century Greco-Roman world.

This verse introduces yet another group, the merchants of the earth, who are explicitly said to be made wealthy from their relationships with the great prostitute. They form the second of three (or more, depending on one's reading of 18:17) groups who lament the fall of Babylon from a distance; the kings of the earth being the first mentioned.

The latter part of the verse is most difficult to translate. The Greek word *strēnos* that John uses here is found nowhere else in the New Testament. The verb form *strēniaō* is used at 18:7, 9, and only once in the Greek version of the Jewish Scriptures (2 Kgs 19:28). Kittel's monumental *Theological Dictionary of the New Testament* does not list either the noun or the verb form of this word. Conybeare and Stock translate it "haughtiness."[34] This translation appears to be followed by most English versions of the Jewish Scriptures. The NASB, RSV, REB and NRSV translate the word as "arrogance" in 2 Kgs 19:28, as does T.R. Hobbs in the *Word Biblical Commentary*. The ASB renders it "arrogancy." The NIV uses the synonym "insolence." The KJV translates it "tumult" and the DRV renders it "pride." From this brief survey of translations, it is obvious that there is widespread agreement that *strēnos* in 2 Kgs 19:28 denotes arrogance or pride. In examining the translations of this word in Rev 18:3, however, the following sampling appears: "sensuality"(NASB), "wantonness" (RSV, ASV, Barclay), "luxury" (NRSV), "luxurious living" (LNT), "delicacies" (KJV, DRV), "bloated wealth" (NEB), "wealth and luxury" (REB), "unrestrained lust" (TEV), "excessive luxury and wantonness" (Amp), "dissipation" (Phillips), and "luxury" (Williams, Beck). The economic dimension of the word is most obvious in this sampling.

Perhaps this observation calls for an explanation of my own translation. In rendering the word as "sensuality," I had in mind the broadest sense of that term, anything that appeals to the five senses. That the mer-

---

33. Beale, *Book of Revelation*, 895.
34. Conybeare and Stock, *Grammar of Septuagint Greek*, 376.

chants are said explicitly to be made wealthy from the "power of her sensuality" and that they are linked with the "kings of the earth" in lamenting the fall of Babylon may lend further support to Beale's interpretation of "fornication" as emphasizing the economic dimension.

Clearly the same negative appraisal of the kings of the earth that we observed in 6:15, 17:2, and 17:18 is continued in this chapter of Revelation. The same language of committing fornication with the great prostitute is repeated from 17:2. As we move to 18:9, we find the beginning of a dirge over the destruction of Babylon. The kings of the earth are joined by the merchants of the earth (v. 11) and the shipmasters, along with those associated with them (v. 17). Little new is found here concerning the kings of the earth. For the third time they are said to have committed fornication with the great prostitute. They are further said to have lived sensuously with her. We encountered the noun form *strēnos*, or "sensuality," in v. 3. Here we encounter one of only two usages of the verb form *strēniaō* in Revelation, the other appearing in v. 7. Beckwith has captured the full force of the usage of the word better than any other commentator with whom I am familiar. He says the noun and verb forms together convey the idea of ". . . excessive luxury and self-indulgence with accompanying arrogance and wanton exercise of strength."[35] The kings of the earth are possibly listed first in the dirge because they received both political power and economic wealth from their fornication with the great prostitute. They stand off at a safe distance (v. 10) as they view the source of their power and wealth disappearing. As Sweet notes, "The smoke of her burning . . ." echoes the fate of Edom (Isa 34:10) and Sodom (Gen 19:28).[36] Also, as several commentators have pointed out (e.g., Aune, Kealy, and Ford[37]), Leviticus 21:9 prescribes burning as the punishment for a daughter of a priest who becomes a prostitute. Thus we have a precedent in the Jewish Scriptures for the idea of burning both a prostitute and a city as judgment for sin.

This passage adds little if anything to the identity or character of the kings of the earth. Their negative character may be heightened by the company of merchants and seafarers who join them in lamenting the destruction of the great prostitute. All three groups are clearly governed

---

35. Cited in Mounce, *Revelation*, 324, n. 10.
36. Sweet, *Revelation*, 271; cf. Beale, *Book of Revelation*, 905.
37. Aune, *Revelation 17–22*, 957; Kealy, *Apocalypse*, 206; Ford, *Revelation*, 303.

by self-interest in that they all keep their distance from her rather than attempting to come to her aid.

As we consider the next passage, Rev 19:19, we confront preparations for a great battle, although no actual battle scene is ever described. The beast is the beast from the sea described in 13:1. He is probably also to be identified with the beast from the abyss of 11:7.[38] The beast's description in 13:1 clearly links him to the dragon, Satan (Rev 12:3.). He is prepared to do battle with the one riding upon a white horse, who has been previously described in such a way that he can be no other than the exalted Christ. Considerable difference of opinion may be noted as to whether this rider is a picture of Christ at the *parousia* (second coming) or whether it describes his coming to the aid of his beleaguered followers throughout history, but that need not detain us here. For this study the major point of interest is the kings of the earth, who are here depicted as leaders of one part of the armies amassed against the forces of Christ.

In the final passage that mentions the kings of the earth (21:24), I will argue for a positive connotation to that term. This passage is an elaborate description of the New Jerusalem or bride of Christ that descends from heaven (Rev 21:2–3, 9–10.). That city has no need of the luminaries of the present creation because the glory of God and the Lamb provide all the light that is necessary. As is widely recognized, the Seer relies heavily at this point on Isa 60, especially vv. 3, 5, and 11, which in turn develop further Isa 2:2, 5.[39] The writer of Revelation adjusts his source material so as to convey something different from what it meant in the original source(s), however. As Krodel aptly notes, "John uses here the traditional image of the pilgrimage of the Gentiles to a renewed Jerusalem within history (Isa 60:3–11) in order to show its fulfillment beyond history."[40] Probably the dominant picture in all the prophets in the Jewish Scriptures is one in which the Gentiles will be made subservient to the Jews.[41] All traces of subservience have been laid aside in the present text, however.

---

38. So Krodel, *Revelation*, 249; Mounce, *Revelation*, 250; Metzger, *Breaking the Code*, 70; Kealy, *Apocalypse*, 172; Boring, *Revelation*, 147; Wall, *Revelation*, 145; Sweet, *Revelation*, 186; for a *contra* position see Aune, *Revelation 17–22*, 616.

39. Cf. Beale, *Book of Revelation*, 1094; Bauckham, *Climax*, 315; Robbins, *Revelation*, 241; Mounce, *Revelation*, 384; Krodel, *Revelation*, 364–65.

40. Krodel, *Revelation*, 365.

41. See for example Isa 18:7, 55:5; Jer 3:17–18; Zech 8:20–23, 14:14–19 and elsewhere.

The second half of this verse presents several exegetical difficulties. First of all, the kings of the earth have been destroyed prior to the present passage (19:19–21). Second, after the destruction of all evil people and the forces of evil itself, how can there be anyone "outside" the holy city to come into it? Third—and most significantly for this study, since the dominant picture of the kings of the earth has been one of hardened opposition to God, how can they be said to bring their glory into the New Jerusalem? Let us approach each of these questions in turn.

With regard to the first, we have ample evidence that chronological sequence and logical consistency were not a concern for the Seer. A few examples will serve to demonstrate this fact. In Rev 8:8 all the green grass of the earth is burned up, yet in 9:4 the demonic locusts are commanded not to hurt the grass. Summers's argument that 8:8 refers only to all the green grass on the one-third of the earth affected by the first trumpet falls into the category of special pleading, in my judgment.[42] In Rev 14:14–20 we have a picture of judgment that appears to be total in scope, yet this passage precedes the bowl judgments of 16:1–7. Furthermore, Rev 15:1 says the wrath of God is finished with the seven last plagues and the bowl judgments; and this declaration is reemphasized in 16:17—yet the judgment of the great prostitute does not come until chapters 17 and 18. Many other examples could be cited. Charles's well-known argument that the discrepancies are to be attributed to a "faithful but unintelligent" disciple of the Seer writing after the latter's death has not won wide acceptance.[43]

With regard to the second question raised above, we must again consider language versus reality and recognize the limitations of the former. Mounce's comment is appropriate here: "The imagery of the Apocalypse must of necessity be concrete and spatial, but its significance is inevitably spiritual."[44] In a similar vein Beale writes, "'Bringing glory' into the city in vv. 24 and 26 is spatial language, but it conveys a nonspatial notion."[45] Krodel has made perhaps the most important point succinctly: "The spatial images of bringing into or entering the city mean to participate in the city's life."[46]

---

42. Summers, *Worthy Is the Lamb*, 154.
43. Charles, *Critical and Exegetical Commentary*, 2:147; cf. Krodel, *Revelation*, 365.
44. Mounce, *Revelation*, 385.
45. Beale, *Book of Revelation*, 1098.
46. Krodel, *Revelation*, 365.

As to the final question, the problem of the "kings of the earth" participating in the New Jerusalem began to be felt even by some scribes copying manuscripts of the Apocalypse. A few late manuscripts add "of them that are saved" after "nations." The manuscript support for this phrase is so slight that modern critical editions of the *Greek New Testament* do not even mention it, yet it was accepted into the *Textus Receptus* ("received text") of the sixteenth century and hence was included in the KJV.[47] This inclusion is a measure of the difficulty of regarding the kings of the earth, heretofore referred to so negatively in the Apocalypse, as participating in eschatological salvation. Here, as well as at many other points in the Apocalypse, however, I will be arguing repeatedly that the author is intentionally using counterimaging. Verse 27 precludes taking the kings of the earth in this passage in any fashion other than as redeemed people whose names are in the Lamb's book of life. As Beale notes, John has left room for some good kings of the earth in 1:5. He concludes that both "nations" and "kings of the earth" "are best identified with those in 5:9–10 who were 'bought . . . from every tribe and tongue and people and nation,' were made a 'kingdom,' and reigned as kings throughout the church age."[48] In a similar vein Bauckham affirms that the present passage presents a positive destiny for the nations and kings of the earth. He sums up the matter in these words: "The kings of the earth offer their own glory to God's glory. In place of their old idolatrous allegiance to the beast, they now give glory to God."[49] Ewing adds a significant point to the discussion by saying, "In Revelation's picture of the kings entering the gates of the New Jerusalem, we finally find an image of forgiveness. God's purpose for all humanity, including the kings and merchants, is to bring them into the divine unity and enable them to offer their gifts for the whole."[50] Other commentators who affirm the positive use of "kings of the earth" in this passage include Jeske, Aune, Kealy, Boring, Wall, Sweet, Robbins, Maxwell, and Royalty.[51]

In summary, John begins with an ambiguous use of the phrase "kings of the earth" in 1:5. That text *may* be read as referring to kings who

47. Cf. Mounce, *Revelation*, 384.
48. Beale, *Book of Revelation*, 1097.
49. Bauckham, *Climax*, 314–15.
50. Ewing, *Power of the Lamb*, 151.
51. Jeske, *Revelation for Today*, 118; Aune, *Revelation 17–22*, 1172; Kealy, *Apocalypse*, 229; Boring, *Revelation*, 221; Wall, *Revelation*, 252–53; Sweet, *Revelation*, 308; Robbins, *Revelation*, 241; Maxwell, *Revelation*, 196; Royalty, *Streets of Heaven*, 231–32.

choose to accept the sovereignty of the exalted Christ and voluntarily align themselves with him, or as kings opposed to him who will be forced to accept his sovereignty in the end. This verse is followed by six references in which "kings of the earth" are unambiguously on the side of the forces of evil (6:15, 17:2, 18; 18:3, 9; and 19:19). Then follows the positive counterimage in 21:24 in which the kings of the earth bring their glory into the holy city, New Jerusalem.

2

The Sword

... and having in his right hand seven stars, and a sharp, two-edged sword coming out of his mouth; and his appearance was like the sun shining in its strength.

(Rev 1:16)

And to the messenger of the church in Pergamum write, Thus says the One having the sharp, two-edged sword ...

(Rev 2:12)

Repent therefore; otherwise I am coming to you quickly and I will do battle with them by means of the sword of my mouth.

(Rev 2:16)

And the rest were killed by the sword which came out of the mouth of the one sitting upon the horse, and all the birds were filled from (eating) their flesh.

(Rev 19:21)

And another horse went out, (a) fiery red (one), and it was given to the one sitting upon it to take peace from the earth so that (people) might slay one another; also a large sword was given to him.

(Rev 6:4)

And I looked and behold a sickly green horse (appeared) and one sitting above it whose name was Death; and Hades followed behind him: and authority was given to them over one-fourth of the earth to kill by sword and famine and plague and by the beasts of the earth.

(Rev 6:8)

> *If anyone (is destined) for captivity, he goes into captivity. If anyone (is destined) to be killed by sword, he is to be killed by sword.*
>
> (REV 13:10)
>
> *And he leads astray those dwelling upon the earth because of the signs which were given him to do before the beast, commanding those dwelling upon the earth to make an image for the beast who has the wound of the sword, but lived.*
>
> (REV 13:14)

THE FIRST MENTION OF a sword in Revelation comes in what is often called the inaugural vision. "One like a son of man" is depicted as being in the midst of the seven lampstands (Rev 1:13), which are later identified as the seven churches (Rev 1:20). A few scholars have espoused the view that this identification is an allegorical interpolation, such as Malina,[1] or have regarded it as a marginal gloss that has been incorporated into the text,[2] but this view has not been widely accepted. Further description of the "one like a son of man" points to his identity as the resurrected and exalted Christ. Such is the interpretation of Bauckham, Beasley-Murray, Courts, Krodel, Boring, Mounce, and others.[3] The fact that the sword issues from the mouth of the one like a son of man prompts the reader to think of the word of God, and rightly so in my judgment. As Kiddle expresses it, this sword "represents the Gospel in all its sternness."[4] The appropriateness of the symbol lies partially in the fact that the Roman short sword was tongue-shaped.[5] Krodel takes the matter one step further by suggesting that the sword represents more specifically the word of God in Christ's function as the ultimate judge of the church.[6] Mounce likewise speaks of the sword as representing "the irresistible power of divine judgment."[7] Wilson says of the sword that ". . . this vigorous image points to the executive power of his Word, which renders any other weapon unneces-

---

1. Malina, *Genre and Message*, 75.
2. Cf. Giblin, *Book of Revelation*, 49.
3. Bauckham, *Climax*, 166; Beasley-Murray, *Revelation*, 67; Court, *Revelation*, 24; Krodel, *Revelation*, 95; Boring, *Revelation*, 80; Mounce, *What Are We Waiting For?*, 79.
4. Kiddle, *Revelation*, 15.
5. *Hastings Dictionary of the Bible*, as cited in Morris, *Revelation*, 57.
6. Krodel, *Revelation*, 95–96.
7. Mounce, *Revelation*, 79.

sary."[8] Mounce also points out that sword symbolism is not at all unusual. He cites examples from Isa 49:2, Wis 18:15–16, and 2 Esd 13:10.[9]

The interpretations of Krodel and Mounce, namely that the sword is related to judgment, appears to be supported by the next two occurrences of the word. Both are found in the address to the church at Pergamum. This city was the provincial capital. It also had the dubious distinction of being the official center in Asia for the imperial cult. In 29 B.C.E. it had received permission from Caesar Augustus to erect a temple to him and the goddess Roma.[10] Kiddle claims that Pergamum was ". . . a stronger fortress of pagan life than any other of the seven cities."[11] Lilje echoes this point, stating that the young church faced a stronger challenge from Hellenism in Pergamum than in any other city in the Empire.[12]

The speaker identifies himself to the church at Pergamum as the one having the sharp two-edged sword (Rev 2:12), i.e., as the exalted Christ. As Mounce points out, this sort of language would not have been lost upon the citizens of a city to which the proconsul was granted the *ius gladii*, or "right of the sword".[13] This expression would have reminded the church there that the right of the proconsul to execute people by means of the sword was only a pale imitation of the power and rights of the "one like a son of man."[14]

A call to repentance follows in the body of the address to the church at Pergamum. Christ then issues the warning that unless they repent, he will come and do battle with them (the Nicolaitans) by means of the sword of his mouth (Rev 2:16). Little is known about the Nicolaitans, but they seem to have been an antinomian group within the churches of Ephesus and Pergamum. Smalley suggests that they may represent a Gnostic heresy ". . . which gave rise to idolatry as well as immorality."[15] Many commentators associate the Nicolaitans with those holding the teachings of Balaam (Rev 2:14).[16] There are two major reasons for this association: first, because

8. Wilson, *Revelation*, 23.
9. Mounce, *Revelation*, 80, n.
10. Ibid., 96.
11. Kiddle, *Revelation*, 30.
12. Lilje, *Last Book*, 78.
13. Mounce, *Revelation*, 96.
14. Cf. Morris, *Revelation*, 66.
15. Smalley, "John's Revelation," 567, n. 62.
16. E.g., Mounce, *Revelation*, 98–99; and Beasley-Murray, *Revelation*, 85.

both are mentioned in close proximity in the addresses to the churches; and second, because of the similar etymology of the two terms. *Nicolaitan* literally means "conqueror of people," and *Balaam* means something like "lord of people." This address to the church at Pergamum transparently portrays a judgment by the word of God unless the church—or at least the Nicolaitans and those following the teachings of Balaam—there repents. Kiddle goes too far in saying that they will doubtless die like Ananias and Sapphira unless they repent.[17] This assertion goes beyond anything that the text will support.

The fourth usage of the word *sword* in the arena of God's operation is in the context of the rider on the white horse, who is unambiguously identified as the Word of God (Rev 19:15).[18] The two-edged sword in this context comes out of the mouth of the rider in order that he might smite the Gentiles ("nations") with it. This statement is followed by a paraphrase of Ps 2:9, which further supports the identity of this rider as the Messiah. This identification, however, leads us into a logical difficulty. The rider on the white horse is the Word of God; and also, if my previous arguments have any merit, the two-edged sword is the word of God. I doubt that the author of the Revelation was troubled by such anomalies. As modern Westerners we are often handicapped in the understanding of the Scriptures by our heritage of Aristotelian logic, which prompts us to think in terms of either/or. The author of the Revelation was a citizen of the ancient Eastern world and was comfortable with paradox, i.e., both/and. To think of Christ as personifying the Word of God and also as speaking the word of God would not likely have presented a problem to him.

As Charles has effectively shown, the reference to smiting the nations has overtones of Isa 11:4 and the non-canonical writings Ps Sol 17:26–27, 39; Wis 18:22, and *1 Enoch* 62:2.[19] He argues further that all these passages support the idea that the sword from the mouth of the Messiah is a metaphor of forensic or judicial condemnation.[20] While I would personally prefer terms other than *forensic* or *judicial*, I agree that these passages portray divine judgment. Kiddle in a similar vein referred to this sword

---

17. Kiddle, *Revelation*, 34; Cf. Acts 5:1–11.

18. Cf. Goldsworthy, *Gospel in Revelation*, 95–96. I shall argue later that the rider on the white horse in Rev 6:2 is a counterfeit and imposter.

19. Cf. also Wilson, *Revelation*, 159.

20. Charles, *Critical and Exegetical Commentary*, 2:136.

as the "punitive power of Christ."[21] For the author of Revelation, as well as the author of the Fourth Gospel (e.g. John 5:22), Christ is the one who effects that divine judgment.

Beasley-Murray and others have called attention to the fact that, though the heavenly armies are said to be following Christ (Rev 19:14), in the execution of the judgment Christ acts alone. The armies are no more than passive witnesses to the judgment.[22]

Two other matters in this passage require attention. Who are the Gentiles or "nations" who will be smitten by the two-edged sword, and what is the significance of the treading of the wine vat? In answer to the former, I think we must recognize a figurative use of the terms *Jew* and *Gentile* that had developed by the time Revelation was written. "Jew" had become a symbol for Christian believers, and "Gentile" had come to signify unbelievers. Partial evidence for this development is found in the address in the letter of James to "the twelve tribes scattered abroad" (Jas 1:1). A comparison of 1 Pet 2:12 and 4:3 points in the same direction.[23] There is no ethnic connotation involved here—the nations to be smitten by the sword of the exalted Christ are any and all nations hostile to God.

The smiting of the nations is inseparable from the treading of the wine vat that follows. As usual, the author is drawing his symbolism from the Jewish Scriptures. Joel 3:13 and Lam 1:15 provide the symbolism for God's judgment being likened to treading grapes in a wine vat.

In view of the often-heard protest that the Christ portrayed in Revelation is a bloody warrior unworthy of the Christ of the Gospels, what the author does with Ps 2:9 is most interesting. That text reads, "Thou shalt break them with a rod of iron, Thou shalt shatter them like earthenware" (NASB). John has used the Greek version, which reads "You will shepherd (*poimaneis*) them with a rod of iron," and has omitted the harsh reference to shattering them like earthenware, thus evoking memories of Ps 23. Smalley attributes this translation to John's limited knowledge of Greek and assumes that John thought that *poimanei* could mean both "destroy" and "rule." He goes on to argue that it can only mean "rule" here, but that the word "makes bad sense."[24] Interestingly enough, in Rev 7:17

---

21. Kiddle, *Revelation*, 385.

22. Beasley-Murray, *Revelation*, 281; Boring, *Revelation*, 197; cf. also Morris, *Revelation*, 225; Wilson, *Revelation*, 159.

23. Cf. Giblin, *Book of Revelation*, 458–59, n. 47.

24. Smalley, "John's Revelation," 563.

the same word is used of the Lamb in relation to the martyrs in heaven. I doubt that anyone would want to argue that the Lamb will destroy the martyrs! Despite the claims of Mounce[25] that "shepherd" in this context means to destroy rather than to rule with sternness; and Smalley's similar claim cited above, I believe the substitution of "shepherd" should be seen as a mitigation of the harshness of the Hebrew version of Ps 2:9. And though the rider on the white horse wears a robe dipped in blood, it is his own blood, not that of his enemies, as Boring, Krodel, Sleeper, Metzger, Jeske, Kealy and others have noted.[26] According to Beasley-Murray, "most" modern commentators interpret the blood as that of Christ's enemies, in accordance with Isa 63:1–3. He does cite Swete as suggesting that the blood is both Christ's own and that of his enemies, and Caird as suggesting that martyr's blood is the referent.[27] Charles is another commentator who denies in the most forceful language that the blood is that of Christ, and interprets the blood as that of the Parthian kings and their armies whom Christ had previously destroyed.[28] Boesak has likewise argued that the blood is that of Christ's enemies.[29] Lilje asserts in similar fashion that the symbol of the bloody garment and the treading of the wine vat are both drawn from Isa 63:1–3, hence the blood would be that of the ungodly.[30]

Two considerations, however, point to the blood as being shed by Christ himself: First, in Rev 19:13 the robe is said to be dipped (*bebammenon*) in blood. While a few manuscripts support the reading "sprinkled" (*hrerantismenon*) instead of "dipped," the support is relatively weak. *Bebammenon* is from the same root as the word for baptism, *baptizō*. That anyone would read or hear this text without thinking of baptism is highly unlikely; and according to the Gospels Jesus referred to his death as a baptism (Mark 10:38–40, Luke 12:50). Second, in the kindred passage, Rev 14:20, we read, "And the wine-vat was trodden outside the city, and blood went out of the wine-vat up to the bridles of the horses for 1600 stadia." The phrase "outside the city" seems to be a thinly veiled reference to the

---

25. Mounce, *Revelation*, 96.

26. Boring, *Revelation*, 196; Krodel, *Revelation*, 323; Sleeper, *Victorious Christ*, 64, 117; Hanson, *Wrath of the Lamb*, 175–76; Metzger, *Breaking the Code*, 91; Jeske, *Revelation for Today*, 112; Kealy, *Apocalypse*, 215.

27. Beasley-Murray, *Revelation*, 280.

28. Charles, *Critical and Exegetical Commentary*, 2:133.

29. Boesak, *Comfort and Protest*, 124.

30. Lilje, *Last Book*, 244.

sufferings of Christ "outside the gate" (Heb 13:12, cf. Mark 12:39 = Luke 20:15). This phrase establishes a link between the treading of the wine vat and the sufferings of Christ. Christ's suffering establishes the basis for the judgment of God in that one's response to Christ determines whether one is cast into the wine vat, but this expression does not mean that Christ is the one who does the treading. The passive voice ("was trodden") is more likely to be a divine passive, with God understood as the one who does the treading. There is therefore no good reason to see the garments of Christ as splattered by any blood except his own. Royalty has affirmed this position in a recent work that the blood is Christ's own, though arguing the point from a slightly different perspective than I have done.[31]

The final occurrence of the term *sword* in the realm of divine operation comes from the same general context as the previous one. It merely takes us one step further in the picture of unfolding judgment by the returning Christ. The judgment upon the essence of evil begins to unfold in the seizing of two members of the "unholy trinity."[32] They are cast alive into the lake that burns with fire and sulfur. "The rest" are killed by means of the sword coming out of the mouth of the rider on the white horse. "The rest" are the kings of the earth and their armies (v. 19), and the rider is clearly the one described in vv. 11–13.

Beale concedes that the sword could be interpreted literally (though I am not sure I would make the same concession) but argues that it is best viewed as "the accusatory word of God."[33] In favor of this interpretation is the picture of judgment in Matt 25, in which the judgment is conveyed by the words, "Depart from me, accursed ones, into the eternal fire which has been prepared for the devil and his angels" (Matt 25:41, NASB), or "Come, you who are blessed by my Father, inherit the kingdom prepared for you from the foundation of the world" (Matt 25:34, NASB). Metzger likewise interprets the sword as the word of God and argues further, "That sword is his word: it is his only armament. By it he convicts, convinces, and exonerates."[34]

Given the association of "sword" with the word of God (cf. Eph 6:17, Heb 4:12) and especially the positive reference in Ephesians, some

---

31. Royalty, *Streets of Heaven*, 214.
32. See Part II, chapter 2 for further discussion.
33. Beale, *Book of Revelation*, 970.
34. Metzger, *Breaking the Code*, 91.

have interpreted the "slaying" as conversion of the nations by the Gospel message. Beale cites Chilton, Swete, and Pieters as supporting this position.[35] Beale himself rejects the position, however, on the grounds that it is incompatible with the picture of final judgment which permeates this section of Revelation. If, as most interpreters seem to agree, this passage depicts events accompanying the *parousia* of Jesus (see for example Beale,[36] Wall,[37] Mounce [apparently],[38] Maxwell,[39] Krodel,[40] Boring,[41] and Aune[42]) the time for conversion of unbelievers is now past. In vivid and emotion-stirring terms the Seer is presenting the finality of God's judgment, a judgment effected by his word alone. All those who have allied themselves with the beast and the false prophet are dealt a fatal blow by God's word. It should be noted, however, that this passage describes only the negative side of God's final judgment. The positive side will be depicted in 21:1–22:5.

To sum up what I have presented thus far, the sharp two-edged sword is a symbol of the word of God; particularly as that word is applied in judgment on evil (cf. 19:20). That weapon is wielded solely by the exalted Christ, who has conquered through shedding his blood and has thereby earned the right to execute judgment on all humanity (cf. Rev 5:5).

When we turn to consider the symbol of the sword as it operates in the arena of evil, the first text we encounter is Rev 6:4. The setting is the opening of the sealed scroll by the "Lion of the tribe of Judah," who alone has conquered and won the ability to open the scroll. With the opening of the first four seals, the infamous four horsemen emerge. Contrary to appearances, the rider on the white horse is not the exalted Christ but a symbol of military conquest. The second horse is fiery red *(purros)*, the same color as the dragon (Rev 12:3). As Mounce[43] and others have noted, his color matches that of his mission. It is the rider on this horse who is given a great sword, along with the ability to take peace from the earth

---

35. Beale, *Book of Revelation*, 971.
36. Ibid., 948ff.
37. Wall, *Revelation*, 233.
38. Mounce, *Revelation*, 349.
39. Ibid., 162.
40. Krodel, *Revelation*, 317.
41. Boring, *Revelation*, 194.
42. Aune, *Revelation 17–22*, 1053.
43. Mounce, *Revelation*, 154.

and incite people to kill one another. Wilson aptly notes that the removal of peace from the earth leaves humanity's destructive instincts to run unchecked. He goes on to say, "War is one of the judgments of God upon an apostate race," and quotes an appropriate statement of Friedrich von Schiller that "The history of the world is the judgment of the world."[44] Kiddle has argued that this horseman represents internal dissensions, civil war, and the like, and that the turmoil following Nero's death would have influenced the understanding of this passage.[45] In similar fashion Lilje states that this rider depicts ". . . civil war, indiscriminate fighting and bloodshed, every man against everyone else, ruin and collapse."[46] Certainly the events following the death of Nero would have been remembered by the first readers of Revelation, but interpretation should not be limited to those events. Kiddle's view is too narrow at this point.

The verb *sphazō*, whose normal significance is "to slaughter" or "to murder," is used in this passage. The four horsemen depict a logical progression from military conquest to internal strife and bloodshed to famine to death and *hadēs*—a progression that inevitably follows military conquest.[47] As Boesak has appropriately noted, death in this scene is not peaceful natural death, but death resulting from cruelty and inhumanity.[48] Barclay claims that in the thirty years preceding Herod the Great, i.e., approximately the years 67–37 B.C.E., a hundred thousand people died in revolutions and rebellions in Palestine and another one hundred fifty thousand died in the revolt in Britain.[49] Hence Morris's comment that such events form "a sombre background to Revelation" appears to be fully justified.[50]

Charles has called attention to the fact that the symbol of the sword belongs to eschatological tradition. It is wielded by Yahweh himself in Isaiah 27:1, 34:5, and Ezekiel 21:3-5 against Leviathan, Edom, and Jerusalem respectively. In a later stage of development, represented by *1 Enoch* 90:19, 34; 91:12, the sword is given to God's faithful people so that they may destroy their enemies (cf. also Esther 8:7—9:5). In the third

44. Wilson, *Revelation*, 65.
45. Kiddle, *Revelation*, 114.
46. Lilje, *Last Book*, 125.
47. Beasley-Murray, *Revelation*, 131; Krodel, *Revelation*, 172-75; Boring, *Revelation*, 122; Charles, *Critical and Exegetical Commentary* 1:164; Court, *Revelation*, 31.
48. Boesak, *Comfort and Protest*, 64.
49. Cited in Mounce, *Revelation*, 154 n; cf. Morris, *Revelation*, 103.
50. Morris, *Revelation*, 103.

stage of the tradition, represented in *1 En*och 88:2, the sword is given to the enemies of God so that they may destroy themselves with it.[51] The latter appears to be the stage of eschatological development that we find in Rev 6:4.

The next usage of "sword" comes in Rev 6:8. The opening of the fourth seal produces a rider on a sickly green (*chlōros*) horse ridden by death, with the place of the dead (*hadēs*) following—whether on the same or another horse is not specified. Morris notes that we should probably understand a horse the color of a corpse here.[52] The text contains an ambiguity in the statement that it was given to "them" to kill with sword, famine, and pestilence, and by the wild beasts of the earth. Kiddle seems to understand this text as meaning that death uses all the weapons mentioned.[53] Charles attempts to clear up the ambiguity by claiming that the text is corrupt here. To see the riders on all four horses as the antecedent to "them" is much simpler and does not involve subjective judgment concerning the text.

Wilson notes that *death* in this passage does not represent death in general but rather the deaths brought about by the events that follow the breaking of the seals. He further comments appropriately that these judgments should be seen as warning judgments, since they affect only one-fourth of the earth.[54] Kiddle also argues that the limit imposed on these judgments indicates that they are still preliminary warnings of the end.[55]

Except in this one instance, the writer of Revelation uses a different word for *sword* within the arena of the forces of good from the one he uses within the arena of the forces of evil. In all the passages we have examined in which the sword is wielded by the exalted Christ, the word *hromphaia*, which implies a short, sharp, dagger-like sword, is used. The other word, *machaira*, a broad sword normally used in battle, is used when the sword appears within the arena of the forces of evil. The question then arises as to why John departs from his normal usage here. The answer may lie in the sources on which he is relying.

---

51. Charles, *Critical and Exegetical Commentary*, 1:165.
52. Morris, *Revelation*, 104.
53. Kiddle, *Revelation*, 117.
54. Wilson, *Revelation*, 66.
55. Kiddle, *Revelation*, 117; cf. also Lilje, *Last Book*, 126.

Charles argues rather cogently for a dependence of Rev 6:1–8 upon Ezek 14:21, in which "four severe judgments" are to be sent against Jerusalem: sword, famine, wild beasts, and plague. He further argues that the original text of 6:8b read, "He that sat upon him was named Pestilence, and there was given to him authority over the fourth part of the earth." He sees the reference to *hadēs* and the sword as interpolations based on Ezek 14:21.[56] Kiddle advances the similar argument that ". . . sword and famine and plague and wild beasts of the earth, is merely an allusion to the eschatological threat in Ezek. xiv.21 [sic]."[57] One is driven to admit that a description of death and *hadēs* as killing by the use of a sword is more than a little awkward. As noted above, making all the riders the antecedent of "them" does much to mitigate the awkwardness, however. Whether or not we would agree with Charles that the text is corrupt here, his argument for the influence of Ezek 14:21 is rather compelling. Not only would this influence explain the reference to the wild beasts, which are otherwise unconnected with the vision of the four horsemen, but it would also explain the occurrence of *hromphaia* instead of *machaira* at this point.[58]

The next occurrence of the negative use of the sword symbol follows the appearance of the beast from the sea in Rev 13. According to Charles, the beast is the Roman Empire, and 13:1–10 are from a Jewish apocalypse originally written in Hebrew either just before or just after the fall of Jerusalem.[59] Hence the reference to the sword in v. 10 would be related to the Jewish wars of 66–70 C.E. Beasley-Murray is another commentator who identifies the beast from the sea with the Roman Empire.[60] Krodel, though interpreting the beast as the empire of the last days, nevertheless sees a special application to Rome and its emperor. He also suggests the influence of Jeremiah 15:2 on the troublesome v. 10.[61] Boring differs from these three interpreters by identifying the beast from the sea as "the inhuman arrogance of empire which has come to expression in Rome, but not only there."[62] Kenneth Durkin offers the similar explanation that

---

56. Charles, *Critical and Exegetical Commentary*, 1:169–71.
57. Kiddle, *Revelation*, 117; cf. also Lilje, *Last Book*, 126.
58. Cf. Morris, *Revelation*, 104.
59. Charles, *Critical and Exegetical Commentary*, 1:341.
60. Beasley-Murray, *Revelation*, 209.
61. Krodel, *Revelation*, 249–50.
62. Boring, *Revelation*, 156.

the beast symbolizes "the magnitude and inter-relation of the developed human rebellion against God."[63] Perhaps Giblin has taken the safest position in his claim that there is no need to identify the beast beyond the fact that "he figures as an image of the diabolical, super-human power of evil at its worst—which never succeeds against the faithful beyond being able to inflict death on them for a short time."[64]

Lilje[65] and others have noted the reminiscences of Jer 15:2 in this text. That passage reads in the NASB:

> And it shall be that when they say to you, 'Where should we go?' then you are to tell them, 'Thus says the Lord:
> Those destined for death, to death;
> And those destined for the sword, to the sword;
> And those destined for famine, to famine;
> And those destined for captivity to captivity.'

In its original context, this passage was a prophecy of inevitable judgment upon Jerusalem because of the sins of Manasseh. Exactly how the Seer is using the passage is not clear, however. There are several textual variations in the Greek manuscripts. There is no word for "destined" in the text, and this omission has apparently prompted scribes to amend the text. Some, as noted by Mounce,[66] have supplied a verb meaning "to lead" (*apagei* or *sunagei*), thus making the verse emphasize that the enemies of God's people would receive a *lex talionis* (law of punishment in kind) retribution for their persecution of believers. In the same context Mounce notes that Codex Alexandrinus (which Charles supports as being the best manuscript of the Apocalypse[67]) substituted a passive infinitive and made both couplets of the verse stress the inevitability of persecution for God's faithful people.[68] Morris argues that the first couplet relating to captivity is simply an exhortation to accept the realities of life, whereas the second relating to the sword has to do with requital. He further argues—correctly in my judgment—that the kingdom of God cannot be established or de-

---

63. Cited in Court, *Revelation*, 59.
64. Giblin, "Revelation 11:1–13," 443.
65. Lilje, *Last Book*, 193.
66. Mounce, *Revelation*, 257.
67. Charles, *Critical and Exegetical Commentary*, 1:clxxi–clxxii.
68. See also Lilje, *Last Book*, 193.

fended with the sword.[69] In similar language Wilson sees here a warning against the folly of resorting to violence; he connects this passage with Jesus' words, "All that take the sword shall perish with the sword."[70]

The identification of the beast with Rome as advocated by Charles and Beasley-Murray leaves the passage with only antiquarian interest to anyone living beyond the first century C.E., and hence falls short of the parameters for interpretation established at the beginning of this study. Boring's interpretation is more appropriate in that it allows the passage to speak both to the immediate recipients and to future generations as well.

In v. 7 we read that it was given to the beast to make war with the saints and to conquer them. The next verse states that all the people dwelling on the earth whose names are not written in the book of life will worship the beast. This statement is followed by a call to attention similar to that found in all the addresses to the seven churches: "If anyone has an ear, let him hear . . . " (13:9). This admonition brings us to the passage so reminiscent of Jer 15:2, in which we have a reference to the sword. The victory of the beast over the saints will result in the use of the sword comparable to that of the Babylonian captivity. Such would be the implication to anyone who was familiar with this prophecy of Jeremiah. In Kiddle's words, "All those who wield the unhallowed sword of Imperial power will be killed by the 'sharp sword with a double edge' (1.16), the sword of God's anger."[71] If the killing be understood metaphorically as eternal separation from God, then Kiddle's words are on target.

The final occurrence of the symbolism of the sword is in reference to the beast from the sea. By this point the third member of the "unholy trinity" has appeared—the beast from the earth (13:11). He is said to exercise all the authority of the first beast (13:12) and to deceive those dwelling on the earth to make an image of the first beast who had been wounded by the sword but lived (13:14). His deceitful actions will even include doing miracles but, as Morris correctly notes, only unregenerate humanity can be taken in by the false miracles that this beast performs.[72]

In 13:3 one of the heads of the beast is said to have been smitten with a deadly wound. Now it becomes clear that the beast itself, not just

---

69. Morris, *Revelation*, 165.
70. Wilson, *Revelation*, 114. Matt 26:52.
71. Kiddle, *Revelation*, 251–52.
72. Morris, *Revelation*, 167; cf. Wilson, *Revelation*, 115.

one of its heads, had received a lethal wound from the sword. This fatal wound is most often interpreted as a reference to the death of Nero. Lilje notes this interpretation, but expresses skepticism as to whether John was referring to the Nero legend.[73] Other interpreters have suggested that the death of Julius Caesar is the background. Whether or not we associate the passage with any individual emperor, the passage suggests that we should think of damage to the empire, not the individual ruler.

In summation, we have four passages in which the sword is something which operates within the arena of the forces of evil. In all these passages the sword is an instrument of warfare and bloodshed. These stand as a sharp counterimage to the four passages in which the sword is a symbol of the word of God. The word of God disciplines and purifies the churches (cf. 2:16) and ultimately destroys all the forces of evil (cf. 19:21).

---

73. Lilje, *Last Book*, 196.

3

Out of the Mouth

> ... and having in his right hand seven stars,
> and a sharp, two-edged sword coming out of his mouth;
> and his appearance was like the sun shining in its strength.
>
> (Rev 1:16)

> Thus because you are tepid, neither hot nor cold,
> I am about to vomit you out of my mouth.
>
> (Rev 3:16)

> And if anyone wants to harm them, fire goes out of their mouth
> and consumes their enemies; indeed, if anyone wants to harm them
> it is necessary for him to be killed in this manner.
>
> (Rev 11:5)

> And a sharp sword is coming out of his mouth in order that by it
> he might smite the nations; and he will 'shepherd them with an iron rod,'
> and he is treading the wine-vat of the wine of the wrath of the anger
> of God the Almighty.
>
> (Rev 19:15)

> And in this manner I saw the horses in the vision and the ones sitting
> upon them, as having breastplates (the color) of fire and hyacinth and
> sulphur; and the heads of the horses (were) like heads of lions:
> and fire and smoke and sulphur are going out of their mouths.
>
> (Rev 9:17–18)

And the serpent cast water like a river out of his mouth after the woman, in order that she might be carried away by the river, and the earth helped the woman, and the earth opened her mouth and swallowed up the river which the dragon cast out of his mouth.

(Rev 12:15–16)

And I saw (coming) out of the mouth of the dragon and of the beast and of the false prophet three unclean spirits like frogs.

(Rev 16:13)

We find a total of five passages in Revelation in which something coming out of the mouth is in the arena of God's actions. The first is the sword issuing from the mouth of the exalted Christ (1:16). This passage was discussed in Chapter Two. I will not repeat that material here but simply note that what comes out of the mouth comes from the exalted Christ, and hence this passage clearly belongs to the arena of God's operation. The second passage is in the address to the church at Laodicea. "The amen, the faithful and true witness, the beginning of the creation of God" speaks to a church that has no effective witness. The descriptive phrases clearly identify the speaker as the exalted Christ. As Beale notes, the witness of this church was ineffective either because it did not exist or because it had been compromised. He also notes the possibility of a more literal understanding of the metaphor: ". . . there is evidence that Laodicea had access only to warm water, which was not very palatable and caused nausea."[1] Aune notes that the verb *emein*, "to vomit," is a coarse term meaning "to utterly reject." He further notes the use of this verb in the Septuagint of Lev 18:25, 28; 20:22 in reference to the fate of the Canaanites and the potential fate of the Israelites themselves.[2] Sweet aptly notes that the use of the verb *mellō*, "to be about to do something," implies God's being at the point of rejecting the Laodiceans, but with repentance yet being a possibility.[3]

The third passage under consideration is related to the account of the two witnesses of Rev 11:5. What comes out of their mouths is fire that consumes those who attempt to harm them. As Morris appropriately

---

1. Beale, *Book of Revelation*, 303; cf. Sweet, *Revelation*, 107.
2. Aune, *Revelation 1–5*, 258.
3. Sweet, *Revelation*, 107.

notes, physical destruction is not in view here. The "fire" is the message of the faithful witnesses that, like the word of God in the mouth of Jeremiah (Jer 5:14), has a fiery aspect.[4] Kiddle appropriately points out that that the witnesses are not protected as individuals but as the heralds of a faith which both includes and transcends the Law and the Prophets as represented by Moses and Elijah.[5]

Wilson, however, appears to take a more literal view, based on Elijah's calling fire down from heaven to consume his enemies.[6] Perhaps Wilson needs to take note of Jesus' response when his disciples wanted to call fire down upon the Samaritans "as Elijah did" (Luke 9:51–56).

The identity of the two witnesses is much debated. Charles is among those who interpret the witnesses as Moses and Elijah.[7] Krodel, after mentioning various people who had interpreted the witnesses as Peter and Paul, James the Lord's brother and John the apostle, John the Baptist and Jesus, Enoch and Elijah, Jeremiah and Elijah, or Moses and Elijah, concluded, "John clearly indicated that the 'two witnesses' are not two individual persons but symbols representing the Christian community."[8] Boring similarly argues that the witnesses are ". . . the whole church of the eschatological times."[9] Giblin suggests that the witnesses are neither individuals nor individual communities but rather that the number two meets the requirement for a juridically valid testimony. He further characterizes the witnesses in a most interesting way as identical twins with prophetic functions of a worldwide scope.[10] Mounce agrees with Boring that the witnesses represent ". . . the witnessing church in the last tumultuous days before the end of the age." He further suggests, with Giblin, that the number two is symbolic, based on the requirement in Deut 19:15 for a second witness in order for testimony to be valid.[11]

The fourth passage in this category depicts the two-edged sword issuing from the mouth of the conquering Christ (19:15). As Beasley-Murray has noted, Christ's judgment is here presented in a threefold imagery

4. Morris, *Revelation*, 144.
5. Kiddle, *Revelation*, 196.
6. Wilson, *Revelation*, 96; cf. 2 Kgs 1:10–12.
7. Charles, *Critical and Exegetical Commentary*, 1:270.
8. Krodel, *Revelation*, 222–23.
9. Boring, *Revelation*, 145.
10. Giblin, *Book of Revelation*, 112–14.
11. Mounce, *Revelation*, 223; cf. Giblin, *Book of Revelation*, 112–14.

drawn from the Jewish Scriptures: the sharp sword, reminiscent of Isa 11:3–5; the rod of iron, reflecting Ps 2:9; and the treading of the wine vat of God's wrath, possibly drawing on Isa 63:1–6.[12] The sword imagery was discussed in the preceding chapter. In that chapter I also noted that slaying with the sword must surely be taken in a figurative manner. As Caird has noted, the Davidic king was supposed to be a prophet who could redress the grievances of the poor and break the power of the unscrupulous by the "rod of his mouth," the latter having given way in the present passage to the sharp two-edged sword.[13]

Opinion among interpreters is deeply divided on the meaning of the sword imagery and the allusion to Ps 2:9. Mounce notes and promptly rejects Swete's suggestion that conversion of unbelievers as well as their judgment is in view here. He then quotes approvingly Ladd's argument that "the radical spiritualization of this concept which sees a conflict of human ideologies in human history and the triumph of Christianity does not accord with the nature of apocalyptic thought."[14] Ladd has made the questionable assumption that John's thought as well as his language is apocalyptic. I have argued earlier that John saw himself as a prophet. If that argument be valid, then room must be left for a prophetic understanding that the purpose of God is continually being worked out on the plane of human history, not just brought about by supernatural intervention in a cataclysmic fashion at the end of history. The language of the verse under consideration points in this direction. Caird notes the sudden shift from the future to the present tense in the reference to treading the wine vat.[15] If the verb for treading (*patei*) be given its normal force in the present tense, then the treading of the wine vat is already taking place, not reserved for the future. Caird goes on to argue quite cogently that the treading of the wine vat is not the judgment itself but the place where the judgment is prepared, and that ". . . it becomes reasonable to suppose that the winepress, like the Cross, is a place where God has turned the murderous acts of men into the means of their own judgment." He also notes that the robe of Christ is already bloody before the final judgment

---

12. Beasley-Murray, *Revelation*, 281; cf. Mounce, *Revelation*, 346–47; Wilson, *Revelation*, 158; Kiddle, *Revelation*, 385.

13. Caird, *Commentary on Revelation*, 245.

14. Mounce, *Revelation*, 346–47.

15. Caird, *Commentary on Revelation*, 245.

ever begins.[16] This observation further supports the position taken earlier that the blood is Christ's own, not that of his enemies.

The fifth and final passage using the phrase "out of the mouth" in the arena of divine action appears in the context of the climactic battle between the forces of evil and the forces of God (19:21). I dealt with this passage in the previous chapter. I will simply note here that just as at 1:16 and 19:15, we again are dealing with the sharp two-edged sword coming out of the mouth of the exalted Christ.

In summation, we have seen the sharp two-edged sword coming out of the mouth of the exalted Christ in three passages. We have also seen fire issuing from the mouths of the two witnesses that "consumes" their enemies. Obviously the killing of these enemies is not to be taken in a literal physical sense because the witnesses themselves are later "killed" by their enemies (Rev 11:7–10). Given the Old Testament background of God's words becoming fire in the mouth of Jeremiah (Jer 5:14), the fire in the mouth of the witnesses may be the same fire. If so, we have the same reality being depicted as the two-edged sword of Rev 1:16, 19:15, and 19:27. Regardless of one's conclusion on that particular point, what proceeds from the mouth represents divine action. In the remaining passage God is said to be at the point of figuratively vomiting the Laodiceans out of his mouth. In Greek, the expression "out of his mouth" is literally "out of the mouth of him"—hence whether it is spoken in the first, second, or third person, the phrase "out of the mouth" would remain constant. However one may interpret the fire coming out of the mouth of the two witnesses or the sharp two-edged sword coming out of the mouth of the exalted Christ, all these passages describe action emanating from either divine forces or God's witnesses. I will leave the matter there.

When we look for the counterimage of the mouth, we first confront the phrase in connection with the sixth trumpet and the demonic army of two hundred million who are released at the Euphrates (Rev 9:17–18). As Caird has noted, "This is an army straight from the jaws of hell."[17] Without denying that the location—the Euphrates River—would have evoked pictures of the Parthian armies, we are not dealing here with any literal Parthian invasion, as some have argued. The text is ambiguous as to whether it is the horses or their riders, or both, who wear breastplates

---

16. Ibid., 245–46.
17. Ibid., 122.

the color of fire and hyacinth and brimstone. Beasley-Murray, following Gunkel, suggests that two traditions are interwoven here: one portraying squadrons of cavalry and the other depicting mythological creatures that spit out fire, sulfur, and smoke. These two themes seem to have been melded into a unity along with the additional feature of the serpent-like tails. Beasley-Murray then concludes, "The picture is meant to be inconceivable, horrifying, and even revolting."[18] Kiddle speaks of this scene as giving the wicked a foretaste in this world of what they are to face hereafter.[19] As Farrer has noted, John is probably still using Joel's account of the locust plague, as he did in the preceding vision. "St. John makes two pictures of it—cavalry-like locusts, and locust-like cavalry. He does not even wish to contrast them strongly."[20] Mounce notes that the detail of fire and smoke coming out of the mouth was probably inspired by Leviathan in Job 41:19–20, and that the brimstone (sulfur) is reminiscent of the destruction of Sodom and Gomorrah. He also notes that this plague resembles the torment of the "unholy trinity" and those who bear the mark of the beast.[21]

The repetition of the phrase "out of their mouths" in v. 18 borders on redundancy, and is possibly intended to tell us that the Seer wanted to place special emphasis on this phrase. Whereas the demon locusts in the first plague were allowed to torment only those not having the seal of God for a limited period of five months (vv. 4–5), now one-third of humanity is killed by the plagues spewed from the mouths of the demonic cavalrymen.

The next passage containing the phrase is 12:15–16. The context is the sign of the woman who gives birth to the Messiah, and of the dragon who attempts to destroy the son. After being unsuccessful in doing so he turns his fury upon the woman herself. The identity of the woman will be explored more fully in Chapter 23. I will note here only that at least by this point in the text she appears to represent the church.

In the statement that the dragon cast water like a river after the woman, but that the earth opened its mouth and swallowed the river, the Seer has in typical fashion drawn from multiple images in the Jewish

---

18. Beasley-Murray, *Revelation*, 165.
19. Kiddle, *Revelation*, 164.
20. Farrer, *Revelation*, 121.
21. Mounce, *Revelation*, 203.

Scriptures. The onset of enemies being likened to a flood is a common metaphor in the Jewish Scriptures (cf. Pss 18:4, 32:6, 124:4–5; Isa 43:2). The earth opening up is reminiscent of Korah's rebellion against Moses (Num 16:31–37), although that passage sheds little or no light on the present one. Beasley-Murray thinks the passage was directly related to the drying-up of the Red Sea.[22] Kiddle notes the Exodus motif and also the prophecies of Isaiah 42:15, 43:2, and 50:2; which he thinks John has used in a figurative fashion to depict divine help in overcoming evil.[23] But what was there in the historical situation that could be compared to this satanic river swallowed up by the earth? Mounce notes the attempt by some interpreters to connect this text with actual rivers that ran underground at some geographical point, or to the attempt to cut off all possibilities of escape for Christians during the Jewish wars of 66–73 C.E.[24] Farrer is even more explicit: "What else can this Satanic stratagem be, than the destruction of the Jewish state in the war of A.D. [sic] 66–70?"[25] If my dating of Revelation be reliable, these events are too far in the past to represent a threat to the churches at the time the book was written. Caird is probably on the right track in noting the references in the addresses to the churches to false teachings and to those calling themselves Jews who were really a synagogue of Satan. He suggests that the "river" was the river of lies coming from the mouth of the dragon.[26] Christians standing steadfastly for the truth without being taken in by the dragon's lies would probably be the meaning of the metaphor of the earth opening its mouth and swallowing the river. Caird's interpretation has the further merit of being applicable to any period of time in which the church is threatened by false teachings.

The final appearance of the phrase "out of the mouth" in the arena of the forces of evil comes in Rev 16:13. The setting is the pouring-out of the sixth vial, which is followed by the drying up of the Euphrates to make way for the kings of the east (16:12). After commenting that vv. 13–16 are sometimes taken as an interlude between the sixth and seventh vial, Mounce suggests that these verses "should be viewed as a topical ex-

---

22. Beasley-Murray, *Revelation*, 205–06; cf. also Farrer, *Revelation*, 148; Morris, *Revelation*, 159.

23. Kiddle, *Revelation*, 237.

24. Mounce, *Revelation*, 246; cf. also Caird, *Commentary on Revelation*, 159.

25. Farrer, *Revelation*, 250.

26. Caird, *Commentary on Revelation*, 159.

pansion of v. 12."²⁷ This interpretation may be correct; however, a direct connection between vv. 12 and 13 is not easily found. Given the pattern of interludes between the sixth and seventh seals and trumpets I suggest along with Robbins²⁸ that the pattern continues here. We have this brief interlude just before the finality of God's judgment.

We have met the dragon and the beasts before, but this is the first mention of the false prophet. There can be little doubt that he is the beast from the earth of 13:11. There his religious function of inducing all to worship the beast from the sea is clearly evident, and thus the transition to the title of false prophet was quite easy for John to make.²⁹

There are several possible connotations to the unclean spirits like frogs coming out of the mouths of the unholy trinity. As Mounce notes, according to Lev 11:10 frogs were classified as unclean creatures.³⁰ Beasley-Murray refers to Moffat as pointing out the sinister ideas connected with frogs as agents of the evil spirit Ahriman in Iranian religion.³¹ Most commentators see an allusion to the second plague inflicted on Egypt.³² Commentators are also generally agreed that the "unclean spirits like frogs" refer to the propaganda coming from the unholy trinity. The shift in title from beast from the earth to false prophet may indicate a more specifically religious propaganda, although other types of propaganda should not be excluded.³³ The propaganda summons the forces of evil to the climactic battle of Armageddon (v. 16). Morris notes the possible model of the "lying spirits" of the prophets used to entice Ahab into battle.³⁴

To summarize the findings of this chapter, we have noted two passages in which fire comes out of the mouths of the two witnesses and two in which a sharp two-edged sword issues from the mouth of the victorious Christ. The latter is clearly the word of God, and the former may be

---

27. Mounce, *Revelation*, 299.

28. Robbins, unpublished classroom lecture, 1965; cf. also Summers, *Worthy Is the Lamb*, 187.

29. Cf. Mounce, *Revelation*, 299; Caird, *Commentary on Revelation*, 206.

30. Mounce, *Revelation*, 199, n.

31. Beasley-Murray, *Revelation*, 244; cf. Kiddle, *Revelation*, 328.

32. E.g., Mounce, *Revelation*, 199; Farrer, *Revelation*, 177; Caird, *Commentary on Revelation*, 206; Beasley-Murray, *Revelation*, 244.

33. Cf. Summers, *Worthy Is the Lamb*, 189; Mounce, *Revelation*, 299; Beasley-Murray, *Revelation*, 244; Caird, *Commentary on Revelation*, 206.

34. Morris, *Revelation*, 192; see 1 Kgs 22:21–23.

as well. At any rate what comes out of the mouth of the two witnesses and of Christ has a positive function of protecting the witnesses and defeating the enemies of Christ. In sharp contrast with these passages stand three in which what comes out of the mouth represents evil forces. In the first of these, fire, smoke, and brimstone come out of the mouths of the demonic cavalry and destroy one-third of humanity (Rev 9:17–18). In the second, the dragon sends forth water like a river out of his mouth in an attempt to destroy the woman who had given birth to the Messiah. In the third, lying propaganda comes out of the mouths of the unholy trinity to deceive humanity and gather the forces of evil for one climactic battle against the forces of God (16:13). The unnecessary or redundant repetition of the phrase "out of their mouth" in 9:18 lends support to the argument that these latter passages were intended as a counterimage to the fire coming out of the mouth of the two witnesses and the two-edged sword issuing from the mouth of Christ.

4

The Keys

Stop being afraid—I am the first and the last and the living One;
I also became dead: but look, I am living forever and ever;
and I have the keys of death and Hades.

(Rev 1:17c–18)

And to the messenger of the church in Thyatira write,
Thus says the holy One, the true One, the One having the key of David;
the One who opens and no one will shut, and when he shuts no one opens.

(Rev 3:7)

And I saw an angel coming down out of heaven having the key
of the abyss and a large chain upon his hand.

(Rev 20:1)

And the fifth angel sounded (his) trumpet; and I saw a star
which had fallen from heaven into the earth: and the key
to the shaft of the abyss was given to him.

(Rev 9:1)

THE CONTEXT OF THE first appearance of the term *key* in the Apocalypse is the inaugural vision, at the point where John has fallen at the feet of Christ like a dead man (1:17a). Christ raises him up with the exhortation to stop being afraid (*mē* plus present imperative). Christ then identifies himself as the first, the last, and the living One who died but now lives forever, and who has the key to both death and the realm of the dead (*hadēs*). One view of the keys treats them as a symbol of authority. As Wilson notes, this symbol indicates that Christ controls both the entrance to death and the subterranean world of departed spirits. "As

Christ's power thus extends even to the unseen realm of the dead, his people need not fear that the death threatened by their persecutors will be able to separate them from his love."[1] As Morris puts it, the exalted Christ has authority to consign to or deliver from death and its realm.[2]

Since death and *hadēs* are personified in the vision of the fourth horseman (Rev 6:8), some commentators suggest that they are personified in this passage as well. In this view the genitive nouns would be possessives and the meaning would be that Christ now has the keys once held by death and *hadēs*.[3] A closely related interpretation sees this passage in relationship to Hellenistic mythology, in which the goddess Hekate was thought to have the keys to the underworld, including death and *hadēs*. This interpretation regards Christ as replacing Hekate.[4] What is beyond doubt is that Christ has obtained these keys by means of his death, resurrection, and status as the ever-living One. If the personification of death and *hadēs* be accepted, the implication is that through his death and resurrection Christ has wrested the keys from the powers of death and the realm of the dead.[5] If the genitives be taken as objective, then by his death and resurrection Christ has obtained the keys to death and the realm of the dead so that they can never again hold human beings captive.[6]

Charles claims that this passage is one of the earliest appearances in Christian literature of the idea of Christ's descent into *hadēs*.[7] Beasley-Murray concedes that the image of Christ wresting the keys from a personified death and *hadēs* would be congenial to this idea but questions whether the text requires such an interpretation.[8]

Regardless of the way in which one interprets the genitive nouns in this passage, the symbol of the keys clearly refers to something that Christ controls for his purposes, even if the "keys" may have once been in other hands. I, however, take the position that the influence of such Hellenistic mythology as the Hekate myth on Revelation is slight to nonexistent.

---

1. Wilson, *Revelation*, 24–25; cf. Kiddle, *Revelation*, 16.
2. Morris, *Revelation*, 56.
3. Charles, *Critical and Exegetical Commentary*, 1:32.
4. e.g., Aune as cited in Boring, *Revelation*, 84; Krodel, *Revelation*, 97.
5. Beasley-Murray, *Revelation*, 68; Boring, *Revelation*, 84.
6. Cf. Krodel, *Revelation*, 97.
7. Charles, *Critical and Exegetical Commentary*, 1:32–33.
8. Beasley-Murray, *Revelation*, 68.

The next occurrence of the word *key* is in the context of the address to the messenger of the church at Thyatira. For the first time the speaker to one of the seven churches identifies himself without using descriptive terms taken from the inaugural vision in Rev 1. Here he describes himself as the holy One, the true One, and the One holding the key of David. The designations "holy" and "true" are used in common with *1 Enoch* 1:3 and 14:1. Also, "the Holy One" was a well-known Jewish title for God.[9] If the word *true* is understood in the sense of "genuine," there may be the intent of refuting those Jews at Philadelphia who would claim that Christ was a false messiah. If the word *true* be taken in the Jewish Scriptures sense of "faithful," the meaning would be that not only was Christ set apart—the root meaning of *hagios*, or "holy"—to carry out the messianic task, but that he could be counted on to carry it out faithfully.[10] The same two designations are applied to God in Rev 6:10. Applying titles to Christ that would normally be applied only to God in the Jewish Scriptures is a repeated pattern in the Apocalypse. As Boring has noted, this pattern is especially true of passages taken from Daniel and Ezekiel.[11]

The reference to the key of David is generally agreed to be derived from Isa 22:22, in which Eliakim, the steward in David's house, is promised the key to that house with undisputed authority to admit or exclude people.[12] Charles also calls attention to the messianic overtones of this passage. Christ now holds the undisputed authority to permit or forbid entrance into the new city of David, the New Jerusalem.[13] Mounce makes the very plausible suggestion that the first recipients of this book would have been reminded of the unbelieving Jews who excommunicated Christian Jews from the synagogue.[14] Although Jewish excommunication could serve to deprive Christians of their legal rights and leave them the horrific choice of denying their Lord or being put to death, these faithful Christians need not fear.[15] Those Jews who thought of themselves as having the authority to include or exclude from the synagogue would find

---

9. Charles, *Critical and Exegetical Commentary*, 1:85.

10. Mounce, *Revelation*, 116.

11. Boring, *Revelation*, 266.

12. So Charles, *Critical and Exegetical Commentary*, 1:86; Beasley-Murray, *Revelation*, 100; Krodel, *Revelation*, 127; Lilje, *Last Book*, 94.

13. Charles, *Critical and Exegetical Commentary*, 1:86; cf. Morris, *Revelation*, 76.

14. Mounce, *Revelation*, 116.

15. Cf. Kiddle, *Revelation*, 49.

themselves excluded from the kingdom of God.[16] Morris also notes this interpretation as the view of "some" commentators but thinks the view expressed by Charles above is more likely.[17] Both Charles and Beasley-Murray note echoes of the keys of death and *hadēs* in 1:18.[18]

The third and final appearance of the word *key* in the arena of God's operation is again reminiscent of the keys of death and *hadēs*. The context is the binding of Satan for a thousand years. In Rev 20:1 an angel comes down from heaven holding the key of the abyss. Mounce argues that this is probably the same angel as the one in 9:1 who opens the shaft of the abyss.[19] This is a difficult argument to accept because the angel in Rev 9 is releasing the forces of evil whereas the angel in Rev 20 is *restraining* the chief of the powers of evil. Morris notes the lack of specific detail regarding this angel and suggests that the ultimate unimportance of Satan may be suggested, in that an unnamed angel rather than God controls him.[20] Kiddle is another commentator who notes the fact that neither God nor Jesus but an "unnamed servant of the throne" casts the dragon into prison.[21] Caird has put the issue in proper perspective in my judgment by saying, "There is all the difference in the world between this fallen angel, to whom **was given the key to the shaft of the abyss** [sic], and the angel of xx. I [sic], whom John sees descending from heaven with the key of the abyss in his hand. . . . The one is an evil agent acting by divine permission—he was given (*edothē*) the key, the other a good agent voluntarily carrying out the beneficent purpose of God."[22]

Two-thirds of the so-called unholy trinity, the beast and the false prophet, have already been consigned to the lake of fire (19:20). Now only the dragon remains to challenge God. The moment to join his colleagues in the lake of fire has not yet arrived. He is only temporarily neutralized before being released to face his final destiny. The abyss in this passage would appear to be the abode of demonic powers, not the place of departed

---

16. Wilson, *Revelation*, 45.

17. Morris, *Revelation*, 76.

18. Charles, *Critical and Exegetical Commentary*, 1:86; Beasley-Murray, *Revelation*, 99–100.

19. Mounce, *Revelation*, 351.

20. Morris, *Revelation*, 228.

21. Kiddle, *Revelation*, 399.

22. Caird, *Commentary on Revelation*, 117–18.

human spirits.[23] Satan is therefore being shut up with his own kind.[24] The idea of the binding of evil powers in a place of temporary punishment is already present in Isa 24:22. A similar notion, the binding of fallen angels, is found in *1 Enoch* 18:12–16. Kiddle notes that the abyss is but a symbol of restraint, "restraint for a purpose."[25] Boring has called attention to the similar motif of the binding of the evil serpent Asi-Dahaka in Iranian religion, which probably predates the passage from Isaiah cited above.[26] Kiddle has noted parallels, though inexact, from Persian and Egyptian eschatology for this account of the capture of the dragon.[27] Whatever may have been the specific source of this image for the author of Revelation, what is significant for the purposes of this study is that the key is used by an angel from heaven to lock up the chief of the powers of evil until the appropriate time for his final disposition. If Wilson be correct at this point, the angel does not act on his own initiative but like Michael (cf. Rev 12:7.), he acts as the agent of the victory of Christ.[28]

The negative use of the word *key* is limited to a single occurrence, Rev 9:1. Here John sees a "star" that had fallen from heaven holding the key to the shaft of the abyss. When the star unlocks the shaft, smoke from the abyss pours out and darkens the sun and the air in a manner reminiscent of Joel 2:10. Out of the smoke comes a huge army of bizarre demonic locusts. These locusts are commanded not to touch green plants and trees—the normal diet of locusts—but instead are given authority to torment people who do not have the seal of God upon their foreheads (Rev 9:2–5).

As one would expect, the fallen star has been interpreted in a variety of ways. One of the more interesting is that of T. F. Torrance, who interprets the fallen star as the Word of God that falls out of heaven; and the bottomless pit as human nature. He then goes on to say, "So terrible are the evils that emerge out of the abyss of the human heart that the Apostle hardly knows how to describe them. At one time he calls them locusts like

---

23. Bauckham, *Climax*, 436.
24. Beasley-Murray, *Revelation*, 285.
25. Kiddle, *Revelation*, 379.
26. Boring, *Revelation*, 201.
27. Kiddle, *Revelation*, 398.
28. Wilson, *Revelation*, 161.

scorpions; at another time he calls them fiery horsemen like serpents."[29] This interpretation may make good preaching, but quite obviously it falls into the category of allegory more than exegesis.

Others have identified the star as none other than Satan himself.[30] Krodel, though conceding that John knew the tradition of the fall of Satan from heaven, does not think he draws on that tradition here.[31] He, along with Charles, Beasley-Murray, Boring, and Court interpret the star as an angel.[32] For Court and Boring the star represents a *fallen* angel. Kiddle concurs in this interpretation and cites as evidence the origin—fallen from heaven—and function of the star.[33] Lilje refers to the star as being "like a fallen angel" and notes its function of releasing the powers of evil.[34] Charles, on the other hand, thinks the word *fallen* means nothing more than descending, and has no reference to the character of the angel.[35] Mounce, like Charles, argues that we are not dealing with an angel of evil character, thinking it more likely that "the star-angel is simply one of the many divine agents who throughout the book of Revelation are pictured as carrying out the will of God."[36] Krodel goes a step beyond Charles and agrees with Mounce in suggesting that this is the same angel as the one who binds Satan in Rev. 20:1.[37] Beasley-Murray argues that even if we are dealing here with an evil angel, he is yet an instrument of the divine will in that he *was given (edothē)*—a divine passive—the key to the shaft of the abyss.[38] In making this statement, Beasley-Murray has made the precise point that establishes this angel as likely belonging to the forces of evil. John uses *edothē*, "it was given," twice as often in the arena of evil as in the arena of good. The reader is referred to Rev 6:2, 4, 8; 9:1, 3, 5; 11:2, 13:5, and 13:7, 14, 15 for usage in the arena of evil; and 6:11, 7:2, 8:3, 11:1, 16:8, 19:8, and 20:4 for the opposite. The star of 9:1 *was given* the key to

---

29. Torrance, *Apocalypse Today*, 75–76.

30. E.g., Robbins, *Revelation*, 123; McDowell, *Meaning and Message*, 104.

31. Krodel, *Revelation*, 201.

32. Ibid.; Charles, *Critical and Exegetical Commentary*, 1:238; Beasley-Murray, *Revelation*, 160; Boring, *Revelation*,136; Court, *Revelation*, 157.

33. Kiddle, *Revelation*, 155.

34. Lilje, *Last Book*, 146.

35. Charles, *Critical and Exegetical Commentary*, 1:239.

36. Mounce, *Revelation*, 192.

37. Krodel, *Revelation*, 201.

38. Beasley-Murray, *Revelation*, 160.

the shaft of the abyss, whereas the angel of 20:1 is seen as *having* the key to the abyss.

In addition to the suggestions mentioned above, a startling variety of interpretations of the star have been advanced. Various interpreters have identified it as Nero, the "angel of the abyss," an evil spirit, Uriel, Apollyon, and even Jesus Christ himself.[39]

Treating the release of evil destructive forces into the world as the will of God creates serious problems, in my judgment. It is one thing to say that God allows evil forces to operate; it is quite another to maintain that he *causes* them to operate. I take the position that the star in the present passage represents either Satan himself or one of the angels who was said to be cast down from heaven along with Satan (Rev 12:9). I agree with Wilson's assessment (who gives credit to Caird): "There is a vast difference between this fallen angel who 'was given' the key of the abyss, and the angel of 20:1, who descends from heaven with this key in his hand as the willing agent of the divine purpose."[40]

The idea of the abyss as a place of intermediate punishment for evil powers has a long tradition. Both Beasley-Murray[41] and Charles[42] cite several passages from *1 Enoch* dealing with the abyss and fallen angels. As noted above, Rev 20:1 does not seem to focus on punishment but only restraint of the dragon, however. The key is in the hands and under the control of the exalted Christ. In the third passage the key is in the hands of an angel coming down from heaven. In these three occurrences the key is in the realm of God's workings. Over against these as a counterimage is set the star fallen from heaven who was given the key to the shaft of the abyss, by which he unleashes manifold demonic powers upon the earth. For the purposes of this study we need only to establish the fact that the abyss harbors a multitude of evil forces that are let loose when the star that had fallen (or descended) from heaven uses his key to unlock the shaft. The key symbolizes the release of these evil forces on humanity.

In summation, we have observed references to the keys of death and Hades, the key of David, the key of the abyss, and the key to the shaft of the abyss. The first two keys are in the hands and under the control of the

---

39. Morris, *Revelation*, 124; cf. Wilson, *Revelation*, 83.
40. Wilson, *Revelation*, 83.
41. Beasley-Murray, *Revelation*, 160.
42. Charles, *Critical and Exegetical Commentary*, 1:238–41.

exalted Christ. In the third instance, the key is in the hands of an angel coming down from heaven. In these three occurrences the key is in the realm of God's workings. Over against these as a counterimage is the star fallen from heaven who was given the key to the shaft of the abyss, a key that allowed him to unleash manifold demonic powers upon the earth.

5

The Mystery

The mystery of the seven stars which you saw upon my right hand and the seven golden lampstands: the seven stars are the messengers of the seven churches and the seven lampstands are the seven churches.

(Rev 1:20)

But in the days of the voice of the seventh angel, whenever he is about to sound (his) trumpet, then the mystery of God is complete, as he announced beforehand to his servants the prophets.

(Rev 10:7)

. . . and upon her forehead a name having been written, a mystery: Babylon the Great, the Mother of the Prostitutes and the Abominations of the Earth. . . . And the angel said to me, Why do you marvel? I will tell you the mystery of the woman and the beast which is carrying her, the one having the seven heads and the ten horns.

(Rev 17:5, 7)

Following the inaugural vision in Rev 1, John has the mystery of the seven stars and the lampstands revealed to him (Rev 1:20). He apparently is using the term *mystery* in a manner very similar to Paul; that is, not as something impossible to understand but rather as something that God must reveal (cf. 1 Cor 15:51, Rom 11:25, Col 1:26–27 and others). Morris refers to the mystery as something that human beings could never decipher but that God makes known. "Here it means that Christ makes known the meaning of certain symbols which we could not have guessed."[1] Instead of the word *mystery*, Kiddle has used "secret purpose."

---

1. Morris, *Revelation*, 56.

He concurs that this secret purpose is beyond human discovery and is being revealed by the exalted Christ.[2]

John is apparently making use of the seven-branched lampstand of Zech 4. He has transformed the one lampstand with seven branches into seven individual lampstands, however, perhaps to facilitate the picture of the exalted Christ moving among the congregations and examining the quality of their witness, as well as offering comfort and hope to the struggling congregations. Another possibility for John's transformation as suggested by Caird is that there are seven lampstands because each local congregation was thought to contain the fullness of the church universal.[3] Each of the addresses to the seven churches bears out the fact that Christ is in fact examining their witness.[4] In accordance with the symbolism of the number seven throughout Revelation, the seven churches symbolize the whole church. Such an interpretation is encountered as early as the late second century C.E.[5]

The interpretation of the lampstands as representing the churches is generally accepted. An occasional commentator will argue that this passage is an allegorizing interpolation or gloss (e.g., Kraft and Malina[6]), but this interpretation has not thus far commanded wide assent. Rowland,[7] Beasley-Murray,[8] Boring,[9] and Charles[10] are but a sampling of commentators who consider the interpretation of the lampstands as the churches to be a legitimate part of the text.

When we turn to the seven stars in the right hand of Christ, however, the scholarly consensus disappears. An almost endless variety of interpretations has been advanced. Beasley-Murray, though pointing out that *angelos* or "angel" in both the Jewish Scriptures and the Christian Testament is sometimes used in reference to human beings, nevertheless argues that the simplest explanation is the one that regards the stars as guardian angels entrusted with the welfare of the congregations.[11] Mounce likewise

---

2. Kiddle, *Revelation*, 16.
3. Cited in Moyise, *Old Testament in Revelation*, 42.
4. Cf. Rowland, *Revelation*, 60.
5. Krodel, *Revelation*, 98; Charles, *Critical and Exegetical Commentary*, 1:25.
6. Cited in Aune, *Revelation 1–5*, 106.
7. Rowland, *Revelation*, 60.
8. Beasley-Murray, *Revelation*, 66.
9. Boring, *Revelation*, 84–85.
10. Charles, *Critical and Exegetical Commentary*, 1:35.
11. Beasley-Murray, *Revelation*, 68–69.

concedes the possibility of *angelos* referring to human beings, and thinks that if so, the *angeloi* should probably be seen as prominent members of the congregations or their emissaries sent to Patmos who were entrusted with the letters.[12] While Krodel does not use the term "guardian angel," he does, like Beasley-Murray, understand the stars as angels. He interprets them in the light of the ancient belief that stars control the fate of human beings.[13] This vision would then constitute an ironic reversal—instead of the stars controlling human fate, the exalted Christ controls the stars.[14] Charles cites unnamed scholars who regard the stars as literal messengers entrusted with delivering the messages to the churches. He then cites Lightfoot, Schoettgen, and Bengel for the interpretation that the stars are subordinate synagogue officials; and Primasius and Volter for the interpretation that the stars are prominent officials in the churches. Then, in a typically dogmatic fashion, he says, "If used at all in Apocalyptic [sic], *angelos* [sic] can only represent a superhuman being."[15] Charles then discusses the possibilities of interpreting the stars as angels. He says they could be guardian angels, based on the idea in Daniel of angelic guardians of the nations. He also cites Sir 17:17 and the LXX of Deut 32:8 as containing the same idea. He further claims—though I personally am not convinced—that in the Christian Testament people are thought to have guardian angels. He finally concludes, "Hence the only remaining interpretation is that which takes these angels to be heavenly doubles or counterparts of the Seven Churches [sic], which thus come to be identical with the churches themselves."[16] Unless I am missing something here, this argument moves in a circle!

Morris concludes after discussing most of the views noted above, "There are difficulties in the way of all views, but perhaps the fewest in that of seeing the angels as the spirits of the churches, standing for and symbolizing the churches."[17] Mounce, after conceding the possibility of the stars being human messengers, cannot quite seem to make up his mind. He points out, as many others have done, that the use of *angelos* in

12. Mounce, *Revelation*, 82.
13. Krodel, *Revelation*, 95.
14. For a thoroughgoing astral interpretation, not only of this vision but of the entire book of Revelation, see Malina, *Genre and Message*.
15. Charles, *Critical and Exegetical Commentary*, 1:34.
16. Ibid.
17. Morris, *Revelation*, 57; see also Wilson, *Revelation*, 25–26.

Revelation favors the interpretation that the messengers are heavenly beings. He goes on to mention the possibility that they are guardian angels or heavenly counterparts of the churches. Finally he says, in words very similar to those of Morris, "The most satisfactory answer, however, is that the angel of the church was a way of personifying the prevailing spirit of the church."[18]

Charles and the other scholars cited above notwithstanding, a significant number of scholars have interpreted the stars as the human leaders of the churches. These include Robbins,[19] Summers,[20] McDowell,[21] Pinn,[22] Hamstra,[23] and Billerback.[24] Enroth is more specific, suggesting that the angel of the community could be its prophet, and that this identification would make John the leader of the prophets working in each community.[25] Beasley-Murray's objection that the letters are concerned with the churches themselves and not just their leaders betrays a Westernized way of thinking that does not take into account the Hebrew notion of community and corporate personality. Separating the leaders from the congregations would have been unthinkable to a person from a Hebrew background.

In my judgment, interpreting the angels either as heavenly counterparts to the churches or as guardian angels faces a virtually insurmountable difficulty. John is instructed to send what he writes to the seven churches (Rev 1:11). Each letter is addressed to the *angel* of that particular church. How does one send a written communication to a guardian angel presumably residing in heaven, or to the heavenly counterpart of the churches, and get the message to the churches themselves? I think the circularity of Charles's argument cited above, and Mounce's hesitancy to take a stand, strongly reflect this difficulty. The least difficult interpretation may after all be the one that sees the angels as human leaders, thought of as inseparable from the churches themselves.

I am well aware of the argument that apart from the addresses to the churches, the word *angelos* in the Apocalypse always refers to a superhu-

18. Mounce, *Revelation*, 82.
19. Robbins, *Revelation*, 49.
20. Summers, *Worthy Is the Lamb*, 108.
21. McDowell, *Meaning and Message*, 31.
22. Pinn, *Revelation Today*, 31–32.
23. Hamstra in Pate, *Four Views*, 102.
24. Cited in Beasley-Murray, *Revelation*, 69.
25. Enroth, "Hearing Formula," 604.

man being—but who would dare claim that this writer could not have used a term in more than one way? Furthermore, has this argument been examined carefully enough? In Rev 22:16 we read, "I, Jesus, sent my *angelos* to bear witness to you (concerning) these things." Two verses later we read, "I (emphatic) am bearing witness to everyone hearing the words of the prophecy of this book." While I readily concede the difficulty of knowing who the speaker is in Rev 22:10–22, this passage *could* be read as designating John the *angelos*. Readily conceding that mine is a minority position, I still maintain that the angels are the human leaders of the churches.

To return to the word *mystery*, which is the focal term for the purposes of this study, the primary meaning appears to be a revelation from God given to the churches. Bornkamm describes mystery in apocalyptic as "God's counsels destined finally to be disclosed."[26] God has willed the final and complete destruction of evil; and although all the details have not yet been worked out, God has revealed the substance of that destruction to his prophets.[27] This revelation defies all appearances of the circumstances of the struggling Christian congregations. The fate of the churches is neither "written in the stars" nor is it controlled by the seemingly invincible power of Rome. Christ is very near to the churches, and he holds their leaders in the hand of his power—the right hand. He, not Rome or any other self-deifying human power, controls the destiny of the people of God.

The next appearance of the word *mystery* in the arena of God's workings is the point at which the seventh angel is about to blow his trumpet (Rev 10:7). The last three trumpets are also said to be three woes to come upon the "dwellers upon the earth" (Rev. 8:13). Just prior to the vision of the seventh trumpet, John sees an angel standing with one foot on the land and the other on the sea lift his right hand and swear that there will be no more delay (*chronos*) [Rev 10:5–6]. As Krodel points out, the oath seems to be modeled on the angel of Dan 12:4–9, who swore that it would be for "a time, two times, and half a time" until the end, when the oppression of God's people would cease.[28] Now, in the Seer's mind, there is not to be even that brief delay. John is then told that with the sounding of the seventh trumpet, the mystery of God is to be completed (Rev 10:7). This

26. Cited in Mounce, *Revelation*, 212.
27. Mounce, *Revelation*, 213.
28. Krodel, *Revelation*, 214.

verse presents more than one difficulty of interpretation. As Charles has pointed out, if the verb *mellō* be taken in its usual sense, then the mystery of God is said to be completed before the sounding of the seventh trumpet.[29] (For Charles this is actually the third trumpet, since he considers the first four to be interpolations by the "unintelligent editor."[30])

Another difficulty of interpretation is the simple fact that the seventh trumpet is followed by a series of unnumbered visions and then the seven vials before we finally get the announcement of the completion of God's judgment (Rev 16:17). Perhaps the simplest approach is to regard the seven seals as a transition into the vision of the seven trumpets that in turn leads into the vision of the seven vials. To put the matter in a different way, we might visualize the seventh seal as containing within itself the seven trumpets and the seventh trumpet as containing within itself the seven vials.[31]

Charles is probably correct when he says that we should abandon the usual sense of *mellō* and interpret Rev 10:7 as meaning that the mystery of God is completed after or with the sounding of the seventh trumpet because the Greek preposition *meta* can mean either "after" or "with."[32] Now comes the significant question: What is this mystery of God? Charles cites Bousset as linking it with the casting down of Satan from Heaven (Rev 12:8–9); and Vischer, Volter, and Holtzmann as linking it to the birth of the Messiah. He then says that the first view is inadequate and the second impossible.[33] He finally concludes that the mystery is the whole purpose of God toward the world.[34] Wilson accepts this definition and adds the detail that this mystery was once kept secret but is now being revealed.[35] In a similar vein Krodel writes, "The mystery of God is not identified with mysterious calculations or reading heavenly tables or scrolls about the end. It is the revelation of Jesus Christ (1:1) in judgment and in salvation."[36] Beasley-Murray takes essentially the same position, saying, "*The mystery of God* [sic] is not to be limited to the appearance of the Antichrist

---

29. Charles, *Critical and Exegetical Commentary*, 1:264–65.
30. Ibid., 1:218–23; 2:238, 264.
31. So Torrance, *Apocalypse Today*, 125.
32. Charles, *Critical and Exegetical Commentary*, 1:264–65.
33. Ibid., 1:265.
34. Ibid.
35. Wilson, *Revelation*, 91.
36. Krodel, *Revelation*, 214.

[sic] and the beginning of tribulation, as Charles inferred from chapters 10 and 13. Rather it is the completion of God's purpose in creation, and in the history of man in particular, which is to be fulfilled when the seventh angel sounds his trumpet."[37] I am not quite sure what Beasley-Murray read in Charles. Here are the latter's exact words on the issue: "*to mysterion tou theou* [sic] ("the mystery of God") in our text embraces the whole purpose of God in history. The manifestation of evil in the Antichrist [sic] is only a part of this all-embracing purpose, which issues in the complete triumph and manifestation of goodness."[38] Bauckham espouses essentially the same position, stating that the mystery is the secret purpose of God for the coming of his kingdom.[39]

The statement in v. 6 that there will be no more delay presents another difficulty for interpreting this passage. To begin with, does it mean that there will be no more delay before the seventh trumpet sounds? Or that there will be no more delay in the execution of God's purpose for the world? Bauckham takes the position that the delay refers not to the trumpet but to the beginning of the final period of history before the kingdom of God is accomplished.[40] Charles takes a similar position, referring the delay to the coming of the Antichrist [sic], which is a prelude to the coming kingdom of God.[41] Kiddle treats the delay as conditional, dependent on the completing of the number of the martyrs.[42]

A second question that insinuates itself into the discussion is whether the idea of delay exhausts the meaning of *chronos* here. Rowland is very emphatic in saying, "It is unlikely that the message proclaims an end of time."[43] In a more dogmatic fashion Beasley-Murray writes: "There is no question of time being suspended to give way to an eternal and timeless order, but rather an end being made to the all but intolerable waiting for the fulfillment of the divine promise."[44] Morris also strongly advocates the meaning "delay" instead of "time."[45] Torrance offers the interesting

37. Beasley-Murray, *Revelation*, 174.
38. Charles, *Critical and Exegetical Commentary*, 1:266, n.
39. Bauckham, *Climax*, 261; cf. Morris, *Revelation*, 37.
40. Ibid., 260–61.
41. Charles, *Critical and Exegetical Commentary*, 1:263.
42. Kiddle, *Revelation*, 172–73.
43. Rowland, *Revelation*, 97.
44. Beasley-Murray, *Revelation*, 173.
45. Morris, *Revelation*, 137.

interpretation that God suspended time between the sixth and seventh trumpets. He then goes on to say, "Because time is suspended no man can calculate the arrival of the fateful moment."[46] While I readily concede that most commentators stress the idea of delay here, a double meaning would not be unusual in this writing, to say the least. I am not convinced that a late first-century congregation, hearing the word *chronos* read, would not have thought of the cessation of time as well as delay in the execution of God's purpose.

The last phrase of v. 7 requires a brief comment. Most commentators detect overtones of Amos's statement that God does nothing without revealing his secret to his servants the prophets (Amos 3:7). Krodel briefly mentions this passage, then goes on to say that while John never explicitly referred to himself as a prophet, he saw himself in continuity with both the prophets of the Hebrew Scriptures and the Christian prophets who preceded him.[47] Charles on the other hand argues that only Christian prophets contemporary with John are in view because the prophets of the Hebrew Scriptures dealt only slightly or not at all with most of the problems that concern the Seer.[48] This argument is rather weak, in my judgment. Regardless of the specific issues that concerned the prophets of the Jewish Scriptures, both they and the Seer were in the business of proclaiming God's purposes for humanity. I agree with Mounce at this point that there is no reason to identify the term *prophet* with either the prophets of the Hebrew Scriptures or those of the Christian Testament.[49] Morris appears to concur with this judgment, suggesting, "We should probably understand prophets here to mean the New Testament prophets as well as the great prophets of the Old Testament."[50]

Bauckham, after mentioning the passage from Amos, points to a significant difference between Amos and the Seer: "Unlike Amos, Revelation does not say that God revealed (*galah*) his secret to his servants the prophets, but that he announced (*euangelisen*) it. This makes it clear that

---

46. Torrance, *Apocalypse Today*, 82.
47. Krodel, *Revelation*, 215.
48. Charles, *Critical and Exegetical Commentary*, 1:266.
49. Mounce, *Revelation*, 213.
50. Morris, *Revelation*, 137.

to the prophets themselves it remained a secret, while also suggesting its character as the good news of the coming of God's kingdom."[51]

In summation, if the word *mystery* refers to the complete purpose of God in bringing about his kingdom, then it may be seen as complementary and supplemental to the earlier use of the term in Rev 1:20. There the mystery concerned God's dealings with the churches. Now it is broadened to include God's dealings with all of humanity and in fact, the entire cosmos.

When we turn our attention to the usage of the word *mystery* in the arena of the operation of evil, we find the word used twice, with both instances having the same referent (Rev 17:5, 7). The context is the judgment pronounced against the "great prostitute," Babylon or Rome. Commentators are generally agreed that Babylon is a cipher for Rome.[52] Beasley-Murray speaks of Babylon as the "anti-Christian city," but seems to have Rome in mind as well.[53] Rowland offers a more satisfactory explanation in my judgment. He concedes that the city of Rome was the immediate inspiration for the Seer, but that "The image can be of universal application because of the description of the city as Babylon, a symbol of military power and oppression . . . it also was the place of exile and alienation (Ps 137 & I Peter 5:13) where the people of God do not feel at home and are always exiles."[54] In similar fashion Boring writes, "It is arrogant human empire as such that is condemned, not just its embodiment in Rome in John's time."[55]

As is his custom, the Seer draws his symbolism from the Jewish Scriptures in depicting Rome as the great prostitute. As Charles notes, the term is applied to Nineveh in Nah 3:4 and to Tyre in Isa 23:16–17.[56] Reference to the prostitute as sitting upon many waters appears to be derived from Jer 51 (LXX 28):13. This is a detail that literally described historical Babylon but does not fit Rome. Hence (possibly) the further explanation that the "waters" upon which the prostitute sits are "peoples

---

51. Bauckham, *Climax*, 261; cf. 1 Pet 1:10–12 for the notion that the message of God spoken by the prophets of the Jewish Scriptures likewise remained a mystery to them.

52. So Charles, *Critical and Exegetical Commentary*, 2:65; Garrow, *Revelation*, 97; Boring, *Revelation*, 185; Bauckham, *Climax*, 343; Court, *Revelation*, 64, 101; Krodel, *Revelation*, 292; Wilson, *Revelation*, 139.

53. Beasley-Murray, *Revelation*, 252.

54. Rowland, *Revelation*, 129.

55. Boring, *Revelation*, 184; cf. Stagg, "Interpreting Revelation," 340.

56. Charles, *Critical and Exegetical Commentary*, 2:62; cf. Kiddle, *Revelation*, 343.

and multitudes and nations and tongues" (Rev 7:15).[57] Rowland makes the apt comment that the reference to sitting upon many waters also alludes to the inherent instability of the prostitute and the beast on which she sits.[58] Charles makes the further comment that in the depiction of the prostitute we have an indirect contrast to the woman clothed with the sun in Rev 12.[59] This woman will be discussed more fully at a later stage in this study.

The prostitute is depicted as having her name written on her forehead in the style of typical Roman prostitutes.[60] The name of the prostitute is preceded by the word *mystery*. Her name is then given as "Babylon the Great, the Mother of Prostitutes and Abominations of the Earth" (Rev 17:5). Krodel connects the phrase "mother of prostitutes" with the imperial cult that spread from Rome throughout the empire. He further makes the interesting though unsupported statement that some believed the name of the goddess Roma should be spelled backwards to make it convey the idea of *amor* (*amour*).[61] Charles interprets "mother of prostitutes" as a reference to both harlotry and to the world's idolatries.[62] Lilje takes a similar approach, arguing for a metaphorical use of adultery as "a symbol of the undisciplined character of the world-power."[63] Beasley-Murray writes, "What ancient Babylon was to the world of its day so the city represented by the woman is to John's day, the cause of earth's apostasy from God and devotion to devilish ways."[64]

The woman is also described as being drunk with the blood of saints and the witnesses of Jesus (v. 6). This detail may be both backward- and forward-looking. It is unlikely that a first-century audience would fail to remember the bloody persecution of Nero after the great fire of Rome in 64 C.E. Mounce aptly points out that, though that specific persecution

---

57. Cf. Charles, *Critical and Exegetical Commentary*, 2:62–63.
58. Rowland, *Revelation*, 17.
59. Charles, *Critical and Exegetical Commentary*, 2:64.
60. So Beasley-Murray, *Revelation*, 253; Krodel, *Revelation*, 293; Mounce, *Revelation*, 310; Wilson, *Revelation*, 139; Lilje, *Last Book*, 222–23—although some recent commentators have questioned whether there is any solid historical evidence to support this custom.
61. Krodel, *Revelation*, 293–94.
62. Charles, *Critical and Exegetical Commentary*, 2:65.
63. Lilje, *Last Book*, 222.
64. Beasley-Murray, *Revelation*, 253; cf. also Mounce, *Revelation*, 310.

may have been in the back of John's mind, the picture of the harlot was also intended to depict persecution at the end of the age.[65]

As John contemplated the external splendor of the prostitute he said, "I marveled a great marvel when I saw her (Rev 17:6)." Porter suggests translating *ethaumasa*, "I marveled," here as meaning something like "I was appalled."[66] Boesak suggests that it refers to ". . . the devastation of mind and feeling one experiences when confronted with the *mysterium iniquitatis*."[67] Ruiz seems to interpret John's marveling as something like admiration and says that John should have known better.[68] Whether there is any way of interpreting John's attitude and feelings at this point must be considered doubtful, in my judgment, although the suggestions of Porter, Wilson, and Boesak are admittedly appealing.

The next development is that the interpreting angel volunteers to tell John the mystery of both the woman and the beast upon which she sat (Rev 17:7). As Morris notes, to know one is to know the other—they are inseparable.[69] The woman is the great city who rules over the kings of the earth (Rev 17:18). Kiddle seems to have missed this point and has interpreted the woman as the empire rather than the city.[70] As for the beast, the reference to his having seven heads and ten horns (possibly intended to symbolize complete knowledge and humanly complete power) establishes his identity with the beast from the sea (13:1) and his link with the dragon (12:3). The heads are then interpreted in an allegorical fashion as seven mountains on which the woman sits and also as seven kings; and the ten horns as ten kings who have not yet received a kingdom, but who are destined to receive authority as kings from the beast (*meta tou theriou*) for one hour (17:12). The beast is also described as one "who was, and is not, and is about to come up out of the abyss (17:8)," a rather obvious parody of the God ". . . who is, who was, and who will come". . . . (1:8 and elsewhere).[71]

---

65. Mounce, *Revelation*, 310–11.
66. Porter, "Language of the Apocalypse," 585.
67. Boesak, *Comfort and Protest*, 121.
68. Ruiz, *Ezekiel in the Apocalypse*, 340.
69. Morris, *Revelation*, 202.
70. Kiddle, *Revelation*, 345.
71. This parody will be discussed more fully in Part II of this study.

Revelation 17 is a veritable minefield of exegetical difficulties that I will not attempt to negotiate at this point. My primary focus is on the word *mystery* in the context of 17:5, 7. The mystery is an open secret as to the nature and destiny of the "great prostitute" and the beast. As Mounce and Morris have noted, we have here a single mystery—neither the beast nor the woman can be understood apart from the other.[72] In the immediate situation of the late first century c.e., these represented the city of Rome and the Roman Empire as a whole. Outside that context they may represent the nation and capital city of any self-deifying human nation. Other examples one might cite would include Mussolini's Italy, Hitler's Germany, or Stalin's Russia.

The Seer depicts the destiny of the beast with the simple statement that the "ten horns" will make war with the Lamb, and the Lamb will overcome them because he is "Lord of lords and King of kings" (17:14). Strangely enough, the ten horns and the beast will also turn on the prostitute, will make her desolate, and will eat her flesh and burn her with fire (17:16). This is one of several images by which the Seer conveys the idea that evil is ultimately self-destructive. As Goldsworthy has expressed it, "Then the logic of evil emerges again as the beast wars against the harlot (17:16–17). Evil cannot preserve order but only consume it. It is the judgment of God which condemns evil to self-destruction."[73]

In summary, we have examined one passage in which *mystery* refers to the open secret of the lampstands as the churches, and the stars as the angels of those churches. In the next passage (10:7), the mystery is the open secret of the completion of God's purpose. In the third and fourth passages (17:5, 7), the mystery is the revelation of the great prostitute and the beast supporting her as the capital city of an ungodly empire and the empire itself, respectively. While one could argue that these latter passages also belong in the realm of God's activities, since ultimately they reflect God's judgment upon the prostitute and the beast, I am looking at them from the standpoint of the content of the word *mystery*. From this standpoint the first two usages of the term are positive, while the last two are negative and therefore qualify as counterimages.

---

72. Mounce, *Revelation*, 312; Morris, *Revelation*, 202.
73. Goldsworthy, *Gospel in Revelation*, 122.

6

The Crown

Do not go on fearing what things you are about to suffer. Look, the devil is about to cast (some) of you into prison in order that you might be tested; and you will have tribulation lasting ten days. Become faithful (even) unto the point of death, and I will give to you the crown of life.

(Rev 2:10)

I am coming quickly; keep holding on to what you have so that no one may take your crown.

(Rev 3:11)

And around the throne (were) twenty-four thrones, and sitting upon the thrones (were) twenty-four elders who had been clothed with white garments; and golden crowns (were) upon their heads. . . .
The twenty-four elders fell before the One sitting upon the throne and they worshiped the One living forever and ever, and they cast their crowns before the throne, saying . . .

(Rev 4:4, 10)

And a great sign appeared in Heaven; a woman who had been clothed with the sun, with the moon underneath her feet, and a crown of twelve stars upon her head.

(Rev 12:1)

And I looked, and behold a white cloud (appeared), and One like a son of man (was) sitting upon the cloud, having upon his head a golden crown and in his hand a sharp sickle.

(Rev 14:14)

> *And I looked, and behold a white horse (appeared) with the one sitting upon it holding a bow; and a crown was given to him, and he went out conquering and in order that he might conquer (more).*
>
> (Rev 6:2)
>
> *And the appearances of the locusts (was) like horses having been prepared for battle, with something resembling golden crowns upon their heads, and with faces like the faces of men.*
>
> (Rev 9:7)

WE FIRST ENCOUNTER THE word *crown* in Revelation in the address to the church at Smyrna. This church is commended for being poor, yet rich; and for living with the blasphemy of those claiming to be Jews but who are in reality the synagogue of Satan (Rev 2:9). This commendation is followed by an admonition not to be fearful of the things these believers are about to suffer. The Devil will cast some of them into prison. They will have tribulation for a brief but limited time ("ten days").[1] Kiddle compares this expression to our common phrase "a week or so."[2] Summers, on the other hand, takes the position that the number ten symbolizes completeness, and therefore the meaning is extreme or complete tribulation.[3] Morris cites Niles as saying that the tribulation would not last long but that endurance would be tested to the limit. Faithfulness even to the point of death will be rewarded by a crown of life (Rev 2:10).[4]

The first phrase of v. 10 literally says, "Do not go on fearing what you are about to suffer" (*medēn* plus present infinitive). As Krodel remarks, such an admonition ". . . is sheer madness unless faith in the God who raised Christ from the dead opens up a new vision of truth and reality."[5] After all, the Devil, probably in the form of the Roman authorities, was about to cast some of the church members into prison and were probably using Jewish slander to do so.[6] For the Seer, the Jews had forfeited the right to the title by refusing to acknowledge Jesus as Messiah and had thereby

---

1. So McDowell, *Meaning and Message*, 47; cf. Morris, *Revelation*, 64; Aune, *Revelation 1–5*, 166; Beale, *Book of Revelation*, 242–43; Sweet, *Revelation*, 86.
2. Kiddle, *Revelation*, 28.
3. Summers, *Worthy Is the Lamb*, 113.
4. Morris, *Revelation*, 64.
5. Krodel, *Revelation*, 112–13.
6. So Krodel, *Revelation*, 112; cf. Boring, *Revelation*, 92.

become the synagogue of Satan. The probability that the synagogue had expelled many of the Christians is rather high (cf. John 9:22, 34.). Once outside the synagogue, the Christians were members of a *religio illicita*, or illegal religion, and thus open to persecution by the Roman state. This situation was shaping up into a severe testing of anyone's Christian faith. Although the tribulation would last only for a brief time, it quite probably would be very severe.

The word *thlipsis*, "tribulation," comes from a verb meaning most literally "to compress," or to apply external pressure to someone or some thing.[7] As Sleeper and others have noted, *thlipsis* can have a variety of meanings.[8] The tribulation of which John spoke was not some spectacular event in the future but oppression that was already a reality at the time he wrote.[9] Probably he viewed the escalation from simple harassment of a despised minority into active persecution as a signal that the end was near. Quite possibly this was the reason for his belief that the tribulation would last for "ten days." There are at least two possibilities as to the source of this specific designation. The first is the trial of Daniel and his friends (Dan 1:8–15), who asked to be given vegetables and water instead of the delicacies from the king's table as a test to see whether they would be in as good condition as their fellow Israelite captives who ate from the king's table.[10] The other obvious possibility appears in the story of Isaac when he was trying to persuade Bethuel and Laban to allow him to return home with his wife Rebekah. Laban and his mother asked Jacob to delay his journey for perhaps ten days (Gen 24:55). The latter text, and possibly the former, would support the meaning of "ten days" as being a brief but limited time.

The specific use of the word *crown* appears in an exhortation to faithfulness even to the point of death, and the promise of the crown of life for those who are thus faithful. Much has been said on the subject of persecution at the time Revelation was written. Relying upon Eusebius of Caesarea, many commentaries have taken the position that Domitian (r. 81–96 C.E.) viciously persecuted Christians. More recent commentators have become increasingly skeptical on this issue. Moyise, for example, has

7. Cf. Pinn, *Revelation Today*, 110.
8. Sleeper, *Victorious Christ*, 120.
9. Boring, *Revelation*, 91.
10. Dan 1:12–14; cf. Morris, *Revelation*, 64; Sweet, *Revelation*, 86; Beale, *Book of Revelation*, 242; Aune, *Revelation 1–5*, 166; and others.

thoroughly examined the evidence of Eusebius and has rather conclusively shown that that evidence is "deeply ambiguous" at best.[11] Krodel is another recent commentator who has argued that Revelation contains no real evidence of any widespread persecution. He further argues that Tacitus, Suetonius, and Dio Chrysostom, all of whom have been cited in support of a Domitianic persecution, were strongly biased against Domitian because of the treatment they had received from him.[12] This view has come to be accepted by a number of modern commentators.[13] Adela Yarbro Collins is probably on the right track in suggesting that we should think in terms of *perceived* rather than actual persecution.[14] What a minority group such as the churches of Revelation perceived may be very far from an objective appraisal of the situation. As long as persecution was perceived, however, John's readers had to be challenged to remain faithful unto death. The promised crown of life, as Krodel has noted, has value only as a symbol of victory. It was used to honor winners of athletic contests and benefactors of cities, among other things. Krodel goes on to say that the crown symbolizes the gift of final salvation.[15] Morris notes that the *stephanos* ("crown") of victory would have been especially significant to the residents of Smyrna because of its famous games.[16] If the phrase "of life" is treated epexegetically it yields the meaning, "the crown that is life," and supports Krodel's interpretation.[17] I believe that interpretation is also in harmony with the Seer's intention at this point. Faithful endurance means bestowal of the gift of life (cf. Rev 2:7).

The word *crown* appears next in the address to the church at Philadelphia (3:11). Are we dealing with the same crown as in 2:10? Krodel thinks not. He argues that the crown here represents the redemption already received, whereas in 2:10 the crown is in the future.[18] McDowell, in similar fashion, says, "In the case of Philadelphia the crown is won and in possession of the faithful. In the case of Smyrna the crown is yet to be

---

11. Moyise, *Old Testament in Revelation*, 49.
12. Krodel, *Revelation*, 36–37.
13. Cf. Barr, *New Testament Story*, 408.
14. A. Collins, *Cosmology and Eschatology*, 165; see also Thompson, *Apocalypse and Empire*, 237, n. 10; McDowell, *Meaning and Message*, 59.
15. Krodel, *Revelation*, 113.
16. Morris, *Revelation*, 64–65; cf. Lilje, *Last Book*, 76.
17. Cf. Morris, *Revelation*, 65.
18. Krodel, *Revelation*, 139.

won."[19] Kiddle takes a both/and position at this point. He notes that John speaks of the crown as already possessed by the faithful at Philadelphia, whereas at Smyrna the crown is yet to be won. He then concludes, "In a sense John clearly thinks of both ideas as being true."[20] Both McDowell and Krodel would seem to agree that the crown represents life, either now or in the future. The admonition to the church at Philadelphia to hold fast is echoed throughout the addresses to the churches, combined with the warning, "Behold, I am coming quickly." Morris rightly points out that no one could take their crown from them, but they could forfeit it, as Esau, Reuben, and Saul forfeited their places to Jacob, Judah, and David respectively.[21]

Wilson argues that the advent of Christ in this passage is not his final coming in glory but rather his coming to give succor to his struggling and oppressed people; and that it is also a warning of judgment.[22] A similar warning shows up in 2:16: "I will come like a thief." The threat of Christ's coming to remove the "lampstand" that appears in 2:5 is another reference to Christ's entry into the historical situation rather than his eschatological coming.

We meet the crown symbolism next in connection with the twenty-four elders who surround the throne of God (Rev 4:4, 10). As Charles points out, these elders have been variously interpreted as glorified men, a college of angels, angelic representatives of the twenty-four priestly orders, and angelic representatives of the entire body of the faithful.[23] Beasley-Murray opts for the interpretation that they are related to the twenty-four priestly and twenty-four Levitical orders.[24] Wilson, after noting that "many" commentators interpret the elders as the church in its totality, argues that they are angelic princes who exercise priestly functions and are ". . . the heavenly counterparts of the twenty-four priestly orders in 1 Chronicles 24:9–19."[25] Kiddle strongly argues that their origin was ultimately the twenty-four star-gods worshiped in Babylon who were altered to angels by later apocalyptic writers because of monotheistic as-

---

19. McDowell, *Meaning and Message*, 61.
20. Kiddle, *Revelation*, 52–53.
21. Morris, *Revelation*, 79; cf. Kiddle, *Revelation*, 53.
22. Wilson, *Revelation*, 46–47.
23. Charles, *Critical and Exegetical Commentary*, 1:129.
24. Beasley-Murray, *Revelation*, 114.
25. Wilson, *Revelation*, 55.

sumptions.²⁶ Krodel interprets the elders as angelic counterparts of the patriarchs and apostles representing the true people of God.²⁷ McDowell, followed by Robbins, suggests that they represent the twelve patriarchs of the Old Testament and the twelve apostles, i.e. the combined people of God of the Hebrew Scriptures and the Christian Testament.²⁸ Mounce argues against this position, claiming that the song of the elders in Rev 5:9–10 definitely sets them apart from those purchased from every tribe and tongue and people and nation, although the logic of this argument escapes me.²⁹ Why could not the elders be included in this song?

Fortunately this study does not require a solution to the problem of the identity of the elders. Whomever they represent—though I personally understand them as designating the complete people of God—the crowns they wear are clearly a sign of royalty, of sharing in the sovereign reign of God. The fact that the elders cast them down before the throne (v. 10) probably implies that the crowns are God's gift and therefore should be returned to God. The elders have no sovereignty of their own but only that derived from God.³⁰

We next encounter the positive use of the crown symbol in relation to the "woman" who gives birth to a male child (Rev 12:1). She is referred to as a great *sēmeion*, or "sign." As Morris noted, this word is used in the Fourth Gospel to refer to Jesus's miracles, but here the meaning seems to be more along the lines of a significant person rather than an act. Morris also notes that the word translated as "heaven" in this passage should probably read "sky."³¹ The Greek word *ouranos* may mean either, and is used in both senses numerous times in the Christian Testament. The woman is wearing a crown of twelve stars. Charles claims that the original author of Rev 12 could not have been a Christian or a Jew because the mythological features "could not have been the original creations of a Jew or a Christian."³² Lilje seems to accept the mythological interpretation of the woman by designating her the "Queen of heaven."³³ Beasley-Murray

26. Kiddle, *Revelation*, 84.
27. Krodel, *Revelation*, 155.
28. McDowell, *Meaning and Message*, 76; Robbins, *Revelation*, 86.
29. Mounce, *Revelation*, 135.
30. Wilson, *Revelation*, 56; cf. Morris, *Revelation*, 90; Kiddle, *Revelation*, 84.
31. Morris, *Revelation*, 152.
32. Charles, *Critical and Exegetical Commentary*, 1:299–300.
33. Lilje, *Last Book*, 170.

suggests that the woman was originally an astral figure, and the crown of twelve stars would have represented the twelve signs of the zodiac.[34] Wilson suggests that the description simply represents the dignity of her position.[35]

Both Beasley-Murray and Charles may have too quickly resorted to ancient mythology for their explanations. The resemblance to Joseph's dream in which the sun, moon, and eleven stars bow down to him (Gen 37:9) can scarcely be accidental. Transparently this dream referred to his father, mother, and eleven brothers, as the next verse makes clear. How could anyone familiar with the Jewish Scriptures fail to think of this woman as Israel? Morris is one who connects this scene with Joseph's dream and argues, "In view of this Old Testament [sic] *symbolism* it is unnecessary to see a reference to pagan mythology."[36] Furthermore, the symbolism of Israel as a woman in travail about to give birth is commonplace in the Jewish Scriptures (e.g. Isa 26:17, 66:7–8; Mic 4:10). As Krodel and McDowell point out, this woman represents the true Israel from whom the Messiah came.[37] In similar fashion Smalley argues that the woman is the messianic community.[38]

We must be careful not to make our interpretation so limited that it cannot be applied to all that is said about the woman. As Boring suggests, "The woman is not Mary, nor Israel, nor the church but less and more than all of these."[39] She is the true people of God, including Mary who gave birth to the Messiah.[40] Her crowns remind us, among other things, of God's promise of a people who would be a kingdom of priests (Exod 19:6).

One passage in which *crown* is used in the arena of God's operation remains to be considered. In Rev 14:14, "One like a son of man" appears on a cloud, having a golden crown upon his head and a sharp sickle in his hand. The allusion to Dan 7:13 can scarcely be missed. Krodel and McDowell interpret the One like a son of man as Jesus Christ.[41] Wilson

---

34. Beasley-Murray, *Revelation*, 197.
35. Wilson, *Revelation*, 103.
36. Morris, *Revelation*, 152.
37. Krodel, *Revelation*, 238; McDowell, *Meaning and Message*, 130.
38. Smalley, "John's Revelation," 556.
39. Boring, *Revelation*, 152.
40. Cf. Boesak, *Comfort and Protest*, 79; Moyise, *Old Testament in Revelation*, 88.
41. Krodel, *Revelation*, 274; McDowell, *Meaning and Message*, 150; cf. Lilje, *Last Book*, 205–6.

also supports this interpretation and quotes Beckwith's statement, "The figure is comprehensive, including in a word the whole process of the winding up of the ages, and the recompense of both the good and the bad."[42]

Others interpret the figure as an angel, based on the phrase *allos angelos* in 14:17. Aune gives an extensive listing of reasons for suggesting this interpretation.[43] Among the most frequently raised arguments is that the figure on the cloud is here given a command by an angel, and that Christ would not be portrayed as taking orders from angels. Morris argues this point extensively, concluding, "It is best to think of the holder of the sickle as an angel, albeit an important one."[44] Kiddle, though admitting that Christ appears in the guise of "One like a son of man" in Rev 1, nevertheless argues that the figure here is an angel, and that the only harvest in view is that of the wicked.[45] As I have pointed out elsewhere, there is support in the Gospel tradition for both Jesus and angels as "reapers" at the end of the age. Boring has probably steered us in the right direction here by saying, "We do not have to decide whether or not this figure is Christ. John's evocative language conjures up associations of Daniel 7, of Jesus's words about the coming judgment in the Gospel tradition, and of the vision of Christ in 1:12–16."[46] Charles, after noting that in Dan 13 the "one like a son of man" is a collective figure designating righteous Israelites, points out that in *1 Enoch* 37–71 the figure has been individualized as the Messiah. He concludes that this usage paved the way for the title Son of Man as it was applied to Jesus.[47] The golden crown, therefore, would symbolize the sovereignty of the resurrected Christ in his function as judge.

The first appearance of the crown in the arena of evil forces comes with the vision of the rider on a white horse in Rev 6:2. That he is not, as his color would suggest, the exalted Christ must now be demonstrated. I previously referred to him as a counterfeit and an imposter. The reasons for this assessment are as follows: first, he is in the company of horsemen

---

42. Wilson, *Revelation*, 123.
43. Aune, *Revelation 6–16*, 839–42.
44. Morris, *Revelation*, 178–79.
45. Kiddle, *Revelation*, 285–89.
46. Boring, *Revelation*, 170.
47. Charles, *Critical and Exegetical Commentary*, 2:20.

who bring bloodshed, famine and death,[48] and the Seer in his visions of judgment (the seals, trumpets and vials) always ties the meaning of the first four in each series together. Second, this rider's weapon is a bow—a weapon never associated with Christ. Third, a crown "was given" (*edothē*) to him. Nowhere else in the Apocalypse is this verb used with reference to Christ. It is, on the other hand, used with some regularity in reference to the forces of evil (Rev 6:4, 8; 9:1, 3, 5; 11:2; 13:5, 7, 14–15). It is also used of heavenly martyrs (Rev 6:11), of angels (Rev 7:2, 8:3), of the Seer himself (Rev 11:1), of the sun (Rev 16:8), of the bride of the Lamb (Rev 19:8), and of reigning martyrs (Rev 20:4)—but never of Christ. Fourth, Christ is the one opening the seals, and even in an apocalyptic writing, having him both opening the seals and riding out as the first horseman is more than a little awkward. In Wilson's words, ". . . the Lamb who opens the seal cannot be expected to reappear as the rider thus sent forth."[49]

Fifth, he rides out at the command of one of the "four living creatures." Presenting Christ as under the command of one of these creatures places him in a position unparalleled in the Apocalypse—or of any other writing in the Christian Testament, for that matter. This rider on the white horse is the counterimage of the rider on a white horse in Rev 19:11-21. Court suggests that the term *parody* does justice to the relationship between the horsemen of 6:2 and 19:11-21. He later speaks of a "polemical parallelism" intentionally devised by John between the first horseman of Rev 6 and the exalted Christ on the white horse in Rev 19.[50] Morris notes the "surprising number" of commentators who have failed to recognize this fact, and have identified this horseman with the one in 19:11; and rightly concludes that about all these riders have in common is the color of the horses.[51] Lilje argues strongly that we must on no account confuse this rider with the one in 19:11–21, as is often done by devotional commentaries on this passage.[52] This tendency is by no means limited to devotional works. Oman, for example, goes so far as to transpose Rev 6:2 to a location following the rider on the white horse in 19:11–21 in his

---

48. Cf. Morris, *Revelation*, 102.
49. Wilson, *Revelation*, 65.
50. Court, *Revelation*, 62–63, 157.
51. Morris, *Revelation*, 101.
52. Lilje, *Last Book*, 125.

eagerness to identify the two riders.[53] Kiddle notes that in both cases the white horse is symbolic of victory, "But Christ is to win the final victory, over all kings of earth and all powers of darkness."[54] This victory would include victory over the other rider on a white horse. Stagg summarizes the matter well in stating that the white horse in Rev 6:2 ". . . probably symbolizes triumphant militarism or the world in its unending will to conquer."[55] The crown this rider wears represents the temporary sovereignty of military conquest that God allows,[56] just as he allows the unholy trinity to operate for a time.[57]

The next and final usage of the word *crown* in the arena of evil relates to the bizarre locusts released when the shaft of the abyss is opened (Rev 9:1-12.). Their detailed description leaves little doubt that they represent demonic forces.[58] Only one phrase of the description need concern us here—the reference to a crown. Krodel interprets the phrase to mean that the locusts had golden crowns on their heads,[59] but Charles accurately points out that the phrase *hōs stephanoi homoi chrusō*) ("as crowns in gold" does not mean they had crowns but rather only the semblance of crowns.[60] This semblance may imply that the forces of evil can have only an imitation, a copy, of real sovereignty. Boring asserts that all earthly claims to sovereignty are only pale imitations and parodies of the One who sits upon the throne.[61] Thus in Rev 6:2 we saw a delegated sovereignty, and here we have an imitation of sovereignty. This is all that the forces of evil can ever have. What a contrast with the crown of life (Rev 2:10, 3:11), the crown of the twenty-four elders sharing in the sovereignty of God (Rev 4:4 and elsewhere), the woman with the crown of twelve stars, and the sovereignty of the resurrected Christ!

53. Oman, *Book of Revelation*, 127–30.

54. Kiddle, *Revelation*, 114.

55. Stagg, "Interpreting Revelation," 338. The riders on white horses will be discussed more fully in a later chapter.

56. Cf. Morris, *Revelation*, 101.

57. See Rev 13:5, 7, 14–15; also Lilje, *Last Book*, 125.

58. Boring, *Revelation*, 136; cf. Lilje, *Last Book*, 147–48.

59. Krodel, *Revelation*, 203.

60. Charles, *Critical and Exegetical Commentary*, 1:244; cf. Morris, *Revelation*, 147; Lilje, *Last Book*, 147.

61. Boring, *Revelation*, 103.

7

The Thrones

I will grant to the one conquering to sit with me upon my throne as I also conquered and I sit with my Father upon his throne.

(Rev 3:21)

And immediately I became "in spirit" and behold a throne was lying in heaven, with One sitting upon the throne... and around the throne (were) twenty-four elders who had been clothed with white garments; and golden crowns (were) upon their head.... And before the throne (was) a glassy sea like crystal.... The twenty-four elders fell before the One sitting upon the throne and they worshiped the One living forever and ever, and they cast their crowns before the throne, saying...

(Rev 4:2, 4, 6, 10).

And he came and took (the scroll) out of the hand of the One sitting upon the throne.

(Rev 5:7)

And they continually cry out in a loud voice, saying, "The salvation (is) by our God who is sitting upon the throne and by the Lamb".

(Rev 7:10)

And another angel came and was placed near the altar, having a golden censer; and much incense was given to him in order that he might offer (it) upon the golden altar which is before the throne, with the prayers of all the holy ones.

(Rev 8:3)

*And I saw thrones and (people) sat upon them
and judgment was given for them.*

(Rev 20:4a)

*And I saw a great white throne and the One sitting upon it,
from whose face the earth and the heaven fled, and a place
was not found for them. And I saw the dead people, the great
and the small, having stood before the throne.*

(Rev 20:11–12a)

*And I heard a loud voice out of the throne saying, "Look, the dwelling place
of God is with the people, and he will dwell with them, and they will be his
people and God himself will be with them." And the One sitting upon the
throne said, "Look—I am making all things new."*

(Rev 21:3, 5a)

*And he showed me a river of water of life, clear as crystal, going out from
the throne of God and the Lamb. . . . And no curse shall be there any
longer; and the throne of God and the Lamb shall be in it, and his servants
will serve him.*

(Rev 22:1, 3).

*I know where you are living, where the throne of Satan (is),
and you are holding fast my name and you did not deny
my faith(fulness) even in the days of Antipas my faithful witness
who was killed alongside you, where Satan is living.*

(Rev 2:13)

*And the beast which I saw was like a leopard, and his feet (were) like
(the feet) of a bear; and his mouth (was) like the mouth of a lion: and the
Dragon gave to him his power and his throne and great authority.*

(Rev 13:2)

*And the fifth (angel) poured out his vial upon the throne of the beast,
and his kingdom became darkened; and people were gnawing
their tongues from the pain.*

(Rev 16:10)

According to Boring's count, the word *throne* appears forty-seven times in Revelation;[1] however, I have chosen only representative passages to discuss, which I believe are sufficient to demonstrate the usage of this term in both arenas. The first of these, Rev 3:21, promises a sovereignty of the Christian believer shared with Christ and God. As both Charles and Beasley-Murray have noted, its fulfillment comes in the millennial reign and beyond it in the final kingdom of God.[2] As Krodel aptly notes, this promise summarizes all prior promises. He then goes on to say, "Just as Jesus by his conquest became the victorious coregent with his Father, just so Christians who persevere in faith shall participate in the messianic reign and share in Christ's sovereignty."[3] As the Seer makes clear at several points, however, the way of conquest for both Christ and the believer is the way of being faithful unto death.[4]

We next examine a cluster of references to *throne* in Rev 4. First of all, we confront the vision of a throne in heaven with one sitting upon it (4:2). This throne symbolizes God's majesty and omnipotence.[5] Kiddle calls it a symbol of absolute power, and appropriately cautions us against visualizing it as a piece of furniture.[6] As most commentators have noted, the Seer is drawing his inspiration from Ezekiel's vision (Ezek 1). The fact that John attempts no description of the one on the throne is our clue that God is the occupant. In contrast with the apparent might of Rome, God is here portrayed as sovereign over the entire universe.[7] He will share that sovereignty only with Christ and with faithful believers. Around God's throne are twenty-four thrones occupied by twenty-four elders. I have previously interpreted these elders as symbolizing the combined people of God of both the Jewish Scriptures and the Christian Testament. A major point of evidence that these elders represent the true people of God rather than angelic beings, as many have argued, is that God's sovereignty is said to be shared with Christ and faithful believers but never with angels. Whatever may be the precise identity of these elders, they each have

1. Boring, *Revelation*, 102.
2. Charles, *Critical and Exegetical Commentary*, 2:101–2, Beasley-Murray, *Revelation*, 107.
3. Krodel, *Revelation*, 145–46; cf. Kiddle, *Revelation*, 60.
4. Morris, *Revelation*, 84.
5. Krodel, *Revelation*, 154; cf. Wilson, *Revelation*, 54.
6. Kiddle, *Revelation*, 81.
7. Cf. McDowell, *Meaning and Message*, 75.

thrones and therefore are kings in their own right. Their white clothing signifies their holiness (cf. Rev 19:8) and also their status as victors.[8] That their sovereignty is subordinate and derivative is indicated by their falling down to worship the one sitting upon the throne and casting down their crowns before him (Rev 4:10).

In Rev 5:7 the Lamb takes a sealed scroll from the one sitting upon the throne. The throne here symbolizes his sovereignty in the unfolding of judgment. His sovereignty in salvation is reflected by the multitude in white robes as they proclaim salvation by (or to) God and the Lamb (Rev 7:10). God, though sovereign, responds to the prayers of his people as they are offered up on the golden altar (Rev 8:3). Morris correctly notes that the incense here is not the prayers of the saints as in Rev 5:8, but is offered with those prayers. He sees this incense as a symbol of the unity of worship in heaven and on earth.[9] Wilson notes Lenski's argument that the incense represents the intercession of Christ that makes the prayers of the saints effective.[10] In all these passages the symbolism of the throne would appear to be much the same—namely God's sovereignty over creation, in redemption, and in judgment. Kiddle makes the further point that "John is expressing the perfect harmony between the will of God and the will of Christ."[11]

A different usage of the term *throne* confronts us in Rev 20:4. There the martyrs in heaven sit on thrones and judgment is given to, for, or by them. Moyise interprets this text to mean that the martyrs are given the authority to judge.[12] Kiddle notes the ironic reversal here, in that Christians who were in this life judged and executed as criminals are now given the authority to judge.[13] Lilje also argues that the martyrs "from the time of the dominion of the beast . . . are brought to life and are allowed to exercise the power of judgment."[14] This interpretation would be consistent with the view expressed by Paul in 1 Cor 6:3 and elsewhere.

---

8. Morris, *Revelation*, 87.
9. Ibid., 117.
10. Wilson, *Revelation*, 78.
11. Kiddle, *Revelation*, 81.
12. Moyise, *Old Testament in Revelation*, 54; cf. Morris, *Revelation*, 23.
13. Kiddle, *Revelation*, 392–93.
14. Lilje, *Last Book*, 248.

Boring notes the possibilities in translating *autois* either as "by them" or "for them," but does not opt for one or the other.[15] Both Boring and Beasley-Murray note the influence of Dan 7:9–14 on this passage. The latter is ambiguous as to whether judgment was given *to* the martyrs or *for* them, however. He notes that in Dan 7:22 the meaning is that the cause of the saints was vindicated.[16]

While Boring, Beasley-Murray, Lilje, and others interpret this scene as including only the martyrs in Heaven, McDowell argues that the phrase "such as worshiped not the beast, neither his image, and received not the mark upon their forehead and upon their hand" is a second category that includes all faithful Christians.[17] Wilson agrees with McDowell that all believers are involved; and along with Moyise and Morris above, opts for the reading "to them"; i.e., that believers are actually given a share in God's judgments.[18] Charles, on the other hand, sides with Boring and Beasley-Murray in interpreting the passage as referring only to the martyrs.[19] His position—that from Rev 20:4 to the end of the book the text has been hopelessly garbled due to the death of the Seer and an unintelligent editor completing the book—is well known.[20]

I will personally take my stand with McDowell and Wilson. I am not convinced by any of the arguments that the martyrs will be given special treatment in distinction from other faithful Christians. Would one who was willing to die for the faith but did not have to do so, for whatever reason, be treated differently from the actual martyr in God's sight? I find a tremendous theological difficulty with that sort of thinking.

There may be no way to decide with any certainty whether judgment is given to or for those mentioned in Rev 20:4; or whether those mentioned include all faithful Christians or only the martyrs. What is significant for the purposes of this study is that the thrones are clearly in the arena of God's working. They represent a sovereignty that God has delegated to the martyrs and possibly to all Christian believers.

---

15. Boring, *Revelation*, 203.
16. Beasley-Murray, *Revelation*, 292–93.
17. McDowell, *Meaning and Message*, 191.
18. Wilson, *Revelation*, 162.
19. Charles, *Critical and Exegetical Commentary*, 2:154; cf. Kiddle, *Revelation*, 393.
20. Charles, *Critical and Exegetical Commentary*, 2:144–47.

To briefly sketch the significance of the other passages quoted above that use the word *throne* in God's arena, I will begin with Rev 20:11–12a. That passage pictures judgment before the "great white throne." The image is again one of God's sovereignty in judgment. While the occupant of the throne is not identified, this is the kind of language John uses normally of God. Lilje would appear to be on target in his claim that "the presence of God is of such transcendent majesty that it can only be described indirectly."[21] Both earth and heaven fled from the presence of the one upon the throne. Kiddle notes that for humanity this is not the end but rather the beginning of rewards for the righteous and punishment for the wicked. He also points out that *4 Ezra* speaks of all irrelevancies [sic] of nature being banished and all people standing before the "Most High."[22]

The possibility that the figure on the throne might be Christ must also be recognized, in that while God is the judge, we have indications in the Christian Testament (e.g., John 5:22) that God has committed the power of judgment to Jesus.[23] The similarity of the language used of God as creator in Rev 4, however, would seem to suggest the same occupant here. This interpretation receives further support from Rev 21:5, which I examine below.

In 21:3 a voice from the throne states that God's dwelling place is with his people. Kiddle notes this verse as a fulfillment of Ezekiel's prophecy that the name of the restored holy city would be *Yahweh shamah*, "the Lord is there".[24] The detail that the voice comes from the throne again points us to the sovereignty of God.

In 21:5 the one on the throne speaks of making all things new. As God was sovereign over the old creation, so he is also in the new. As Lilje writes, "In the image of the new holy city which is adorned like a bride prepared for her husband, the seer creates a dignified and tender picture of the new reality, equally removed from pale abstractions about the future life, as from a heaven of sense enjoyment."[25] Morris aptly notes that

---

21. Lilje, *Last Book*, 255.
22. Kiddle, *Revelation*, 401.
23. Cf. Morris, *Revelation*, 233–34.
24. Kiddle, *Revelation*, 413; see Ezek 48:35.
25. Lilje, *Last Book*, 258–59.

this renewal is not only a feature of the end times, but as the present tense of the verb indicates, God is continually in the process of renewing.[26]

Finally, we get a picture of the river of the waters of life flowing out from the throne (22:1, 3). This passage serves to remind us of God's sovereignty in redemption as in creation. Morris calls attention to the significant fact that the Lamb shares the throne with God in both of these verses.[27] In all of these passages the throne belongs to God, or to God and the Lamb, and the familiar ideas of judgment and redemption are associated therewith.

In considering the use of the word *throne* in the arena of the forces of evil, three passages claim our attention. The first is in the address to the church at Pergamum. The one having the sharp two-edged sword claims knowledge of the location of the throne of Satan (Rev 2:13). The church of Pergamum is commended for holding onto the faith even in the face of the martyrdom of Antipas. That martyrdom is further said to take place where Satan lives. The phrase "where Satan lives" is probably to be identified with his throne. Morris notes that some have interpreted the throne of Satan as a reference to images of Zeus or to Asclepius with its symbol of the serpent, but that Pergamum by no means had a monopoly on the worship of these deities.[28] Beasley-Murray[29] and Kiddle[30] are among several interpreters who have suggested that Satan's throne may have been a large statue of Zeus that overlooked the city. The one area in which Pergamum was preeminent was emperor worship, thus lending support to Krodel's interpretation of that throne as a reference to the local temple of the imperial cult.[31] As early as 29 B.C.E., Pergamum had its temple to the divine Augustus and the goddess Roma.[32]

Lilje thinks all the preceding suggestions are too limited. He interprets Satan's throne as the entire area of the pagan cults, arguing that "the

---

26. Morris, *Revelation*, 239.
27. Ibid., 248–49.
28. Ibid., 66.
29. Beasley-Murray, *Revelation*, 84.
30. Kiddle, *Revelation*, 30.
31. Krodel, *Revelation*, 115; cf. also Morris, *Revelation*, 66; McDowell, *Meaning and Message*, 48; Charles, *Critical and Exegetical Commentary*, 1:61; Wilson, *Revelation*, 34.
32. McDowell, *Meaning and Message*, 47; Charles, *Critical and Exegetical Commentary*, 1:61; Kiddle, *Revelation*, 30.

whole of Pergamum, as the site of famous cults, above all as the seat of emperor worship, was a 'Throne of Satan.'"[33]

In Rev 13:2 we find a reference to the beast from the sea receiving his throne from the dragon, who is unambiguously identified as Satan later on (Rev 20:2). Just as God and the Lamb share a throne (3:21, 22:1), so do the dragon and the beast. Whatever dominion the latter may enjoy, however, is doomed to destruction (cf. 19:20, 20:10). That destruction is partially portrayed in the final passage, which refers to a throne occupied by the forces of evil. In Rev 16:10 the fifth angel pours out his vial upon the throne of the beast, causing people to gnaw their tongues in pain. Lilje defines that throne as "the seat of world dominion, which is at enmity with God."[34] Morris calls attention to the fact that the indefinite "men" who gnaw tongues in pain should be interpreted as adherents of the beast.[35] This text appears to indicate that the throne of the beast, like the throne of Satan (2:13), is located on earth among human beings. Goldsworthy connects the throne of the beast with people in these words: "The connection between the devil and the sinful world is clear from the fifth bowl poured out on the throne of the beast so that men gnawed their tongues in agony and cursed the God of heaven."[36]

In summation, we have two references to the throne of the dragon and two to the throne of the beast. The only authority they have, however, is that given to them (cf. 13:5, 7, 14–15). The so-called divine passive is probably to be understood in these passages. The Seer probably intends for us to understand these verses as meaning that God permits the powers of evil to have a kind of sovereignty, but that he also always limits that sovereignty and will ultimately obliterate the evil powers entirely. These thrones are to be viewed as counterimages to the throne of God, the throne of God and the Lamb, and the thrones of the twenty-four elders.

---

33. Lilje, *Last Book*, 79–80.
34. Ibid., 215.
35. Morris, *Revelation*, 190.
36. Goldsworthy, *Gospel in Revelation*, 122; see also Wilson, *Revelation*, 132.

8

The Star

Just as I received from my father,
so will I give to him the early morning star.

(Rev 2:28)

And the third angel sounded a trumpet—and a great star burning like a lamp fell out of heaven and fell upon a third of the rivers and springs of waters. Now the name of the star is called Wormwood, and a third of the waters became bitter as wormwood; and many of the people died because (the waters) were made bitter.

(Rev 8:10–11)

I, Jesus, sent my angel to bear witness (to) these things unto the churches. I am the root and family of David, the bright, early morning star.

(Rev 22:16)

And the fifth angel sounded (a) trumpet, and I saw a star having fallen out of heaven into the earth; and the key of the shaft of the abyss was given to him.

(Rev 9:1)

THE FIRST APPEARANCE OF the word *star* in the Apocalypse is in the address to the church at Thyatira. The one who is conquering and is keeping unto completion *(achri telous)* the works of the Son of God (2:26) is promised the early morning star (2:28). Beasley-Murray interprets this text as a reference to the planet Venus, the morning star, a symbol of victory and sovereignty; and thus regards the promise as sharing in the victory and sovereignty of Christ.[1] Krodel takes a similar line of argument, concluding that "the conquerors at Thyatira are assured that Christ's victory will be theirs, that nothing can defeat him or them, provided they keep his works."[2] Kiddle takes note of a similar interpretation, without specifying any interpreter in particular, that for the faithful believer the path is not always to be through the darkness of the oppression that he is now suffering, but that the dawn of a new day lies ahead.[3]

The second appearance of the term *star* in the realm of divine operations confronts us at Rev 8:10–11, in the vision of the seven trumpets. With the sounding of the second trumpet, a third of the sea is destroyed. With the sounding of the third trumpet, a blazing star turns a third of the fresh water sources into wormwood. The fact that fire is a symbol of divine judgment is almost universally recognized. In Revelation, *star* always symbolizes an angel except, as previously argued, the stars identified as the angels of the seven churches in 1:16, 20. Sweet, however, argues that the star in the present passage is an aspect of Satan. He goes on to quote approvingly Caird's statement, "Wormwood is the star of the new Babylon which has *poisoned* by its idolatry the *springs* of its own life."[4] Mounce, on the other hand, rejects Caird's statement as "ingenious but overly subtle."[5] While I tend to agree with Mounce at this point, there may be an association of the term *star* in the Jewish Scriptures that he has missed. Isa 14:12 refers to the king of historical Babylon as a star having fallen from heaven. In the Seer's mind there may very well have been an association of the fall from heaven of the king of historical Babylon with the fall he foresaw of the Babylon of his own day. One difficulty with this position is that the star in the present passage is carrying out God's judgment rather than *receiving* that judgment, as would be the case with Babylon or Rome. Here is a major difficulty with Sweet's position that this star is an aspect of Satan. Nowhere in the Christian Testament is Satan depicted in the role of carrying out God's judgment. One might make a case for this role in the Jewish Scriptures but not in the Christian Testament. In my judgment the safer position is to see the fire as symbolizing God's judgment and the star

1. Beasley-Murray, *Revelation*, 93–94.
2. Krodel, *Revelation*, 129–30.
3. Kiddle, *Revelation*, 43.
4. Sweet, *Revelation*, 164.
5. Mounce, *Revelation*, 187 n. 38.

as the instrument of that judgment. The Seer may also have intended a subtle allusion to Isa 14:12. Admittedly this allusion would involve mixing metaphors, in that the star in Isa 14:12 is a person receiving the judgment of God, whereas in the present passage the star is carrying out the judgment of God. This verse would by no means be the only passage in Revelation with mixed metaphors, however.

As Aune has noted, *Sib. Or.* 5:155–61 contain some remarkable similarities to the present passage. There a burning star will destroy the whole earth. Aune goes on to note two important differences, however. In the present passage the star poisons the waters, whereas in the *Sibylline Oracles* it *destroys* the waters. Second, in the present passage the star is a physical instrument causing a plague on earth, whereas in the *Sibylline Oracles* the star is a savior figure.[6] One might quarrel with the word "physical," but otherwise Aune's points are well taken.

Beale notes that *1 Enoch* 18:13 and 21:3 refer to the judgment of fallen angels as "stars like great burning mountains," and that *1 Enoch* 108:3–6 uses the same image in reference to the punishment of sinful people. He goes on to conclude that the present passage is intended "to portray judgment that people and their representative angel(s) endure throughout history and that precedes their final condemnation at the end of history."[7] Because no writing that unambiguously teaches a doctrine of guardian angels was accepted into the canon of the Christian Testament, such interpretations are suspect in my judgment.

A particular difficulty arises in interpreting this text in that wormwood is bitter, but not poisonous. Beale appears to be on the right track in suggesting Jer 9:15 and 23:15 as background. These passages threaten a judgment of feeding with wormwood *and* poisonous water.[8] Krodel aptly speaks of this text as the miracle of Marah (Exod 15:25) in reverse.[9]

Since in Rev 22:16 the star is clearly identified as Jesus, some have interpreted the promise in 2:28 as the gift of Jesus himself. Charles, while stating that no satisfactory explanation has ever been found for the words in 2:28, nevertheless states that the "best" interpretation is the promise that when a Christian has won through strife, Jesus will be the possession of

---

6. Aune, *Revelation 6–16*, 520–21.
7. Beale, *Book of Revelation*, 478–79.
8. Ibid., 479; cf. also Sweet, *Revelation*, 164; Mounce, *Revelation*, 187.
9. Krodel, *Revelation*, 198; cf. also Mounce, *Revelation*, 187–88.

that Christian.[10] In a similar fashion McDowell says, "The morning star, brightest of the heavens, is a symbol of the greatness and glory of the Christ in which all those who love him to the end will share."[11] Morris, though conceding that this is a strange way for Christ to refer to himself, nevertheless sees it as the best way of interpreting these words.[12] Lilje notes that the morning star is Venus and that it was the symbol of world dominion, even among pagans. He goes on to point out Christ's identification of himself as the morning star and concludes, "When he sheds his light upon a soul, he is giving himself to him."[13] Beasley-Murray says this interpretation is "tempting," but rejects it and takes the position noted above.[14]

The single occurrence of the word *star* in the arena of evil forces confronts us at Rev 9:1. This star we have encountered previously. I noted earlier that some interpreters identify the star as a good angel, possibly the same one who "binds" Satan in 20:1. I further called attention to the fact that this star performs the function of releasing evil forces, whereas the angel in 20:1 is restraining the chief of the powers of evil.

Morris notes Charles's position that the abyss in Revelation is the preliminary place of punishment, but rightly argues that no unambiguous reference to punishment exists in any of the passages where John uses this term.[15] For the Seer the abyss is the location of demonic forces.

A major clue that this star is an evil personage is that the key to the shaft of the abyss *was given* (*edothē*) to him. By a two-to-one ratio the Seer characteristically uses this verb for the forces of evil. The high probability, therefore, is that this star should be identified either as Satan himself or one of his angels. Other identifications were previously noted in the chapter on the keys.

In summary, we have a star as the promised reward for the conquering believer and a star that is Christ himself within the arena of God's operation. These stars may be one and the same. This star is set as a counterimage over against a star that, after falling (or, if Charles be correct, descending)[16] from heaven, unleashes all sorts of demonic forces on the earth.

---

10. Charles, *Critical and Exegetical Commentary*, 1:77; cf. Wilson, *Revelation*, 40.
11. McDowell, *Meaning and Message*, 53.
12. Morris, *Revelation*, 74; cf. also Kiddle, *Revelation*, 43.
13. Lilje, *Last Book*, 87–88.
14. Beasley-Murray, *Revelation*, 93.
15. Morris, *Revelation*, 125.
16. See Charles, *Critical and Exegetical Commentary*, 1:238–39.

9

They Are Worthy

But you have a few names in Sardis who did not soil their garments, and they shall walk with me in white (garments), because they are worthy.

(Rev 3:4)

For they poured out the blood of holy ones and prophets, and you gave them blood to drink; they are worthy.

(Rev 16:6)

For the first time in this study we encounter a phrase rather than a single term used in both arenas. After the one having the seven spirits of God and the seven stars addresses members of the church at Sardis as those who have a reputation for being alive but who really are dead, (Rev 3:1), he then says that the church there yet contains a few names who had not soiled their garments. The use of the term *names* here illustrates the inseparability of name and person in Hebrew thought. The speaker promises that these will walk with him in white garments, for they are worthy (*axioi eisin*).

One crucial point of interpretation of this passage is the meaning of "soiling" their garments. Charles interprets soiling as moral stains, especially *porneia* or fornication.[1] He goes on to identify the white garments as the spiritual bodies that believers will possess after the resurrection.[2] Krodel, while agreeing with Charles that the soiling has moral connotations, especially sexual promiscuity, interprets the white robes as symbolizing the forgiveness and purity that Christ offers to believers. He

---

1. Charles, *Critical and Exegetical Commentary*, 1:81.
2. Ibid., 1:82.

then goes on to say, "Their present unsoiled garments (v. 4) are metaphors of the gift of redemption which are received in baptism and retained in conduct."[3] Beasley-Murray, taking strong issue with Charles's position, points to the identification in Rev 19:8 of white linen as the righteous deeds of the saints. He then notes, "The contrast between soiled garments of sinful believers and unsoiled garments of faithful Christians suggests that the white garments have to do with purity or holiness."[4] McDowell takes essentially the same position.[5] David Barr takes the position that white is a symbol of victory rather than purity in the Apocalypse.[6] Morris notes that some have identified the white robes with purity, festivity, and victory; then calls attention to Farrer's interpretation that the parallel in the next verse with not having their names erased from the book of life would seem to identify the white robes as justification. Morris also rightly notes that these who were given the white robes had not earned them but had done nothing to forfeit what was a gift to them.[7]

To sum up the significance of the white garments, they have to do with purity, holiness, victory, and perhaps other aspects of the Christian life. Both grace and works are involved. These faithful believers at Sardis are worthy to walk in white garments because the Lamb is worthy to open the sealed scroll (5:9). The Lamb's worthiness is related directly to his victory achieved by his death and resurrection. The faithful Christian must also become worthy through suffering and death if necessary. As expressed in the present passages, that worthiness is connected with their "not having soiled their garments."

The use of the phrase under consideration in the arena of evil appears in the account of the outpouring of the third bowl (Rev 16:6). As the bowl is poured out, the sources of fresh water become blood, reminiscent of Moses' sign before Pharaoh (16:4; cf. Exod 4:9; 7:17–21).[8] Even the angel in charge of the waters concedes that the judgment is a just one because "they" had poured out the blood of prophets and holy ones

---

3. Krodel, *Revelation*, 133.

4. Beasley-Murray, *Revelation*, 97.

5. McDowell, *Meaning and Message*, 56; see also Wilson, *Revelation*, 43.

6. Barr, *New Testament Story*, 389. When I challenged him in person on this interpretation he reluctantly conceded that there might be grounds for the idea of purity as well. Cf. Lilje, *Last Book*, 91.

7. Morris, *Revelation*, 76.

8. Cf. McDowell, *Meaning and Message*, 159.

(16:5–6). As Krodel notes, giving people blood to drink should obviously be interpreted metaphorically rather than literally. He also notes that the last phrase of 16:6 (*axios eisin*) is identical with the last phrase of 3:4.[9] English translations tend to obscure this fact. For example, the NASB translates the phrase "they are worthy" in 3:4 but renders the same phrase in 16:6 as "they deserve it." As both Krodel[10] and Charles[11] note, this passage describes a punishment in kind for the blood of the martyrs,[12] although Charles "restores to their original context" vv. 5b–7. For him that context is the verses following 19:4.[13]

In summary, the worthiness of those pouring out the blood of martyrs to drink blood is set in sharp contrast with those faithful believers at Sardis and their worthiness to walk with the exalted Christ in white garments. The worthiness in each case is related to the conduct of those to whom it is applied.[14] The use of the exact phrase *hagioi eisin* in both cases would seem to indicate that the Seer was deliberately counterimaging the worthiness of the faithful believers at Sardis to walk with Christ in white garments with the worthiness of those who poured out the blood of martyrs to drink blood.

---

9. Krodel, *Revelation*, 283–84.
10. Ibid.
11. Charles, *Critical and Exegetical Commentary*, 2:121.
12. Cf. Wilson, *Revelation*, 131; Morris, *Revelation*, 188; Lilje, *Last Book*, 214.
13. Charles, *Critical and Exegetical Commentary*, 2:120–22.
14. Cf. comments in Hughes, *Revelation*, 174.

10

They Have No Rest Day and Night

> ... and the four living creatures, each one of them having six wings
> and being full of eyes outside and inside; and they have no rest day
> and night, saying, "Holy, holy, holy Lord God, the Almighty,
> the One who was and who is and who is coming."
>
> (Rev 4:8)
>
> And the smoke of their torment is going up forever and ever,
> and they have no rest day and night, (that is) the ones who are worshiping
> the beast and his image, and whoever is receiving the mark of his name.
>
> (Rev 14:11)

Once again the Seer has used a phrase rather than a single word for his counterimaging. The phrase appears first in the throne vision of Rev 4. The "four living creatures" are said to have no rest day or night from repeating the *trishagion* ("threefold holy") to the Lord God Almighty (Rev 4:8). As Court notes, this threefold acclamation of holiness echoes Isaiah's vision in the temple (Isa 6:3).[1] Who are these living creatures, described as having six wings and being full of eyes outside and inside? Various answers have been given. For Krodel, they represent God's pets around his throne and a symbol of the new creation. He states further, "God's pets in John's vision are the symbol of harmony and worship yet to come, when God shall dwell among his people."[2] Court rightly notes that these creatures have the vision of Ezek 1:5–28 as their background, and also that they are the source of much later Christian symbolism in which the lion, ox, hu-

---

1. Court, *Revelation*, 27.
2. Krodel, *Revelation*, 156–57.

man being, and eagle become the symbols of the four evangelists.[3] Charles considers the four living creatures to be a modification of the cherubim as described by Ezekiel.[4] In similar fashion Beasley-Murray describes them as a second order of angels around the throne that he later refers to as cherubim.[5] Boring writes, "Their descriptions are a collage of details from Ezekiel 1 and Isaiah 6, both of which draw upon the traditional picture of the cherubim." He further traces this imagery to the winged bulls and other similar creatures in Mesopotamian and Canaanite mythology that supposedly guarded the thrones of both heavenly and earthly kings.[6] Kiddle describes these creatures in terms of the abstract theological doctrines of omnivision and omniscience.[7] Wilson notes the resemblance of these creatures to the cherubim and seraphim of Isa 6:1–3, Ezek 1:1, 5:25, and 10:20, and takes the position that they are angelic attendants around the throne "who lead the heavenly hosts in the unceasing praise of God."[8] Morris also emphasizes their function of continuous praise.[9]

McDowell, while agreeing that the symbolism is drawn from Ezekiel, takes a different view of the creatures. He interprets them as representative of all living beings.[10] Robbins, a student of McDowell, after noting that there have been at least thirteen interpretations of these creatures, goes a step further. In view of the symbolism of the number four as the cosmic number, Robbins interprets the creatures as symbolizing the totality of God's creation. He writes, "The whole chapter relates to the majesty of God, so it seems more natural to suppose that the figure is symbolic of all creation fulfilling its proper office; waiting upon God, fulfilling his will, and setting forth his glory."[11] I will take my stand with Robbins at this point. One primary reason is the voice in the center of the four living creatures advertising the exorbitant prices of wheat and barley in 6:7. I doubt that there is much need for wheat and barley in heaven!

3. Court. *Revelation*, 27.
4. Charles, *Critical and Exegetical Commentary*, 1:125.
5. Beasley-Murray, *Revelation*, 116–18.
6. Boring, *Revelation*, 107.
7. Kiddle, *Revelation*, 91.
8. Wilson, *Revelation*, 56.
9. Morris, *Revelation*, 89.
10. McDowell, *Meaning and Message*, 78.
11. Robbins, *Revelation*, 88; cf. Torrance, *Apocalypse Today*, 153.

To return to the passage under consideration, the function of the four living creatures is unceasing praise to God. The Jewish Scriptures contain no scarcity of texts depicting the created order as praising God (e.g. Pss 19:1, 89:5, 145:10, and 148:3–13; and 1 Chr 16:31–33). There is no cessation of creation's praise to the one who sits on the throne. While the idea of the created order continually praising God may seem strange to modern Westerners, it was not unusual to persons of a Hebrew background.

The phrase under consideration occurs in the arena of evil only at Rev 14:11. The context is the first announcement of the fall of Babylon. As McDowell notes, "The victory of God is assured before the carnage of conflict begins."[12] The picture is one of unrelieved torment and suffering. This image has often been challenged as unworthy of the God revealed in Jesus Christ. If taken as an objective picture of the reality following God's judgment, the challenge is probably justified. John is dealing in vivid imagery designed to influence human emotions, not with objective statements of fact. Boring points out that "such language does not function to give an objective picture of what shall in fact happen to God's enemies the outsiders . . . ; it functions to warn insiders who ponder the question, Is it such a terrible thing to participate in Roman worship?"[13] John's vivid imagery replies to such a question with the answer that to worship anyone or anything other than the true and living God has terrible consequences. To those who thought that death for not worshiping the "beast" was the worst that could happen, John points out that the judgment of God on unbelievers leading to eternal separation from God is far worse than physical death.[14] Morris makes the further important point that John is not gloating over or reveling in this picture of unbelievers and their torment but is simply trying to persuade his readers or hearers to face ultimate realities. As tempting as personal escape from martyrdom might be, the writer of Revelation believes a fate worse than death awaits those who deny their faith.[15]

Krodel has called attention to another reason for the widespread negative reaction to such passages as this. As contemporary people, we do

---

12. McDowell, *Meaning and Message*, 149.
13. Boring, *Revelation*, 170.
14. Ibid., 170–71.
15. Morris, *Revelation*, 176.

not like to be presented with the consequences of our actions.[16] We prefer to think of ourselves as victims of our heredity and environment rather than to accept any personal responsibility for what we have done. We cannot claim to be guided by the Bible, whether Revelation or the Gospels, in such thinking. We must not let the exaggerated language of John's picture of God's judgment cause us to miss the reality of which he speaks. Nor should we forget that ultimately God's judgment is self-judgment, in that it is the human response to God that brings about condemnation.

One could well question why I am presenting the phrase "they have no rest day or night" in the arena of evil, because it is presented as the outworking of God's wrath. The reason is that such wrath is understood in the Apocalypse as the result of human choices. As Mounce comments, "After due allowance is made for the place of symbolism in apocalyptic literature, what remains in these verses is still the terrifying reality of divine wrath poured out upon those who persist in following Antichrist [sic]."[17] This statement appears to be fully supported by the text. John, however, is thinking of evil as eventually turning in upon itself and self-destructing. For example, the "ten horns" and the beast "will hate the 'harlot' and will make her desolate and naked, and will eat her flesh and will burn her up with fire" (Rev 17:16). Though the language is slightly different, in all likelihood we are intended to think of it as depicting the same reality as eternal suffering in fire and brimstone. In this sort of framework, therefore, would not the punishment ultimately be self-punishment? Hanson is among those commentators who have pointed out that God's wrath is something people bring on themselves.[18] Paul seems to have thought along these same lines concerning the wrath of God. In Rom 1:18–31, the most thorough discussion of the wrath of God found anywhere in the Bible, he repeatedly says (vv. 24, 26, 28) "God gave them over" (*paredōken*) to the consequences of worshiping the creation instead of the Creator.

Whether or not one would agree with the above assessment of the wrath of God, there can be no doubt that the Seer intended here a sharp contrast in the use of the phrase "they have no rest day and night" in Rev 14:11 with the use of the same phrase in 4:8. As Charles notes, "There it means the deliberate and willing surrender on the part of the Cherubim

---

16. Krodel, *Revelation*, 269–70.
17. Mounce, *Revelation*, 277.
18. Hanson, *Wrath of the Lamb*, 88.

of their entire time to the praise of God, whereas here it denotes the involuntary endurance of ceaseless torment on the part of those who worship the beast."[19] Though I have previously challenged the interpretation of the four living creatures as cherubim, Charles has otherwise well expressed the counterimaging of this phrase.[20] In similar fashion Kiddle has noted the unceasing praise of the four living creatures and has pointed out that "the renegade is to pay a different kind of tribute day and night to Him whose power he has set at nought."[21]

---

19. Charles, *Critical and Exegetical Commentary*, 2:18.
20. Cf. Morris, *Revelation*, 176.
21. Kiddle, *Revelation*, 282.

11

Having Been Slain

And I saw in the vicinity of the throne and the four living creatures and the elders a little Lamb having taken his stand as one having been slain; having seven horns and seven eyes, which are the seven spirits of God which have been sent out into all the earth . . . saying in a loud voice, "Worthy is the Lamb having been slain to receive the power and wealth and wisdom and strength and honor and glory and eulogy".

(Rev 5:6, 12)

And when he opened the fifth seal I saw underneath the altar the souls of those having been slain because of the word of God and the testimony which they had.

(Rev 6:9)

And all those dwelling upon the earth whose names have not been written in the book of life of the slain Lamb who existed from the beginning of the world will worship him.

(Rev 13:8)

And in her was found the blood of prophets and holy ones; that is, of those having been slain upon the earth.

(Rev 18:24)

And one of his heads appeared as having been slain unto death, and the wound of his death was healed.

(Rev 13:3)

OUR INVESTIGATION OF THIS phrase takes us first of all into the vision of the sealed scroll and the appearance of the Lamb. He is paradoxically described as *standing* like one having been slain (5:6). He is described in further paradoxical language as having seven horns and seven eyes. Since horns usually symbolize power in apocalyptic writings and seven is the number of completeness, the symbolism suggests that the Lamb, though having been slain, now possesses complete power and vision.[1]

Charles, along with Caird, discusses at some length the phrase *en mesō*, which I have translated "in the vicinity." Charles, supporting the translation "in the midst," concludes that the Lamb stands between the circles of the four living creatures and that of the twenty-four elders.[2] All these attempts to locate the Lamb in space are wasted effort if one reads John 8:9. There the woman taken in adultery is said to be in the midst (*en mesō*, the same phrase as in Rev 5:6), when clearly no one was present any longer except her and Jesus. The obvious meaning in John 8:9 is that the woman stood before or in the presence of Jesus. I find no reason to look for any different significance to the phrase in Rev. 5:6. The Lamb is simply seen as standing either before the throne or in close proximity to it. In Farrer's words, "The common meaning (of *en mesō*) appears to be 'in the area of'" either one thing, or several."[3] The Lamb's stance is that of the victor over death. As Mounce notes, "In one brilliant stroke John portrays the central theme of NT [sic] revelation—victory through sacrifice."[4]

The seven eyes of the Lamb are further described as the seven spirits of God sent out into all the earth. Mounce interprets this expression to mean that the Lamb possesses completeness of vision leading to perfect knowledge.[5] Morris also, though noting that this phrase might be a reference to the Holy Spirit, chooses rather to interpret the seven spirits as implying perfection of vision.[6] While this interpretation is no doubt true, it does not go far enough. Charles likewise falls short in confining the seven eyes to the concept of omniscience.[7] Sleeper similarly speaks of the

---

1. Cf. Boring, *Revelation*, 110; Mounce, *Revelation*, 145; McDowell, *Meaning and Message*, 83–84; Krodel, *Revelation*, 164; Wilson, *Revelation*, 60; Morris, *Revelation*, 95; Lilje, *Last Book*, 115; Robbins, *Revelation*, 95.

2. Charles, *Critical and Exegetical Commentary*, 1:140; see also Mounce, *Revelation*, 146; Caird, *Commentary on Revelation*, 75–76.

3. Farrer, *Revelation*, 91.

4. Mounce, *Revelation*, 144.

5. Ibid., 146.

6. Morris, *Revelation*, 95.

7. Charles, *Critical and Exegetical Commentary*, 1:143.

seven horns and seven eyes as meaning that the Lamb is all-powerful and all-knowing.[8] Boring, though first referring the seven eyes to the Lamb's fullness of insight, goes on to say: "John wants his hearer-readers to grasp how close the relationship is between Christ, God, and the Spirit, to relate the living Christ to the Spirit who speaks in the churches, and to relate this Spirit to the crucified and exalted Christ."[9] Using the word *spirit* in the singular and capitalizing it seem to imply that the seven spirits designate the Holy Spirit. Kiddle speaks of the seven spirits as a foreshadowing of the Holy Spirit and as part of the elementary thought from which it was derived.[10] McDowell more specifically equates the seven spirits with the Holy Spirit.[11] Krodel likewise speaks of the empowering of the Lamb to send out the Holy Spirit. He further appropriately notes that omnipotence (seven horns) and omniscience (seven eyes) are the possessions of the Lamb because of the victory that he has won through being slain.[12] Rowland interprets the seven spirits of God as the Holy Spirit and comments further, "Already those attributes of God described independently in 4:5 are linked with the Lamb."[13] Wilson argues that this passage is designed to reflect the fact that the Holy Spirit is sent out into the world by the exalted Christ.[14] I agree with those who understand the seven spirits to symbolize the Holy Spirit.

The second occurrence of the phrase "having been slain" appears in the same chapter at v. 12. There the Lamb receives a sevenfold ascription of praise. Morris takes note of this ascription and argues that "the perfect number is probably significant."[15] Wilson is a bit more explicit, stating, "Their sevenfold ascription is a complete unit governed by the definite article before the first item."[16] Though Wilson does not spell it out, his statement seems to imply that the sevenfold ascription symbolizes the complete praise to which the Lamb is entitled. Krodel notes that a sevenfold ascription of praise is directed to God in Rev 7:12 but does not

8. Sleeper, *Victorious Christ*, 22.
9. Boring, *Revelation*, 110–11.
10. Kiddle, *Revelation*, 99–100.
11. McDowell, *Meaning and Message*, 84; cf. Robbins, *Revelation*, 95.
12. Krodel, *Revelation*, 164; cf. Boring, *Revelation*, 111; Pinn, *Revelation Today*, 21.
13. Rowland, *Revelation*, 75.
14. Wilson, *Revelation*, 60.
15. Morris, *Revelation*, 98.
16. Wilson, *Revelation*, 62.

take account of some subtle differences.[17] As Charles notes, the Seer has substituted "thanksgiving" for "riches" in 7:12. He also suggests that the septenary number may imply completeness.[18] What John exhibits here is a tendency seen at other points in Revelation: he will use a numerical grouping repeatedly but will make a subtle change each time. A good example is the fourfold phrase "tribe and tongue and people and nation" (5:9). He uses this phrase a total of seven times (5:9, 7:9, 10:11, 11:9, 13:7, 14:6, and 17:15) but never in exactly the same form. This repetition would seem to indicate that the Seer is consciously and deliberately using these numerical groupings and expects us to grasp the symbolism of the numbers. In the present passage, therefore, the sevenfold ascription of worship and praise should be interpreted as complete worship and praise. As Sleeper[19] and Rowland[20] have noted, the Lamb is entitled to the same worship as God. Kiddle points out that nowhere else in the Christian Testament is Christ adored on such equal terms as the Godhead.[21] The complete worship of creatures in Heaven and on earth rightly belongs to both.

Bousset presents a further refinement of the sevenfold ascription. He notes that the items enumerated fall into divisions of four and three—a pattern that may be observed in the septets of the seals, the trumpets, and the vials. He goes on to say, "The four deal with the power and wisdom that the Lamb assumes; the three with the recognition of the Lamb on the part of mankind."[22] Mounce also divides the ascription into groups of four and three, but speaks of the first four as qualities that the Lamb possesses which make him praiseworthy. He agrees with Bousset and Krodel that the last three relate more specifically to the responses of human beings and angels.[23]

John's image of the slaughtered Lamb is a mind-wrenching paradox.[24] Although the Lamb is led to the slaughter, he is nevertheless the all-conquering Lion who exercises the power of and merits all the praise

17. Krodel, *Revelation*, 167.
18. Charles, *Critical and Exegetical Commentary*, 1:149.
19. Sleeper, *Victorious Christ*, 65.
20. Rowland, *Revelation*, 75.
21. Kiddle, *Revelation*, 105.
22. Cited in Charles, *Critical and Exegetical Commentary*, 1:149; cf. Krodel, *Revelation*, 167; Morris, *Revelation*, 98.
23. Mounce, *Revelation*, 149–50.
24. Cf. Boring, *Revelation*, 108.

of God. As Kiddle points out, "In heaven the slain Lamb is in the midst of the throne, and in the new heaven occupies it along with God."[25]

The two references to the Lamb as having been slain are balanced by two references to the martyrs having been slain (6:9 and 18:24). The setting of the first of these passages is the Lamb's opening of the fifth seal. John is enabled to see into heaven and his vision is that of souls underneath the altar. They cry out for vengeance but, as Wilson points out, "They do not thirst for private revenge, but cry for public justice."[26] Krodel correctly notes that several traditions are woven together by the Seer at this point. For one, there is a clear reminiscence of Ezekiel's vision of the temple (Ezek 40:1—44:3). We also have overtones of the traditional belief that a heavenly temple with its altars existed as a counterpart to the earthly temple and altars. The belief that blood contains life and the tradition of pouring the blood of a sacrificed animal at the base of the altar are also evident.[27] Here the altar would seem to be the altar of burnt offering. Elsewhere, as in Rev 8:3 and 8:5, the altar of incense seems to be in view. Charles has adduced considerable evidence that there is no evidence of a belief in two altars in heaven in Jewish and Christian apocalyptic, but that the two have been collapsed into one that alternately assumes the characteristics of both the altar of incense and the altar of sacrifice.[28]

McDowell takes the description of the souls under the altar as referring to those slaughtered by Nero, but argues that "the martyrs in Heaven are one with the martyrs-to-be upon earth; thus is dramatically illustrated the solidarity of the long line of saints, living and dead, who have loved not their lives unto death."[29] Krodel agrees that Antipas (Rev 2:13) and the martyrs under Nero are included here but also argues that the vision includes future martyrdoms.[30] Boring would include both Jewish martyrs and the martyrs under Nero, but asserts that John has specifically in mind those who were yet to be martyred in the great tribulation that he saw as already beginning.[31] Charles holds that the martyrs in view are "incon-

25. Kiddle, *Revelation*, 105.
26. Wilson, *Revelation*, 67.
27. Krodel, *Revelation*, 177.
28. Charles, *Critical and Exegetical Commentary*, 1:226–30; see also Mounce, *Revelation*, 157; Morris, *Revelation*, 105.
29. McDowell, *Meaning and Message*, 91.
30. Krodel, *Revelation*, 178.
31. Boring, *Revelation*, 124.

testably Christian martyrs, to wit, the martyrs of Neronic times," and that these have been offered up as sacrifices to God on the heavenly altar.[32] Kiddle thinks the reference is to all who have died in the service of God, whether in the Christian or pre-Christian era, since the Seer refers only to "testimony" in general rather than the testimony of Jesus—though he mentions the possibility that only Christian martyrs are included.[33]

Let us now pursue the meaning of the phrase "because of the word of God and the testimony of Jesus which they had." An understandable tendency has been to view this expression as the testimony that the martyrs had given by their death. But, as Charles has pointed out, the verb "had" (*eichon*) lends itself more naturally to the idea of preserving a testimony that Jesus had given. He further says, "The testimony no less than the word is an objective possession of the faithful."[34] Mounce basically agrees with Charles, and quotes Caird's translation of the phrase under consideration, "because of the word spoken by God and attested by Jesus." Mounce goes on to point out, however, that the testimony of the martyrs could hardly be separated from the testimony of Jesus.[35] The genitives "of God" and "of Jesus" are probably best taken as objective genitives and understood with Caird as the word spoken by God and the testimony that Jesus gave.[36] That the testimony is to be upheld by the believer should also be understood.

The next passage for our consideration speaks of those dwelling on the earth worshiping the beast, unless their names are written in the book of life (13:8). As has been widely recognized by interpreters, the phrase "those dwelling upon the earth" refers almost exclusively to unbelievers in the Apocalypse.[37] The syntax of the latter part of this verse is notoriously difficult. The primary difficulty is whether the phrase "from the foundation of the world" should be taken with "slain" or with "written." As Aune notes, the word order would seem to suggest the former. He goes on to cite the AV, the NIV, the REB, Caird, Mounce, Sweet, and Harrington as

---

32. Charles, *Critical and Exegetical Commentary*, 1:174; cf. also Mounce, *Revelation*, 158; Lilje, *Last Book*, 128.

33. Kiddle, *Revelation*, 119.

34. Charles, *Critical and Exegetical Commentary*, 1:174.

35. Mounce, *Revelation*, 158.

36. Cf. Morris, *Revelation*, 106.

37. E.g., Caird, *Commentary on Revelation*, 167; Aune, *Revelation 1-5*, 240; Beale, *Book of Revelation*, 290; Sweet, *Revelation*, 104; Bauckham, *Climax*, 239.

supporting this position.[38] He then notes the possibility of the translation "written from before the foundation of the world" and argues, "This interpretation is preferable since it is logically and theologically impossible to make sense of the statement that the Lamb 'was slaughtered *before* the foundation of the world.'"[39] Wilson, however, is among those who support the latter reading.[40]

Aune next adduces the parallel passage, Rev 17:8, in support of his position. This passage has its own ambiguities, however, and rather than connecting "written" with "from the foundation of the world," it is possible to connect it to "the book of life." Hence the reference would be to those whose names have been written in the book of life that existed from the foundation of the world. The reader may compare Exod 32:32, in which Moses prays that if God will not forgive the Israelites, then God should blot him out of "the book which thou hast written"; and Ps 69:28, which explicitly refers to the book of life. These passages suggest that the book of life is understood as being at least ancient, if not present from the beginning.

Caird, noting the overtones of predestination raised by some interpreters, issues the caveat, "We must not read more into John's doctrine of predestination than he intends. He is not saying that **the inhabitants of earth will worship** [sic] the monster because they have no choice, because this is the fate to which they have been destined from eternity.... Having a Semitic mind, John has no interest in carefully qualified statements, which would show how predestination and free will are related to one another; he simply sets the two beliefs side by side without qualification and allows the one to qualify the other."[41]

While Aune is correct in assessing the grammatical possibilities as far as he goes, and while I have no quarrel with Caird's comment that predestination and free will are set side by side without any attempt to reconcile the two, my translation suggests a third possibility. It is possible to take "from the foundation of the world" with "Lamb," and hence to completely eliminate the specter of predestination. In this understanding it is the existence of the Lamb from the foundation of the world that is affirmed. I will concede that this is not the most natural reading of the Greek syntax

---

38. Aune, *Revelation 6–16*, 746.
39. Ibid., 746–47. Cf. also Beale, *Book of Revelation*, 702.
40. Wilson, *Revelation*, 113.
41. Caird, *Commentary on Revelation*, 168.

here; but as all interpreters have noted, John's use of Greek is irregular at many points. My view finds partial support in the reference to "those having been written in the book of life of the lamb" as used in 21:27 without the troublesome phrase "from the foundation of the world." Furthermore, while I freely admit that no passage in Revelation explicitly refers to the Lamb's existence before the foundation of the world, the common worship of God and the Lamb (as at 5:13) indicates that the Seer thought of the Lamb as existing from eternity along with God. Theologically if not grammatically, seeing in the present passage a reference to the Lamb's eternity is less problematic than connecting either "written" or "slain" with the phrase "before the foundation of the world."

The final reference to "ones having been slain," as meaning those who have given their lives for their faith, appears in Rev 18:24. It follows the announcement of Babylon's final destruction and the lamentation thereupon by all the groups who have profited by her "harlotry." Verse 24 is given as the final reason for Babylon's fall. The other two reasons are leading astray the nations[42] and arrogance based on wealth.[43] As Mounce correctly notes, "prophets and holy ones" are not to be understood as two different groups; instead, the prophets are to be considered only as a special class within the holy ones ("saints").[44]

The commentators again show a tendency to equate Babylon with Rome at this point and hence to limit the meaning of the text to the period of the existence of the Roman Empire. Boring understands that such an interpretation is too limiting, pointing out that Jerusalem could also be "Babylon" and concluding (rightly in my judgment), "Ruthless use of violence by every empire is here included in 'Babylon.'"[45] In a similar vein Morris, after noting the reference to the blood of prophets and saints and all who have been killed on earth being in her, points out that "there is no one city on earth of which this can be said. Babylon is clearly a symbol for all earthly cities."[46]

The one usage of the phrase "having been slain" in the arena of evil appears in the account of the emergence of the beast from the sea (13:3).

---

42. Charles, *Critical and Exegetical Commentary*, 2:112.
43. Krodel, *Revelation*, 308; Mounce, *Revelation*, 334–35.
44. Mounce, *Revelation*, 335.
45. Boring, *Revelation*, 187.
46. Morris, *Revelation*, 217.

As Boring and others have noted, this beast is a composite of the four beasts in Dan 7:1–8.[47] The beast is described as having seven heads and ten horns, thus linking him with the dragon (13:1; cf. 12:3). In 17:10 the heads are also said to be seven kings. In the present passage one of the heads, i.e., one of the Roman emperors, had received a fatal wound that now has been healed.[48] The majority of commentators connect the wounded head with the suicide of Nero and the legend that either he had not actually died, or that he would come to life again and lead the Parthians into battle against Rome. Kiddle thinks the reference to the myth of Nero's suicide and his expected return leading the Parthians against Rome is unmistakably plain.[49] Wilson, after noting the suicide of Nero and the revolution that followed, quotes Moffatt's words, "The vitality of the pagan empire, shown in this power of righting itself after the revolution, only added to its prestige."[50] While I think these interpreters may be correct in seeing a direct reference to Nero, the purposes of this study do not require a conclusion on this issue. Only the stark contrast of the head of the beast as having been slain (*esphagmenēn*) with both the victorious Lamb who conquered by having been slain (*esphagmenon*) and the martyrs having been slain (*esphagmenon*) need be noted. The usage of the perfect passive participle of the same verb in all three cases can scarcely be viewed as accidental. The author intended for us to see this as another counterimage.[51]

---

47. Boring, *Revelation*, 155; cf. Lilje, *Last Book*, 186.
48. This beast will be dealt with more fully later in the chapter on the unholy trinity.
49. Kiddle, *Revelation*, 244–45.
50. Wilson, *Revelation*, 111.
51. I should point out that Revelation contains two other uses of the verb *sphazō*, "to slay," at 5:9 and 6:4. I have dealt only with those passages containing the perfect passive participle of this verb. The sounds of the other forms are so different as to make it unlikely that the author intended them as counterimages.

12

The Lamb

And I saw in the vicinity of the throne and the four living creatures and the elders a little Lamb having taken his stand as one having been slain; having seven eyes, which are the seven Spirits of God which have been sent out into all the earth . . . saying in a loud voice, "Worthy is the Lamb having been slain to receive the power and wealth and wisdom and strength and honor and glory and eulogy."

(Rev 5:6, 12)

And all those dwelling upon the earth whose names have not been written in the book of life of the slain Lamb who existed from the beginning of the world will worship him.

(Rev 13:8)

And I looked and behold the Lamb had taken his stand upon Mount Zion, and with him (were the) one hundred forty-four thousand having his name and the name of his Father written upon their foreheads.

(Rev 14:1)

And I saw another beast coming up out of the earth which had two horns like a little lamb, but he was speaking like a dragon.

(Rev 13:11)

THE POSITIVE USAGE OF the word *lamb* has been dealt with in the previous chapter. The Lamb takes his stand before the throne as one having been slain (5:6) and is proclaimed worthy to receive complete worship and praise along with God (5:12). My interpretation is that the Lamb's existence from the beginning of the world is emphasized rather than his having been slain from before the beginning of the world, as noted above.

We next encounter this same Lamb (apparently, since he is referred to only as "the Lamb") in 14:1. There he has taken his stand on Mount Zion with one hundred forty-four thousand persons who have his name and the name of his Father written on their foreheads. We first encountered the one hundred forty-four thousand in Rev 7 as those who were to be sealed before God's judgment is unleashed on the earth. Is this group the same as that in Rev 14? Commentators are divided on this issue. Charles thinks this entire chapter is proleptic and that the one hundred forty-four thousand, while being identical with those in Rev 7, are now portrayed as risen and sharing the millennial reign with Christ. He further identifies them with the "innumerable multitude" of 7:9–17.[1] Kiddle, like Charles, argues that the one hundred forty-four thousand are the martyrs who have ascended in a cloud to the heavenly Mount Zion.[2] Mounce, along with Charles, identifies them as another portrayal of the "innumerable multitude" of Rev 7:9–17. He also argues that the one hundred forty-four thousand represent the entire number of the redeemed, and that the picture here is of the "Zion above," not the one on earth.[3] McDowell, on the other hand, thinks we are dealing with the same one hundred forty-four thousand as in Rev 7, but that they are still on earth.[4] Krodel argues that the one hundred forty-four thousand symbolize God's people of the last days, and that Mount Zion is "wherever the Lamb is with his followers on earth."[5] Lilje thinks the question of a heavenly or earthly Mount Zion is irrelevant. He speaks of Mount Zion as soaring into the heavens and says "only a very literal mind" will want to know whether this is the earthly Mount Zion or its heavenly counterpart.[6] For Boring this number gives the picture of the redeemed church in the presence of God and of the Lamb as the significant point.[7]

---

1. Charles, *Critical and Exegetical Commentary*, 2:1–3.
2. Kiddle, *Revelation*, 262–63.
3. Mounce, *Revelation*, 267–68; cf. Wilson, *Revelation*, 118.
4. McDowell, *Meaning and Message*, 147–48.
5. Krodel, *Revelation*, 261.
6. Lilje, *Last Book*, 199.
7. Boring, *Revelation*, 168.

To bring the focus back to the Lamb, the one hundred forty-four thousand are said to have the name of the Lamb and his Father on their foreheads. Hence the Lamb must be the Son, identical with the slain but living Lamb of Rev 5. Wilson equates the names on the forehead with the seal of God of Rev 7. He then quotes Lenski as follows: "These two names are the seal because no man comes to the Father save by the Son."[8]

I have made no attempt to deal with all the passages referring to Christ as the Lamb in Revelation. By my count there are 26 other such usages. The passages I have focused on are representative, and for the purposes of this study nothing would be added by dealing with these other passages.

The word *lamb* makes its appearance in the arena of evil at 13:11. The beast from the earth is described as having two horns like a little lamb but speaking like a dragon. Charles cites Mommsen for the view that this beast represents state officials in the provinces and notes that "a number of notable scholars" have identified it with the heathen priesthood. He then takes his stand with Holtzmann, Pfleiderer, Bousset, and J. Weiss by interpreting this beast as the imperial priesthood in the provinces of the Roman Empire.[9] This view is further supported by the reference to the beast as the false prophet (16:13, 19:20, and 20:10). Wilson takes a broader view and interprets this beast as false religion under the aegis of secular power. He agrees that in John's day the particular referent was the priests who propagandized the imperial cult, but without limiting it to this identification.[10]

Others have viewed the beast from the earth as referring to opponents within the church who encourage people to accommodate themselves to Roman culture, political ideology, and cult.[11] Garrow fits broadly into this interpretation, identifying the two horns of the beast as Balaam and Jezebel.[12] He does not seem to recognize that there is no prophet named Balaam mentioned in the Apocalypse, but only people holding (*kratountas*) the teachings of Balaam (2:14).

---

8. Wilson, *Revelation*, 118.

9. Charles, *Critical and Exegetical Commentary*, 1:357; see also Kiddle, *Revelation*, 253.

10. Wilson, *Revelation*, 114.

11. E.g., Boring, *Revelation*, 157.

12. Garrow, *Revelation*, 89.

Both Mounce[13] and Charles[14] have noted the apparent allusion to Jesus's words about false prophets and false messiahs in Matt 7:15. Mounce is probably correct in stating that throughout this section it is the first beast that parodies the Lamb of 5:6, but perhaps goes too far in suggesting that there is no allusion to that lamb in the present passage.[15] When we remind ourselves that the first recipients of the Apocalypse probably heard rather than read this writing, how likely is it that anyone would have heard the phrase "two horns like a little lamb" without remembering the slain but living Lamb of Rev 5? Mounce is to be commended for avoiding the common pitfall of identifying this beast solely with the emperor cult to the exclusion of any other meaning. His conclusion is that "in the final days of Antichrist [*sic*] the false prophet stands for the role of false religion in effecting the capitulation of mankind to the worship of secular power. It is the universal victory of humanism."[16] I cannot, however, agree with Mounce in his assumption (along with probably a majority of commentators) of an individual antichrist to come just before the end of the world. There is no Biblical support for this idea. In the only Biblical references to an antichrist, the antichrist is already present and is not one individual but many (1 John 2:18, 22; 4:7; 2 John 7).

In summation we have on the one hand the Lamb standing as having been slain who can be none other than the crucified, resurrected, and exalted Christ. As the counterimage we have a beast with the deceitful appearance of a lamb but whose speech is that of the chief of the powers of evil. Since, as noted above, not only the same verb, but the same form of the verb is used in reference to the Lamb and the beast, the probability is high that the Seer was deliberately counterimaging the two.

---

13. Mounce, *Revelation*, 258–59.
14. Charles, *Critical and Exegetical Commentary*, 1:358.
15. Mounce, *Revelation*, 259.
16. Ibid.

13

A White Horse

And I saw the heaven having been opened and behold a white horse (appeared), and the one sitting upon it is called faithful and true; and with righteousness he judges and does battle. . . . And the soldiers in heaven were following him upon white horses, having been clothed (with) clean white linen

(REV 19:11, 14)

And I looked, and behold a white horse (appeared) with the one sitting upon it holding a bow; and a crown was given to him, and he went out conquering and in order that he might conquer (more)

(REV 6:2)

AS NOTED IN PASSING earlier, the rider on the white horse in Rev 19 can only be the exalted, victorious Christ. He is called faithful and true, terminology that first appeared in the address to the church at Laodicea (3:14). He judges and does battle in righteousness. As Charles,[1] Krodel,[2] and Mounce[3] have noted, the picture of a warrior Messiah echoes *Ps Sol* 17:22–24, 32. Most modern commentators interpret this scene as the *parousia*—the second coming of Christ—and the supernatural defeat of the forces of evil. Boring is among these, although he admits that this picture of Jesus as a military conqueror is without parallel in any Christian Testament portrayal of the *parousia*.[4] Krodel, after commenting that we might have expected the Messiah to be riding on a donkey

---

1. Charles, *Critical and Exegetical Commentary*, 2:131.
2. Krodel, *Revelation*, 323.
3. Mounce, *Revelation*, 343.
4. Boring, *Revelation*, 195.

in accordance with Zech 9:9 says, "But at his parousia [*sic*] the Messiah appears, not in the lowliness of the suffering servant, but in the majesty of the eschatological warrior whom no one can withstand."[5] In similar fashion Mounce speaks of the rider on the white horse as coming to bring the present age to an end.[6] Kiddle comments that the Lamb has now become a warrior prince. He who shares the throne of God is now ready to assert that unlimited authority which rightfully belongs to him.[7] This line of interpretation is maintained only at the cost of saying that John is mistaken in what he saw, however. The Roman state and the imperial cult were not defeated suddenly by a supernatural army. One could even say that the Roman state eventually bowed to the church rather than being destroyed. Of course futurist interpreters would say that we have misinterpreted the two beasts—that they are yet to come—but such an interpretation leaves the writing meaningless to its first recipients.

McDowell has advanced an interpretation that avoids the difficulty of saying that John was mistaken. He takes the position that although John uses apocalyptic language, he does not envision a sudden, cataclysmic end of the world. Rather than the rider on the white horse representing the *parousia*, the picture is that of Christ's repeated coming with the word of God by which he either wins his way into human hearts or hardens them against him so that they destroy themselves. As I have noted above, Revelation depicts evil as turning inward on and destroying itself. The battle is a spiritual one. "It was by the word of God that Christ conquered the Caesars; it is by the word of God that he continues his conquest in history."[8] In view of McDowell's interpretation it is interesting to note that most of the references in the Apocalypse to the coming of Christ are in the present tense (2:5, 16; 3:11; 16:15; and 22:7, 12, 20). Only in 2:25 and 3:3 do we find a verb in the future tense referring to Christ's coming. Even in these two passages the reference may or may not be to the *parousia*. McDowell's position does not leave out the *parousia*, it only places the emphasis on the present and repeated visitations of Christ. His position is that the text presents both repeated visits and the *parousia* rather than an either/or position.

5. Krodel, *Revelation*, 321.
6. Mounce, *Revelation*, 343.
7. Kiddle, *Revelation*, 384.
8. McDowell, *Meaning and Message*, 185–86.

The appearance of a white horse in the arena of evil occurs in 6:2. I have previously demonstrated that this rider on a white horse is an imposter and a counterfeit of the rider in 19:11–16. Kerkeslager has argued, based on the order of events in the Synoptic apocalypse (Mark 13 and parallels), that the rider on the white horse represents false messiahs and that the bow has its background in the legend of Apollo. He further maintains that the rider is a counterfeit of Christ, and that both false messiahs and false prophets are combined in the symbolism of the white horse and the bow.[9] This symbolism has by no means been consistently recognized by interpreters. Charles cites five different interpretations that have been advocated. Among those who have seen the rider on a white horse solely as a reference to the Parthian armies are Holtzmann, Schmidt, Ramsay, Swete, and Bousset. To this group may be added the names of two more recent interpreters, Boring[10] and Krodel.[11] Lilje accepts the interpretation that the Parthian armies are in view here and says of this first rider that "his whole appearance suggests irresistible victorious power."[12] Ramsay suggests that this rider "describes the Parthian king as seen by Roman apprehension, followed by bloodshed, scarcity and death."[13] Erbest and Volter advance an even more limited interpretation that restricts the meaning to the Parthian general Vologases, who defeated the Romans in 62 C.E. Spitta thought that the rider symbolized Rome. A surprising number have equated this rider with the one in 19:11–16; among them are Victorinus, Primasius, Bede, Bullinger, Paraeus, Grotius, Dusterdieck, and B. Weiss. To this list Mounce adds the names of Hendrickson and Zane Hodges.[14] Even more surprisingly, Hilgenfeld, Zahn, Alford, and Kubel have argued that this horseman represents the victorious march of the Gospel.[15] Rissi is closer to the truth in identifying the rider as the Antichrist [sic], but this is too limited an interpretation.[16] McDowell broadens the interpretation sufficiently to allow it to meet the principles of interpretation presented at the beginning of this study. After pointing out that the white horse and

---

9. Kerkeslager, "Apollo and the Rider on the White Horse," 116–21.
10. Boring, *Revelation*, 122.
11. Krodel, *Revelation*, 173.
12. Lilje, *Last Book*, 125.
13. Ramsay, *Letters*, 44.
14. Mounce, *Revelation*, 153 n.
15. Charles, *Critical and Exegetical Commentary*, 1:63–64; cf. Wilson, *Revelation*, 64.
16. Cited in Mounce, *Revelation*, 154, n.

the bow would probably have reminded any first-century Roman audience of the Parthians, he goes on to say, "He might represent Domitian, who set himself up as a god in opposition to the Lord God of hosts. Or he may stand in our own time for a Napoleon, a Hitler, or some would-be conqueror yet to come."[17] I will note in passing that most modern interpreters would allow at least a secondary reference to the Parthian armies, e.g., Summers,[18] Charles,[19] Krodel,[20] Mounce,[21] and Boring.[22] Kiddle points out that this rider on a white horse depicts a host of invaders—a common expectation in early Christian and Jewish eschatology. He notes the prophecies in Isa 5:26-30 and Jer 40:14; and suggests that the Seer has treated these predictions as applying to his time. Kiddle dissociates the symbolism from any past invasions of the Parthians and insists that the present and future are the Seer's concern.[23]

Let us now take a closer look at the further description of the rider in 6:2. The bow that he carries is part of the reason for the numerous suggestions that he symbolizes the Parthian armies. The Parthians were known like no other ancient people in the ancient world for their archers and white horses. A few interpreters have attempted to relate the bow to the rainbow of the promise to Noah that the world would never again be destroyed by water (Gen 9:12-13). This suggestion is in part an attempt to maintain the interpretation that the rider is Christ. Although the word *toxon* that appears here has sometimes been used for a rainbow, John uses the word *iris* for rainbow (cf. 4:3 and 10:1). The crown that the rider wears—which *was given* to him—is an obvious symbol of conquest and sovereignty, but it is only a counterfeit of the real sovereignty that belongs to God and the Lamb.[24] Instead of a crown (*stephanos*) which *was given* (*edothē*) to the rider in 6:2, the victorious Christ wears *many diademata*, or "diadems." All attempts to equate the two riders on white horses fail to take account of John's love of counterimaging.

---

17. McDowell, *Meaning and Message*, 89.
18. Summers, *Worthy Is the Lamb*, 140.
19. Charles, *Critical and Exegetical Commentary*, 1:163.
20. Krodel, *Revelation*, 173-74.
21. Mounce, *Revelation*, 154.
22. Boring, *Revelation*, 122.
23. Kiddle, *Revelation*, 113-14.
24. Cf. Wilson, *Revelation*, 64-65.

14

From the East

And I saw another angel coming up from the east having the seal of the living God, and he cried out with a loud voice to the four angels to whom was given (authority) to hurt the earth and the sea, saying, "Do not hurt the earth or the sea or the trees until we seal the servants of God upon their foreheads."

(Rev 7:2–3)

And the sixth (angel) poured out his vial upon the great river Euphrates, and its waters were dried up, in order that the way of the kings from the east might be prepared.

(Rev 16:12)

THE POSITIVE USAGE OF the phrase "from the east" occurs in Rev 7:2–3 in the context of the sealing of the servants of God upon their foreheads. The actual phrase is *apo anatolēs hēliou*, "from the rising of the sun." When John is speaking of the gates on the four sides of the city in describing the new Jerusalem (21:13), he uses simply *apo anatolēs* for "east." Whether this usage is anything more than a stylistic feature may be debatable. I will argue, however, that this is another example of the author's counterimaging.

At this point I will limit my comments to the angel from the east. Whatever may be the significance of the phrase, this angel carries out the positive function of sealing the servants of God before the divine judgment and the wrath of the Lamb (6:16–17) begin to unfold. "From the rising of the sun" may signify nothing more than the eastern direction, or it may have something to do with the luminosity of the angel—although this interpretation will not fit the only other passage in which the phrase appears (16:12). Lilje speaks of the east as the "Paradise quarter."[1] Kiddle speaks of it as the region of light and the source of blessing. He also notes that this angel comes from the presence of God.[2]

Since, as Moyise has so clearly demonstrated,[3] the sealing of the servants of God is most clearly paralleled in Ezek 9:4, the author may have intended to remind us of Ezekiel's vision of the glory of the Lord returning from the east (Ezek 43:5–6). Morris mentions several other suggestions. Some commentators have suggested that it relates to the direction from which light originates, and hence the source of blessing (cf. Kiddle above). Others relate the phrase to the coming of the wise men from the east after the birth of Christ. Still others point to the notion in the *Sibylline Oracles* that the Messiah would come from the east. Morris also notes the curious interpretation of Victorinus that this angel from the east was Elijah.[4]

The only other occurrence of the phrase *apo anatolēs heliou* is in Rev 16:12. This verse will be more fully discussed in the chapter titled "River." I will limit my comments here to the phrase in question. In 16:12 the sixth angel pours out the vial of God's wrath on the Euphrates so that it dries up to make way for the kings *apo anatolēs heliou*. The relationship of these kings to the "kings of the whole world" (v. 14), who are gathered at Armageddon through the propaganda of the "unholy trinity" (v. 13), is anything but clear. As noted elsewhere, Charles and others have interpreted the kings from the east as the Parthian armies led by Nero *redivivus*. Kiddle seems also to accept this interpretation.[5] Lilje accepts the allusion to the Parthian armies but takes it as a picture of "great historical horrors" used to illustrate one of the eschatological plagues.[6] Mounce agrees that historically this interpretation has the greater probability, but he also notes the problem of the relationship of the "kings from the east" to the kings in v. 14. He thinks John has woven together two traditions: the Nero *redivivus* myth and another strand of tradition that spoke of a final assault of all the forces of evil against Christ and the armies of heaven.[7] Morris

1. Lilje, *Last Book*, 134.
2. Kiddle, *Revelation*, 132.
3. Moyise, *Old Testament in Revelation*, 71.
4. Morris, *Revelation*, 110–11; cf. Wilson, *Revelation*, 72.
5. Kiddle, *Revelation*, 323.
6. Lilje, *Last Book*, 216.
7. Mounce, *Revelation*, 298; for detailed discussion of this issue, see Kiddle, *Revelation*, 323–32.

calls attention to the fact that in the Nero *redivivus* myth, the late emperor was not coming to ally himself with Rome but rather to attack her. This reading would mean that in the end times a great schism would develop among the forces of evil and a terrible conflict would ensue.[8] Kiddle comments that the simple statement that the Euphrates was dried up to prepare the way for the kings of the east "is a grim foreboding of universal bloodshed, pillage, and ruin."[9]

Another difficulty of interpretation is that John never follows up on these kings from the east in any way, nor does he depict any great conflict among the forces of evil except in the general sense that he portrays evil as inherently self-destructive. The purposes of this study do not require a solution to these knotty interpretive problems. However one may interpret the kings from the east, they are clearly a symbol of evil, destructive forces.

In summary, what we find in the first of these two passages is an angel *apo anatolēs heliou* who accomplishes the positive task of sealing the servants of God in preparation for the unfolding judgments of God. In the other we find kings *apo anatolēs heliou* who are clearly a destructive force. Since John uses simply *anatole* for the direction east in 21:13, I conclude that he has deliberately used the phrase as a counterimage.

---

8. Morris, *Revelation*, 192–93.
9. Kiddle, *Revelation*, 323.

15

I Heard the Number

And I heard the number of the ones having been sealed, one hundred forty-four thusand having been sealed from every tribe of the sons of Israel.

(Rev 7:4)

And the number of the mounted soldiers was two hundred million; I heard the number of them.

(Rev 9:16)

WE COME ONCE MORE to a phrase rather than a single word that John uses in both arenas. First of all, we find in Rev 7 that John heard the number of those who were given the seal of God. The number specified is twelve thousand from each of the twelve tribes of Israel. Interpreters who take this number literally as the salvation of one hundred forty-four thousand Jews have not been lacking. For example, Mounce cites Walvoord and Glasson for this view, among many others who might be mentioned.[1] The Seer gives us a number of clues, however, that this figure is not to be taken literally. His list of the tribes does not agree with any listing found in the Jewish Scriptures. Dan is omitted, but that omission is explained by many interpreters as the result of the idolatry of that tribe and the tradition that the antichrist would arise from it. This interpretation goes back as far as Irenaeus.[2] John also omits Ephraim, however, although the latter was one of the largest and strongest tribes. Third, he includes Levi, which would make thirteen tribes, not twelve, since the Levites as the priestly tribe were disseminated among the other twelve tribes.[3] He lists a tribe of

---

1. Mounce, *Revelation*, 168.
2. Cited in Krodel, *Revelation*, 183.
3. Cf. Wilson, *Revelation*, 73.

Joseph, which never existed. Joseph's two sons, Ephraim and Manasseh, became the heads of tribes to bring the number to twelve, with Levi being omitted as the priestly tribe. As immersed in the Jewish Scriptures as the author of the Apocalypse is, the likelihood that he did not know any better is infinitesimally small. There can, I think, be little doubt that these were clues to the readers or hearers not to take the number literally. Charles (rightly in my judgment) interprets the one hundred forty-four thousand as "purely symbolic," being the number twelve multiplied by twelve and multiplied again a thousandfold. He cites Alford in support of this interpretation.[4] Others who support the interpretation of the one hundred forty-four thousand as a symbolic number including the complete number of God's people on earth include McDowell,[5] Krodel,[6] Mounce,[7] Wilson,[8] Hamstra,[9] and Boring.[10] Charles agrees with the interpreters just cited who interpret those being sealed as "spiritual Israel," not believers descended from literal Israel. He yet has to go to great lengths to make the list of the twelve tribes "correct," because of his position that this passage is derived from a Jewish source.[11]

Kiddle, while accepting the terminology of the new or spiritual Israel, nevertheless strongly insists that the one hundred forty-four thousand are only the martyrs. Taking note of the view that John foresaw a universal martyrdom of the church, he argues that such a view is "quite untenable."[12] Krodel agrees with Charles that the origin of this passage was a Jewish apocalyptic source but takes the twelve tribes as spiritual Israel.[13] Morris notes a number of passages in the Christian Testament suggesting that Christians are the true Israel and adds, "There is thus good reason for seeing a reference here to the church as the true Israel."[14] Before leaving this discussion, perhaps we should observe that the literal twelve

---

4. Charles, *Critical and Exegetical Commentary*, 1:206.
5. McDowell, *Meaning and Message*, 97.
6. Krodel, *Revelation*, 182–83.
7. Mounce, *Revelation*, 168.
8. Wilson, *Revelation*, 73.
9. Hamstra in Pate, *Four Views*, 106.
10. Boring, *Revelation*, 129.
11. Charles, *Critical and Exegetical Commentary*, 1:206–9.
12. Kiddle, *Revelation*, 135.
13. Krodel, *Revelation*, 180–81.
14. Morris, *Revelation*, 111–12; cf. Wilson, *Revelation*, 72.

tribes of Israel had not existed since the eighth century B.C.E., as noted by Mounce,[15] Krodel,[16] and Boring.[17] This fact has not proven to be a deterrent to futurist interpreters of Revelation—they simply assume that God will in some manner reconstitute the twelve tribes before the end. This is a misunderstanding of some of the prophets in the Jewish Scriptures that is long overdue for recognition as such.

As Krodel aptly notes, in the ancient world "Sealing was a mark of property, of protection, and of authentication."[18] The new Israel, the church, is being marked as the property of God. It is also being given protection, but protection from what? Protection from physical harm and death can scarcely be intended. Far from the popular rapture theology accepted by many modern readers of Hal Lindsey, Tim LaHaye, and similar popular interpreters, the seal of God protects through, not from, the developing woes. In Pinn's words, "Those who are sealed will be delivered, not from tribulation in this world, but through it."[19] In similar language Goldsworthy says, "The psalm-like description which follows makes it clear that these redeemed saints did not escape tribulation but rather came through it."[20]

As Boring has noted, this sealing has Ezek 9:3–4 as its background in the Jewish Scriptures. He further aptly says "those who bear the mark of God are kept through (not from!) the coming great ordeal, whatever the beastly powers of evil may be about to do to them."[21] Mounce, in a similar vein says, "Their being sealed does not protect them from physical death but ensures entrance into the heavenly kingdom. It indicates that they will remain faithful in the coming persecution."[22] McDowell echoes the same understanding, saying that "sealed with the seal of God they are secure, not indeed from physical injury, but secure in the protection they have received for their immortal souls from the hands of God."[23] Krodel, in similar fashion, argues that the protection is not from physical injury or

---

15. Mounce, *Revelation*, 168.
16. Krodel, *Revelation*, 180–81.
17. Boring, *Revelation*, 129.
18. Krodel, *Revelation*, 181.
19. Pinn, *Revelation Today*, 105.
20. Goldsworthy, *Gospel in Revelation*, 105.
21. Boring, *Revelation*, 28–29; cf. Kiddle, *Revelation*, 133–34.
22. Mounce, *Revelation*, 168.
23. McDowell, *Meaning and Message*, 97.

death but in spite of and within persecution and death.[24] Charles, although maintaining that in the original source protection meant protection from physical injury and death, goes to great lengths to argue that John meant protection from diabolic and demonic powers.[25]

The use of the phrase "I heard the number" in the arena of evil occurs in Rev 9:16. In the context a "star" has fallen from heaven with the key to the shaft of the abyss, following the blowing of the fifth trumpet (9:1). The identity of the star has been discussed previously. As the shaft of the abyss is opened, smoke pours forth. This smoke symbolizes the powers of evil that cloud people's minds and confuse their judgments.[26] Both Robbins and McDowell interpret this scene in a this-worldly fashion rather than an eschatological one,[27] but the eschatological interpretation is much more frequently seen. Most recent commentators suggest a point of historical contact in the appearance of the "cavalry" coming from the area of the Euphrates. For Jew and Roman alike, this image would have evoked painful and fearful thoughts. The Euphrates was the last natural boundary that stood in the way of the Babylonians and Assyrians in their march into Palestine. For the Romans the Euphrates separated them from the Parthians, of whom the Romans were almost paranoid in their fear. Despite this historical grounding of the symbolism, most interpreters do not think the events described in Revelation take place on the historical plane. Krodel, after noting the evocation of the Parthian threat, says of the Seer, "He was not interested in *historical* manifestations of this plague, but only in its *eschatological* dimension." He goes on to say, "The past tense of John's narration of what he saw should not be confused with the future content of the visions."[28] Boring likewise notes the fear of the Parthians that this scene would evoke, but says that John has elevated this historical anxiety to the level of eschatological myth.[29] Mounce takes a similar view, pointing out that "John's eschatological steeds breathe out fire and brimstone and have serpent-like tails with lethal heads."[30] In Kiddle's words,

---

24. Krodel, *Revelation*, 182.
25. Charles, *Critical and Exegetical Commentary*, 1:194–207.
26. Robbins, *Revelation*, 123.
27. McDowell, *Meaning and Message*, 104–5; Robbins, *Revelation*, 123.
28. Krodel, *Revelation*, 205.
29. Boring, *Revelation*, 138.
30. Mounce, *Revelation*, 201–2.

"Their appearance was as frightful as their number was overwhelming."[31] Charles is in basic agreement with these views, though he brackets the phrase "I heard the number" as a "confused gloss." He notes the occurrence of the phrase in 7:4 but argues that there is no true parallel.[32] In the latter statement he is absolutely correct. There is no parallel, but rather a *counterimage*. The Seer has juxtaposed the hearing of the complete and perfect number of those who receive the seal of God (one hundred forty-four thousand) over against the hearing of the number of the cavalrymen from Hell.[33]

---

31. Kiddle, *Revelation*, 163.
32. Charles, *Critical and Exegetical Commentary*, 1:252–53.
33. Cf. Krodel, *Revelation*, 205.

16

The Smoke

And the smoke of the incense went up out of the hand of the angel with the prayers of the saints into the presence of God.

(Rev 8:4)

And the temple was filled with the smoke from the glory of God and from his power, and no one was able to enter into the temple until the seven plagues of the seven angels could be completed.

(Rev 15:8)

And he opened the shaft of the abyss, and smoke went up out of the shaft like the smoke of a great furnace, and the sun and the air were darkened from the smoke (coming) out of the shaft; and out of the smoke came locusts into the earth, and authority was given to them like the scorpions of the earth have authority.

(Rev 9:2–3)

. . . and the heads of the horses (were) like the heads of lions, and out of their mouths fire and brimstone and smoke were going forth. From these three plagues a third of human beings was killed, from the fire and smoke and brimstone going out of their mouths.

(Rev 9:17b–18)

And the smoke of their torment is going up forever and ever; and those worshiping the beast and his image, and whoever is receiving the mark of his name, are having no rest day and night.

(Rev 14:11)

And the kings of the earth who committed fornication with her and became wanton will weep and mourn whenever they see the smoke of her burning.

(Rev 18:9)

And they were crying out as they were seeing the smoke of her burning, saying, Who is like the great city?

(Rev 18:18)

And a second (voice) said, "Hallelujah!" and her smoke is going up forever and ever.

(Rev 19:3)

THE FIRST POINT AT which the word *smoke* appears in a positive sense is in Rev 8:4. In this scene the throne-room vision of Rev 4 has become the heavenly temple.[1] Kiddle notes that John frequently interchanges his symbols of a royal court and throne with the altar where the worship of God is centralized.[2] The mixing of incense with the prayers of the saints symbolizes the fact that the prayers of the saints are heard and will be answered by God.[3] Mounce sees the smoke from the incense as symbolizing the divine acceptance of the prayers of the saints.[4] This liturgical action of the priestly angel connects the trumpet cycle with the throne-room vision of 5:8 and especially with the cry of the martyrs under the altar for justice in 6:9–11.[5] Wilson quotes Lenski's position that the smoke "represents the intercession of Christ for his church, which adds power and efficacy to the prayers of the church." He then goes on to say, "For it is only as the prayers of the saints are purified by Christ's intercession that they ascend to God as a fragrant offering."[6] As Boring points out, the content of the prayers is never revealed; rather the focus of John's message is that the prayers are heard and, as v. 5 shows, they do have an effect.[7] Charles's words are worth quoting in their entirety: "The prayers are made acceptable by be-

1. Krodel, *Revelation*, 194.
2. Kiddle, *Revelation*, 146.
3. McDowell, *Meaning and Message*, 102.
4. Mounce, *Revelation*, 182.
5. Krodel, *Revelation*, 194–95.
6. Wilson, *Revelation*, 78.
7. Boring, *Revelation*, 133.

ing offered with incense on the altar. All access to heaven lies through the avenue of sacrifice. Whether it be the prayers of the faithful or the martyrs themselves, both alike must be presented or offered on the heavenly altar that they may be cleansed thereby from the last taint of self, and be made acceptable to God."[8]

The only other usage of the word *smoke* in the arena of God's operation appears in 15:8. It appears in the immediate prelude to the outpouring of the seven vials, which I interpret as being the finalization of God's judgment on Babylon.[9] The scene is again the heavenly temple. Smoke from the glory of God fills the temple. We are told that no one can enter the temple until the seven plagues of the seven angels are completed. This scene would remind anyone familiar with the Jewish Scriptures of a number of passages. In the great vision of Isa 6, smoke is said to have filled the "house," i.e., the temple. Ezekiel depicts a scene in which the temple is filled with a cloud and the glory of the Lord (Ezek 10:4). In Exod 40:34–35 we encounter the notion that Moses was not able to enter the tabernacle because a cloud covered it and the glory of the Lord filled it.[10] Boring has presented at great length John's thoroughgoing usage of the Exodus story at this point.[11]

In typical fashion the Seer has transformed these images from the Jewish Scriptures, in which the primary idea seems to be the transcendent nature and the inapproachability of God by the merely human. In Revelation, the symbolism of the smoke or cloud as depicting the glory of God still holds, but a new dimension has been added. Once the time comes for the judgment of God, no one can stop that judgment. Entering the temple to intercede is no longer possible.[12] Charles aptly notes that in the passages from the Jewish Scriptures referred to above, the presence of God is a sign of his gracious purposes, but in Revelation the inability of anyone to enter the temple means that "until the plagues were accomplished, none could avert by prayer the doom about to befall the earth through these plagues."[13] While I would take exception to Kiddle's language, in which he speaks of the fire of God's wrath burning vehemently

---

8. Charles, *Critical and Exegetical Commentary*, 1:231.
9. Cf. McDowell, *Meaning and Message*, 153.
10. Cf. Charles, *Critical and Exegetical Commentary*, 2:39.
11. Boring, *Revelation*, 172–73.
12. Mounce, *Revelation*, 290; cf. Morris, *Revelation*, 185–86; Wilson, *Revelation*, 189.
13. Charles, *Critical and Exegetical Commentary*, 2:40; cf. Krodel, *Revelation*, 280.

and surrounding the divine presence with unspeakable terror, he has appropriately noted the resemblance to the awesome scene at Sinai.[14]

The interpreters cited above, along with the majority of commentators, hold to an eschatological interpretation of this passage. The plagues are interpreted as disorders affecting the whole world and that bring about the end of the world. McDowell takes a different view and argues cogently that these plagues represent God's judgment upon "Babylon," not the entire world. "These plagues are said to be the last in that there can be no expression of the wrath of God in degree beyond its direction toward a heathen world government such as that of the Caesars which denies the sovereignty of God in Christ."[15] Readily conceding that McDowell's is a minority view today, I personally find his arguments rather convincing.

I will briefly summarize the usage of the word *smoke* in these two passages. In the first text, the smoke ascends to God with the prayers of the saints in order to aid the effectiveness of those prayers. In the second, the smoke represents the glorious presence of God as God prepares to act in judgment upon Babylon. In both instances the smoke is clearly a symbol directly related to the activity of God.

Passages in which smoke is a negative symbol representing in some way the operation of evil forces begin with Rev 9:2–3. There the smoke is represented as coming out of the abyss and generating the demon locusts. This passage has already been sufficiently discussed.

The next occurrence of the word *smoke* takes us into the appearance of the two hundred million demonic cavalry from across the Euphrates who emerge after the blowing of the seventh trumpet. In 9:17b–18 we read that one-third of humankind is killed by the smoke, fire, and brimstone coming out of their mouths. The demonic character of this army is depicted in vivid apocalyptic language. The riders on the horses have breastplates the color of fire, hyacinth, and brimstone (v. 17), corresponding to the fire, smoke, and brimstone pouring from the mouths of the horses.[16] Plummer asserts that the punishments depicted here are a foretaste of hell, as indicated by the reference to fire, smoke, and brimstone.[17] The heads of the horses are said to be like the heads of lions, a symbol of the ferocity of the punishments added to the allusions to hell.

14. Kiddle, *Revelation*, 313–14.
15. McDowell, *Meaning and Message*, 153–58.
16. Charles, *Critical and Exegetical Commentary*, 1:252; Mounce, *Revelation*, 202.
17. Cited in Wilson, *Revelation*, 88.

Krodel notes an aspect of the mythological background of this scene by pointing to the smoke and fire said to come out of the mouth of the monster Leviathan in Job 41:1, 19–21.[18] Kiddle notes that monsters breathing fire and smoke were commonplace in ancient mythology, along with reminiscences of volcanoes belching fire and smoke, assumed by the ancients to come from the underworld.[19] Mounce notes and rightly rejects the interpretation that applies John's symbolism to tanks, cannons, and other instruments of modern warfare.[20]

We next encounter a passage about which one might ask whether it belongs in the arena of good or the arena of evil. In Rev 14:11 we find a vivid picture of the ceaseless torment of those worshiping the beast and receiving his mark. I am again taking the position that the Seer understands the punishment of evil as being ultimately self-inflicted, and so I place this scene in the arena of evil. We are told that the smoke of torment goes up forever and ever, and that those punished have no rest day or night. The latter phrase has already been examined as the counterimage to the ceaseless praise and worship of the four living creatures in Rev 4:8. Wilson, in commenting on this passage states "their punishment is endless because their guilt is endless."[21]

Not a few modern readers have taken exception to this picture of the ceaseless torment of the ungodly in the presence of the angels and the Lamb.[22] The Seer, however, is probably drawing on traditional imagery at this point. As Krodel points out, the picture of Hell as a place of eternal torment located opposite Paradise is mentioned in *1 Enoch* 90:26–27, 2 Bar 85:13–15, and 2 Esd 7:36.[23] We should no more interpret the symbolism literally here than in any other passage in the Apocalypse. John is concerned to establish the point that worship of God vs. worship of the beast is a matter of life and death. God's judgment is a reality depicted in symbolism designed to elicit abhorrence in the minds of the readers or hearers of this text.[24] Kiddle likewise advises against reading the reference

---

18. Krodel, *Revelation*, 206; Mounce, *Revelation*, 202; cf. Boring, *Revelation*, 128.
19. Kiddle, *Revelation*, 163–64.
20. Mounce, *Revelation*, 202–3.
21. Wilson, *Revelation*, 122.
22. Cf. Krodel, *Revelation*, 269.
23. Krodel, *Revelation*, 269.
24. Cf. Boring, *Revelation*, 170–71; Krodel, *Revelation*, 269.

to torment in the presence of God and the angels in a literal manner, and exhorts his readers to see that worship of the beast is a life-and-death matter.[25] Mounce cites the interpretations of Preston and Hanson that the truth of this passage lies in its portrayal of the suffering of those who deliberately turn away from the highest good, though he does not endorse their interpretation.[26] In my judgment, however, such an interpretation points us in the right direction. The torment of knowing that one has deliberately chosen a path, the end of which is eternal separation from God, is perhaps greater than the torment of literal fire and brimstone.

Our next passage to consider is Rev 18:9. The context is a chapter devoted to the judgment on Babylon or Rome. In the verses immediately preceding, the plagues of pestilence, mourning, famine, and fire are said to come upon her because of her sensual life and her pride.[27] Then we are told that the "kings of the earth" who had "committed fornication" with her would weep and mourn when they saw the smoke of her burning. Kiddle attributes the famine, pestilence, and conflagration to the assaults of antichrist and the Parthian hordes against the civilized world.[28] This historical reference could have been the understanding of the original recipients, but is meaningless beyond the era of the Roman Empire and hence must be judged an insufficient interpretation.

As Charles has noted, the language here is reminiscent of the lament over Tyre in Ezek 26:16–17. He interprets the "kings of the earth" as heathen nations whose princes are either subject to Rome or have some kind of alliance with the empire.[29] Krodel takes a similar view, stating that the kings are Rome's allies in the provinces. He thinks they are not so much identifiable individuals as types of those "who profited from Roman idolatry, exploitation and luxury."[30] Committing fornication and becoming wanton probably have overtones of both idolatry and illicit trade relations between the "kings of the earth" and Rome.[31] Both Krodel[32] and Mounce[33]

---

25. Kiddle, *Revelation*, 281–82.
26. Mounce, *Revelation*, 276–77.
27. Vss. 7–8; cf. Boring, *Revelation*, 187.
28. Kiddle, *Revelation*, 368–69.
29. Charles, *Critical and Exegetical Commentary*, 2:100–1; cf. Wilson, *Revelation*, 148.
30. Krodel, *Revelation*, 304.
31. Cf. Mounce, *Revelation*, 328.
32. Krodel, *Revelation*, 304.
33. Mounce, *Revelation*, 329.

hint at the attitude of unconcern for the "harlot" by noting that the kings, rather than coming to the rescue, stand off at a safe distance. This behavior indicates that they were concerned for their own loss, not for the welfare of the city itself.

Later in the same chapter (v. 18), we find another reference to the smoke of the burning of "Babylon." Kiddle summarizes this verse and its immediate context in very vivid language: "The Empire's political system, her commerce, her intricate communications, all have been shattered. The kings lament, for there is nothing now for them to rule. The merchants lament, for there is nothing for them to sell, and no one to buy. The seafarers lament, for their livelihood, their rich profit, is at an end. The Dark Ages [sic] contracted to a single day have fallen on the Roman world. The smoke from the funeral pyres of the world's cities clouds the sky with its last gloom."[34] This verse also presents us with a counterimage to the phrase, "Who is like God?" in the question, "Who is like the great city?" This question will be explored more fully in a later chapter.

The final appearance of the word *smoke* in the Apocalypse is in Rev 19:3. The context is that of heavenly rejoicing over the judgment of Babylon. "Hallelujah" is an Old Testament expression that literally means, "Praise ye Yahweh." Just as with the fate of those who worship the beast or receive his mark (14:11), the smoke of Babylon goes up forever and ever. The model for this passage was probably the depiction of judgment upon Edom as recorded in Isa 34:1–10. Charles argues that the passage means that the smoke goes up for a thousand years because we are on the verge of the millennial kingdom, and there will be no further devastation of anything on earth after the conclusion of the millennial reign.[35] One wonders if Charles has not lapsed into a literal interpretation that sometimes afflicts even the best commentators.

Once again we have a passage that could be interpreted as a sub-Christian gloating over the sufferings of others. To interpret the passage in this fashion would be to miss a very important point. Boring states the point succinctly: "The jubilation over the judgment of 'Babylon' (19:2) is thus not gloating but the celebration that God has reversed Rome's judgment against the Christians in a higher court and has made it manifest that he is the true judge."[36] Krodel, though linking the hallelujahs with

---

34. Kiddle, *Revelation*, 369.
35. Charles, *Critical and Exegetical Commentary*, 2:120.
36. Boring, *Revelation*, 192–93.

the destruction of the city, nevertheless prefaces his discussion with the statement, "These hallelujahs are ecstatic exclamations of praise befitting the arrival of the eschatological salvation."[37] Rowland comments, "There is very little cry for vengeance (though 19:3 comes close to it) despite the persecution described in these chapters (18:24). It is a celebration of the just and true judgments of God (19:1)."[38] Torrance, after commenting that the music in this chapter might be called the wedding march of the Lamb, says, "But it is a wedding march that recalls the judgments of God upon Babylon and catches up the authentic gratitude of the true church in her triumph over the counterfeit church of the world."[39] Kiddle takes a similar position, noting that the rejoicing in heaven is as much over the prospect of the marriage of the Lamb as over the execution of the justice of God as reflected in "Babylon's" burning.[40]

All these comments keep the focus where it belongs, in my opinion—on the positive celebration of God's judgment upon all that is evil. Rejoicing over the suffering and torment of any human beings must rightly be labeled sub-Christian. Where John's language points in this direction, the reminder that he lived in a day before Christian theology had taken clear shape might be in order. Certainly we should interpret such passages in light of the serious dangers that the Seer believed confronted the struggling churches of his day.

To summarize briefly the findings of this section, we noted two passages in which *smoke* is used in a positive manner. In the first, it is an aid to the prayers of the saints, and in the second it is a symbol of the presence of God. We then examined six passages in which the imagery of smoke is negative. In the first passage, smoke is a symbol of evil forces released from the abyss. In the second, smoke is one of the three elements issuing from the mouths of the demonic cavalry by which one-third of humanity was killed. In the third, smoke symbolizes the torment of those who worship the beast and receive his mark. The last three passages refer the smoke to the burning of "Babylon." These passages form a strong counterimage to the smoke that ascends with the prayers of the saints and the smoke that represents the beneficent presence of God.

---

37. Krodel, *Revelation*, 310.
38. Rowland, *Revelation*, 143.
39. Torrance, *Apocalypse Today*, 153–54.
40. Kiddle, *Revelation*, 377.

17

The River

And he showed me a river of water of life, clear as crystal, going out from the throne of God and the Lamb. In the midst of her street and on each side of the river (was) the tree of life bearing twelve fruits, each giving its fruit monthly; and the leaves of the tree (were) for healing of the nations.

(Rev 22:1–2)

And the sixth angel sounded a trumpet and I heard a voice from the horns of the golden altar which (was) before God saying to the sixth angel who had the trumpet, "Loose the four angels who have been bound by the great river Euphrates."

(Rev 9:13–14)

And the serpent cast water like a river out of his mouth after the woman, in order that she might be carried away by the river. And the earth helped the woman by opening its mouth and swallowing up the river which the Dragon cast out of his mouth.

(Rev 12:15–16)

And the sixth (angel) poured out his vial upon the great river Euphrates, and its water was dried up, in order that the way of the kings from the east might be prepared.

(Rev 16:12)

THE POSITIVE USAGE OF the term *river* occurs only in Rev 22:1–2, as part of John's vision of the New Jerusalem. Charles has again (without any real evidence, in my judgment) argued that this Jerusalem is one that descends from heaven for the millennial reign, not the permanent New Jerusalem. He does, however, raise a significant question as to whether the river of life in this verse has the same significance as the water(s) of life in 7:16, 21:6, and 22:17. He concludes guardedly that it probably does, though he notes that no explicit spiritual significance is attached to the river, in contrast with the discussion of the tree of life in the following verses.[1] Mounce, on the other hand, takes the description as that "of the people of God in the glorious and eternal age that is to come."[2] Caird notes that John has used here the Old Testament models of Ezekiel's New Jerusalem and the Garden of Eden. In the former, a river of life-giving water flows from the restored temple to the Dead Sea, causing it to bring forth fruit trees along its banks and living creatures in its waters.[3] Goldsworthy highlights the necessity of deviating from the description in Ezekiel, however. The New Jerusalem will have God and the Lamb as its temple (21:23). "That is why the river of life must flow from the throne of God and of the Lamb instead of from the threshold of the temple as Ezekiel originally depicted it."[4] Beasley-Murray notes the introduction of some new symbolic elements here: the throne of God and the Lamb,[5] and "the imagery of the paradise of Eden, linking the end of history to its beginning." He also notes that because the life-giving water in Ezekiel's vision flows from beneath the temple, there might appear to be a major difference. The difference is only apparent, however, because God and the Lamb have replaced the temple in the New Jerusalem that John is describing.[6] Mounce cites Swete as taking the position that the river refers to the Holy Spirit, and Ladd as arguing that it depicts immortality. He then concludes, "Obviously, all this is true, but the central affirmation of the verse is that in the eternal state the faithful will live at the source of the life-giving stream which proceeds from the very presence of God. In the hot and arid climate of Palestine this figure would hold special appeal."[7] Torrance's words on this passage are also worthy of our attention: "The new creation bears all that the former creation possessed, and more, for now there is no barrier to the tree of life. The fruit of it becomes the

1. Charles, *Critical and Exegetical Commentary*, 2:174–75.
2. Mounce, *Revelation*, 386.
3. Caird, *Commentary on Revelation*, 280; see Ezek 47:1–2, and cf. Farrer, *Revelation*, 222; Wilson, *Revelation*, 178; Morris, *Revelation*, 248.
4. Goldsworthy, *Gospel in Revelation*, 145–46; cf. Dumbrell, *End of the Beginning*, 38.
5. Cf. Rowland, *Revelation*, 158.
6. Beasley-Murray, *Revelation*, 330–31.
7. Mounce, *Revelation*, 386.

constant food for God's children, and its leaves perpetuate the power of redemption forever, while the river that makes glad the city of God flows eternally to quench the thirst."[8] Rowland has noted that in *1 Enoch*, with which John was possibly familiar, a river of fire flows from the throne, threatening all who came near. The threatening river of fire has, in John's vision, been replaced with the river of life-giving water flowing from a throne now occupied by both God and the Lamb.[9]

The first occurrence of *river* as a negative symbol is found in Rev 9:13–14, in the context of the sounding of the sixth trumpet. Charles would make this event the second trumpet because he excises the first four as interpolations.[10] In doing so he has made a shambles of the author's careful crafting of three septets (seals, trumpets, and vials), each broken down into groups of four and three, with an interlude between the sixth and seventh in each series. Boring[11] and others have argued that the pattern of an interlude is broken in the vials septet, but I am not fully convinced. The issue is whether Rev 16:13–16 is to be read as resulting from the outpouring of the sixth vial, or whether these verses are an interlude. Although it would admittedly be a much shorter interlude than the ones we find after the sixth seal and the sixth trumpet, the relationship between the "kings from the east" in v. 12 and the "kings of the whole world" in v. 14 is a major interpretive difficulty. I therefore am still inclined, along with Summers,[12] Krodel,[13] Schüssler Fiorenza, and others to treat 16:13–16 as an interlude.

With the sounding of the sixth trumpet, John hears a voice from the horns of the golden altar in the presence of God commanding the release of the four angels who have been bound by the great river Euphrates. Morris argues that their being bound indicates that they are evil angels who have been restrained until now but are presently allowed to operate with God's permission.[14] I see no necessity for such an interpretation.

---

8. Torrance, *Apocalypse Today*, 181.
9. Rowland, *Revelation*, 158.
10. Charles, *Critical and Exegetical Commentary*, 1:247–48.
11. Boring, *Revelation*, 121.
12. Summers, *Worthy Is the Lamb*, 187.
13. Krodel, *Revelation*, 286–87.
14. Morris, *Revelation*, 130.

Equally plausible is the reading that God is simply restraining his own messengers until the appropriate time for them to be released.

The reference to the Euphrates as the "great river" has its precedent in Gen 15:18, Deut 1:7, and Josh 1:4. Farrer notes the literary connection between the sixth unsealing and the sixth trumpet, saying, "What was held back in the unsealings is let loose in the trumpets."[15]

Papyrus Manuscript 47 reads "the four horns" in v. 13, but most manuscripts omit the word *four*. The interpretive significance of this reading is minimal. The real point seems to be the coming of the voice from the location where the prayers of the saints were offered up.[16] John's point is that the prayers of the saints are being answered, and those prayers play a significant role in the unfolding eschatological drama.[17] The voice would appear to be that of God rather than an angel, hence re-emphasizing the notion that God is responding to the prayers of the saints.[18] As Charles notes, this demonic plague appears to be in some way connected with the prayers of the saints, since the voice commanding the plague arises from the altar where those prayers were offered.[19]

The moral issue of a Christian prayer leading to the destruction of a third of humanity (9:18) would probably not have occurred to John. Caird notes that if it had been common practice for Christians to pray for the civilized world to be devastated by Satanic hordes, then the Roman charge against them that they were haters of humanity would have some justification. The question as to why horror must be piled upon horror before the coming of the kingdom of God must be faced squarely. Caird goes on to say, "John is determined that his readers shall face this question with the grimmest realism before he is prepared to give the answer."[20] Caird does not expound any further, but I gather he meant something like what Beasley-Murray expresses, namely that "the kingdom comes with judgment."[21] That judgment, as the prophets of the Jewish Scriptures

---

15. Farrer, *Revelation*, 121.
16. See 6:9, 8:3–4; cf. Wilson, *Revelation*, 87.
17. Cf. Mounce, *Revelation*, 199–200; Caird, *Commentary on Revelation*, 121.
18. Beasley-Murray, *Revelation*, 163.
19. Charles, *Critical and Exegetical Commentary*, 1:248.
20. Caird, *Commentary on Revelation*, 121–22.
21. Beasley-Murray, *Revelation*, 163.

repeatedly voiced, is a two-edged sword (cf. Isa 2:12–17, 13:6–13; Amos 5:18–19, Joel 2:11, Mal 3:1–2, and elsewhere).

The identity of the four angels who are to be released has been much debated. Some have attempted to identify them with the four angels in Rev 7:1 who are holding back the four destructive winds. As Beasley-Murray notes, however, about all they have in common is the number four and their connection with destruction. In 7:1 the angels are holding back the winds, whereas in the current passage the angels themselves are being held back. One could argue that Morris's interpretation that the angels are evil is on the right track, though I am not fully convinced. At 7:1 they stand at the "four corners of the earth," whereas here they stand by the Euphrates.[22] After discussing the possible influence of *1 Enoch* and the Gog/Magog prophecies of Ezekiel upon this passage, Charles finally concludes that the identity of the angels cannot be known, "nor can we even conjecture why the number is 'four.'"[23] If he had been able to shake himself out of his literalist mode of interpretation, he might have found a very plausible conjecture in numerical symbolism. The number four is one of John's ways of saying that what he is describing affects the entire created order.

I have previously discussed the Euphrates as the last natural obstacle for the enemies of Jews and Romans alike, and will pursue that issue no further here. For the purposes of this study, noting that *river* in this passage is associated with destruction and with demonic forces will be sufficient. That God commands the release of the angels does not mitigate this fact. That the powers of evil operate only with God's permission is one of the most consistent teachings of the Apocalypse.

The second negative use of *river* depicts the one that the dragon sends out after the "woman" in an attempt to destroy her (12:15–16). Farrer has noted that seeing Old Testament typology in this passage is much easier than finding a corresponding reality in the historical situation. The woman is reminiscent of the delivery of the Israelites from Egypt. The dragon's pursuit typifies in a general way the pursuit of Pharaoh's armies. The river evokes several Old Testament passages in which the onslaught of evil is compared to a flood of waters. The earth's swallowing the river cast after the woman seems designed to remind us of the swallowing up

---

22. Ibid.; cf. also Charles, *Critical and Exegetical Commentary*, 1:248, 250.
23. Charles, *Critical and Exegetical Commentary*, 1:251.

of Pharaoh and his armies by the Red Sea. Farrer then goes on to give an astrological interpretation of some of the symbolism. The eagle, the lady, and the scorpion are all interpreted as astrological figures. The river is the Milky Way. After all this, Farrer comments, "The continued presence of star-lore is perplexing."[24] The reason it is perplexing could be the fact that John had none of these astrological figures in mind when he wrote!

Beasley-Murray accepts the Exodus typology but refrains from any astrological interpretation. He also calls attention to the reference in Judg 5:20 to the stars in their courses fighting against Sisera as another example of the created order coming to the aid of the people of God.[25] Caird connects the referent of these verses to the "river of lies" coming from those who claimed to be Jews but were really a synagogue of Satan.[26] Wilson writes, "This river of lies is the satanic parody of the river of life which flows from the heavenly throne."[27] Mounce suggests the referent as possibly the attempts of the Jerusalem authorities to eradicate the early church as reflected in Acts 8:1–3, for example.[28] Farrer attempts to make a connection with the Jewish wars of 66–73 C.E. and the flight of the church from the armies of Rome. The variety of the explanations offered for the river should remind us that there is no one-to-one correspondence between John's symbols and historical realities. One might even say that there is a deliberate ambiguity in the symbols. More and more scholars are beginning to note the polyvalent character of the symbolism. All the above explanations probably have some merit. Whether any of them, or all of them put together, completely captures the intention of the author must remain an open question.

Mounce remarks, "This river of deceit has as its counterpart the 'river of the water of life' which flows bright as crystal from the heavenly throne (21:1)."[29] The word *counterpart* does not appropriately represent the opposite nature of the two rivers, however. I would change "counterpart" to "counterimage." Wilson's use of "parody" is nearer the mark. One river has Satan as its source and is used in an attempt to destroy the people of God.

---

24. Farrer, *Revelation*, 148–49.
25. Beasley-Murray, *Revelation*, 205–6.
26. Caird, *Commentary on Revelation*, 158–59; see Rev 2:9 and 3:9.
27. Wilson, *Revelation*, 109.
28. Mounce, *Revelation*, 246.
29. Ibid.

The other river has its source in the sovereignty (throne) of God and the Lamb, and is used for the eternal preservation of the people of God.

The final negative use of the word *river* (16:12) is again in connection with the Euphrates. This time that river is dried up, following the pouring out of the sixth vial, to make way for the coming of the "kings from the east." Charles predictably interprets these kings as the Parthian hordes returning under Nero *redivivus* to march against "Rome, the throne of the Beast." The interpretation, however, is not so simple. Walvoord claims that no fewer than fifty different interpretations of these kings have been given.[30] The better part of valor may be to leave the meaning of the kings as an open question.

Farrer notes that the drying-up of the Euphrates has overtones of Jer 1:38 and Isa 11:15. The purpose of the drying-up in the latter passage is to let armies pass, as in the present passage.[31] Sleeper takes note of the river that the dragon spews after the woman (12:15–16) along with the two passages relating to the Euphrates and concludes, "The river then is another symbol of destruction."[32] This is true of the three passages he mentions, but he fails to take notice of the counterimage, the "river of the water of life" in Rev 22:1.

Parenthetically, let me call attention to the fact that *potamos*, or "river," occurs also in Rev 8:10 and 16:4. In both those verses it is plural and a general reference to "the rivers." The passages I have included above are the only ones that refer to a specific river.

---

30. Cited in Mounce, *Revelation*, 298.
31. Farrer, *Revelation*, 176–77.
32. Sleeper, *Victorious Christ*, 30.

18

To Do Battle and to Conquer

These will do battle with the Lamb, and the Lamb will conquer them because he is Lord of lords and King of kings; and those with him (are) called and chosen and faithful (people).

(Rev 17:14)

And when their testimony is completed the beast who comes up out of the abyss will do battle with them and will conquer them and kill them.

(Rev 11:7)

And it was given to him to do battle with the holy ones and to conquer them; and authority was given to him over every tribe and people and tongue and nation.

(Rev 13:7)

THE COUNTERIMAGING EXPLORED IN this section focuses on two key verbs: to make war (*polemeō*) and to conquer (*nikaō*). The first passage in which they appear together is Rev 17:14. The larger context is the description of the "great prostitute" and the beast on which she sits. The beast is described as having seven heads and ten horns, thus linking him with the dragon (Rev 12:3) and the beast from the sea (13:1). The ten horns of the beast are further described as ten kings not yet in power but who will receive authority as kings with the beast for "one hour" (17:12). In the historical context, the ten kings are probably satellite kings under Roman suzerainty, although that detail need not detain us. What is significant for the purposes of this study is that the ten kings will do battle (*polemēsousin*) with the Lamb, and the Lamb will conquer (*nikēsei*) them because he is King of kings and Lord of lords (17:14b). These titles are well-known attestations of sovereignty that appear in both canonical and non-canonical writings. In the former category, Mounce cites Deut 10:17 and Dan 2:47. In the latter he cites 2 Macc 13:4 and *1 Enoch* 9:4.[1] Beasley-Murray calls attention to a Babylonian tradition in which these titles are accorded to Marduk as the conqueror of the monster Tiamat. He concludes that if John knew of this tradition, he has accorded to the Lamb the sole privilege of using these titles because he and he alone is the true conqueror of evil.[2]

Exactly how this battle unfolds we are never told. Beasley-Murray's suggestion that v. 14 "compresses a whole complex of ideas" is well taken.[3] Among the missing details is the role that the followers of the Lamb play in this battle.[4] Beasley-Murray thinks that in Rev 11–13, the saints are allied with the Lamb in the battle; and based on the parallels with 13:7, they conquer by the blood of the Lamb and their own faithful testimony.[5] Kiddle likewise regards the battle as being fought and won by the Lamb and the elect. He interprets the latter as the martyrs coming out of the "great distress."[6] This interpretation is rendered doubtful in that only the Lamb is said to conquer in 17:14. While it is true that the "called and chosen and faithful" are said to be with the Lamb, nothing is said about their taking part in the conquest in any way. We noted the same phenomenon earlier in 19:14. Morris notes that these called and chosen persons are the retinue of the Lamb, not his resources. They do not represent any external auxiliary because the Lamb has no need of such.[7]

The use of the phrases "to do battle" and "to conquer" in the arena of evil appear first in Rev 11:7. The context is the testimony of the two witnesses. This time we have the noun form of the word for *battle* instead of the verb. Their similarity is such that to one listening as this document was being read aloud, the likelihood of associating this passage with the one cited above is considerable. We are told that when the two witnesses complete (*telesōsin*) their testimony, the beast from the abyss will make war (*polēmsei polemon*) with them and will conquer (*nikēsei*) them. Kiddle interprets the

1. Mounce, *Revelation*, 318.
2. Beasley-Murray, *Revelation*, 259.
3. Ibid., 258.
4. Cf. Mounce, *Revelation*, 318.
5. Beasley-Murray, *Revelation*, 258.
6. Kiddle, *Revelation*, 354.
7. Morris, *Revelation*, 206.

completion of the witnesses' testimony as the carrying of the gospel of repentance and the warning of impending judgment to all parts of the earth by the witnessing church.[8] The identity of the witnesses has been discussed earlier. I will add only the comment in support of Kiddle that two individuals would hardly justify a battle on the part of the beast. As Morris has noted, the two witnesses represent a mighty host, not individuals. The beast will do battle with them and will be temporarily victorious.[9] Wilson notes that this passage does not portray the martyrdom of the entire church, but rather that the church will experience ever-increasing opposition by the forces of Satan, which will result in an apparent victory for the forces of evil.[10] The two witnesses are a cipher for the entire witnessing church.[11]

The beast in this passage has been variously interpreted. Farrer is very dogmatic in saying that this beast must be interpreted in the light of Dan 7:2–21, not from the discussion of the beasts in Rev 13 and 17.[12] About all these passages have in common, however, is the beast's defeat of the saints or witnesses. Against Farrer's argument is the fact that all of Daniel's beasts come up out of the sea, not out of the abyss. Mounce is more cautious, suggesting that the beast may be a reference to Dan 7 or may anticipate the discussion of the beasts in Rev 13 and 17.[13] Morris calls attention to the definite article before *beast*, and suggests that this is the same beast who figures so prominently in the second half of the book.[14] Beasley-Murray mentions the Daniel passage but identifies the beast with the one in Rev 13 and 17.[15] Kiddle sees the beast as the Roman emperors collectively, "having the same allegorical shape as the great Dragon himself."[16] Perhaps the best approach is to see this passage as looking back to the opening of the shaft of the abyss in Rev 9:1–2 and forward to Rev 13 and 17. Caird makes the important point that John is not predicting the future emergence of this beast but that "this monster

---

8. Ibid., 198.

9. Morris, *Revelation*, 145.

10. Wilson, *Revelation*, 97.

11. Cf. Mounce, *Revelation*, 225; Farrer, *Revelation*, 133; Caird, *Commentary on Revelation*, 134; Beasley-Murray, *Revelation*, 185; Kiddle, *Revelation*, 198.

12. Farrer, *Revelation*, 135.

13. Mounce, *Revelation*, 225.

14. Morris, *Revelation*, 145.

15. Beasley-Murray, *Revelation*, 185.

16. Kiddle, *Revelation*, 199.

has a long history, and rising from the abyss is not a single episode in its career but the permanent cast of its character."[17] The use of the present participle *to anabainon* ("the one coming up") would appear to support Caird's interpretation. John at this point seems to focus on the death of the two witnesses at the hand of the beast rather than a description of the beast. If the two witnesses have correctly been interpreted as the entire witnessing church, the question naturally arises, Did John think the entire church would have to die at the hand of the beast? As Beasley-Murray notes, we must not take this passage in isolation from the remainder of Revelation. John has indicated that martyrs will die at various periods (cf. 6:9–11) and that not all are marked out for physical martyrdom. He then comments, "The war of Antichrist [sic] is carried out ruthlessly, but we must take it that if many are killed, others are merely repressed—driven underground, as we should say."[18] It is the church in its entirety that John has designated by the phrase "two witnesses," not the church as composed of a large number of individuals. Beginning shortly after Revelation was written, there have been many points in history where the church seemed to have been killed by the "beast." Each time her enemies have begun to celebrate her defeat, however, she has miraculously come to life again. The beast is only allowed, in the providence of a sovereign God, to win limited and temporary victories.

Before leaving this passage, a word about the completion of the testimony of the witnesses is in order. Some translations and interpreters impose a chronological sequence on the completion of the testimony and the conquest by the beast (cf. Kiddle above). Caird's interpretation should provide a word of caution concerning such an interpretation. The word translated "finish" or "ended" in 11:7 is an aorist subjunctive in the Greek (*telesōsin*), preceded by *hotan* ("whenever"). The verb *teleō* means not so much "to end" or "to terminate" as to bring something to fulfillment of its intended goal or purpose.[19] In combination with *hotan* it lends itself most naturally to the interpretation that whenever the testimony of the witnessing church is fulfilled, the beast arises to do battle and to defeat it. This is not a single battle of the end times but an ongoing series of battles on the plane of history. It is precisely at the time when the witness of the

17. Caird, *Commentary on Revelation*, 137.
18. Beasley-Murray, *Revelation*, 185; cf. Farrer, *Revelation*, 134.
19. Cf. Morris, *Revelation*, 145.

church becomes most complete that it inspires a comparable strength on the part of the "beast."

The second and final passage in which the powers of evil are said to do battle and to conquer is 13:7. While there may be some question regarding the identity of the beast in 11:7, in this passage we are dealing with the beast from the sea. Typically the divine passive is used, indicating that the beast has no authority beyond what has been given to him by a sovereign God.[20] The language is almost, though not quite, identical with that in 11:7. The key phrases are "to do battle" (*poiēsei polemon*) and "to conquer" (*nikēsai*). The phrase "it was given" (*edothē*) is used twice in this verse, as if to make sure we remember that the beast has no authority of its own. Although his authority is in one sense universal ("over every tribe and tongue and people and nation"), it yet remains an authority that is exercised only within the permissive will of God. Morris adds that this proves that more than the Neronian persecution of the church was in John's mind because that persecution was not worldwide.[21] Concerning the universality of the beast's authority, Swete comments, "Wherever the Gospel was carried, Rome was there beforehand; the Beast's [sic] authority extended over all the nations and races which surrounded the Mediterranean."[22] Kiddle makes the intriguing comment on v. 7 that "We must do full justice to the vigour [sic] of a faith which saw in the very prevalence of evil the presiding wisdom and might of God."[23]

To briefly summarize this section, the Seer has counterimaged the words for *battle* and *conquer*. Although he has used the verb *polemeō* in 17:14 and the noun form *polemon* in 11:7 and 13:7, the word is so similar in its noun and verb forms that the connection could scarcely be missed when hearing the Apocalypse read aloud. The verb *nikaō* ("conquer"), is used in all three passages. The beast is permitted to win a temporary battle with the saints, but the Lamb is granted permanent and complete victory over the forces of evil. The beast's temporary waging of battle and conquest is counterimaged against the permanent conquest and eternal victory of the Lamb.

---

20. Ibid., 164.
21. Morris, *Revelation*, 164.
22. Cited in Wilson, *Revelation*, 113.
23. Kiddle, *Revelation*, 248.

19

The City

And I saw the holy city, New Jerusalem, coming down out of heaven from God, having been prepared like a bride who has been adorned for her husband. . . . And he brought me in spirit to a great and high mountain, and he showed me the holy city, Jerusalem, coming down from God out of Heaven. . . . And the one speaking to me had a golden measuring rod in order that he might measure the city and its gates and its walls. And the city lies foursquare, that is, its length was the same as its width; and he measured the city with the rod as twelve thousand stadia; the length and width and height of it are equal. . . . And the structure of its walls (was) jasper and the city (was) pure gold like a clean, transparent stone. The foundations of the walls of the city were adorned with every precious stone; . . . And the twelve gates (were) twelve pearls, each gate being one pearl, and the (main) street of the city (was) pure gold like (a) transparent stone. . . . And the city has no need of the sun or of the moon to give light to it, because the glory of God gives it light, and the Lamb (is) its lamp.

(Rev 21:2, 10, 15–16, 18–19a, 21, and 23)

Blessed (are) the ones washing their clothing so that their authority will be over the tree of life, and they will enter into the city by its gates.

(Rev 22:14)

And their body (lay) upon the street of the great city which is called spiritually Sodom and Egypt, where also their Lord was crucified.

(Rev 11:8)

And the great city was split into three parts; the cities of the nations also fell. And Babylon the Great was remembered before God who gave to her the cup of the wine of the wrath of his anger.

(REV 16:19)

And the woman which you saw is the great city, the one having dominion over the kings of the earth.

(REV 17:18)

And the kings of the earth who committed fornication and became wanton with her will weep and lament over her whenever they see the smoke of her burning, having taken their stand from afar because of the fear of her torment, saying, "Woe, woe, the great city; Babylon, the strong city; because in one hour your judgment came." And the merchants of the earth will weep and mourn over her because no one buys their cargoes any longer. The merchants of these things who became wealthy from her will stand far away because of the fear of her torment, weeping and mourning, saying, "Woe, woe, the great city; the one having been clothed (with) linen, and having been gilded with gold and precious stone and pearl." . . . and they were crying out when seeing the smoke of her burning, saying, "Who is like the great city?" And they threw dust upon their heads and were crying out, weeping and mourning, saying, "Woe, woe the great city, by which all those having boats in the sea were made wealthy from her riches; for in one hour she was made a wilderness." . . . And one strong angel took a stone like a great millstone and cast (it) into the sea, saying, "Thus with passion Babylon, the great city, will be thrown; and she will not be found any longer."

(REV 18:9–10, 15–16, 18–19, AND 21)

THE POSITIVE IMAGES OF a city are mostly concentrated in the last two chapters of Revelation. Although the New Jerusalem that comes down out of heaven from God is a reward promised to the victorious in the address to the church at Philadelphia (3:12), I have chosen to focus only on the occurrences of the image in Rev 21 and 22. In 21:2 the New Jerusalem is pictured as a bride adorned for her husband. The bride of the Lamb has already been introduced in 19:7. That we are still dealing with the same symbol is made evident in 21:9–11. There John is invited to come and see the bride, the Lamb's wife, and is then shown the New Jerusalem, which is again described as coming down out of heaven from God. Kiddle makes the important point that the New Jerusalem is not a lure or bribe dangled in front of the struggling Christian communities. This city is one in which only the holy can dwell. "Only those who long for communion with God can drink of the river of the water of Life (xxii.i) [sic]."[1]

Charles's rearrangement theory regarding 21:3—22:21 is well known but should be at least mentioned in passing. According to this theory, John died after he wrote 21:3 and left the remaining material in separate documents that a faithful but unintelligent disciple reassembled in the order he thought best. Charles further argued that this material speaks of two different heavenly cities: one, the capital city of the millennial kingdom; and the other, an eternal city.[2] Charles's rearrangement theory has not met with wide acceptance; however, a wide variety of interpretations of these passages has been advanced by various commentators. After noting that John's vision of the holy city dominates his vision of a new heaven and a new earth, Beasley-Murray continues, "The city fills his vision since it is the centre [sic] of existence for the redeemed and renewed mankind in the new creation."[3] Morris appropriately notes that the adjectives "new" and "holy" emphasize the distinction of the city from this world, whereas "Jerusalem" emphasizes continuity.[4] Ladd interprets the city as the dwelling place of saints between death and resurrection.[5] Walvoord represents those who interpret the city in a completely literal fashion.[6] Lilje takes the city as meaning the church universal.[7] Mounce cites Kiddle and Hunter as supporting an interpretation similar to that of Beasley-Murray, namely that the city is a family, a perfect community of the redeemed in heaven.[8] Morris notes that some interpreters have had difficulty with the two descents of the city. Then, with Charles obviously in mind, he says, "But we need not think of two originally different narratives put together by

---

1. Kiddle, *Revelation*, 410–11.
2. Charles, *Critical and Exegetical Commentary*, 2:144–54.
3. Beasley-Murray, *Revelation*, 308.
4. Morris, *Revelation*, 237.
5. Cited in Mounce, *Revelation*, 370 n. 6.
6. Ibid.
7. Cited in Mounce, *Revelation*, 370, n. 7.
8. Mounce, *Revelation*, 370.

a bungling editor, so obtuse that he forgot what he had included eight verses before."[9]

After depicting the New Jerusalem as coming down out of heaven from God (21:2, 10), the Seer begins to describe her more fully in vv. 15–16. Here an angel begins to measure the holy city. We have previously seen John measure the inner court of the temple, which seems to have been done for its protection (11:1). In the present passage the reason for the measuring is not completely clear. Both Mounce[10] and Beasley-Murray[11] have noted the apparent echoes of Ezekiel's vision in Ezek 40–43. In Ezekiel's vision, however, the measurement seems to have been carried out for the purpose of rebuilding the temple because no temple existed at the time of his writing. Did the Seer intend for us to see in the New Jerusalem the fulfillment of Ezekiel's vision? This concept could have been a part of the message he was trying to convey but not the whole. As most commentators have noted, the perfect cube is reminiscent of the holy of holies, the locus of the special presence of God.[12] As Kiddle points out, the square was a perfect geometrical pattern in Hellenic thought as well.[13] Perhaps the two most important connotations of the measuring of the holy city are the special presence of God—the reminiscence of the holy of holies—and the mind-boggling size of the city. Wilson correctly notes that all the numbers are symbolic, "and simply indicate that there will be plenty of room in the city for the people of God."[14] Mounce, after noting various attempts of scholars to explain away the vast size, quotes approvingly from Beckwith, who says the Seer is "struggling to express by symbols the vastness, the perfect symmetry, and the splendor of the New Jerusalem."[15]

Boesak takes a slightly different viewpoint concerning the four-square city. He says it is "the world, God's world, in which God's permanent presence is the sign of God's blessing and at-homeness [sic]. It is also the sign of the world's redemption."[16]

9. Morris, *Revelation*, 242.
10. Mounce, *Revelation*, 380.
11. Beasley-Murray, *Revelation*, 322.
12. Ibid., Mounce, *Revelation*, 380; Caird, *Commentary on Revelation*, 273; Farrer, *Revelation*, 218; Morris, *Revelation*, 243; Wilson, *Revelation*, 174; Kiddle, *Revelation*, 429.
13. Kiddle, *Revelation*, 429.
14. Wilson, *Revelation*, 174; cf. Kiddle, *Revelation*, 429.
15. Mounce, *Revelation*, 381.
16. Boesak, *Comfort and Protest*, 135.

The Seer gives a further description of the holy city in 21:18–19. The walls are made of jasper, and the city itself is made of pure gold. The foundation stones of the city are every kind of precious stone. As Beasley-Murray[17] and Caird[18] have noted, the jasper in the walls is related to the glory of God.[19] Kiddle mentions a detail from Egyptian mythology that might have influenced John. In the Egyptian Mansion of Life, the four walls are said to be made of jasper and also to face north, south, east, and west.[20] Wilson interprets the jasper walls as meaning that "even [the city's] boundaries were suffused with the glory of God."[21] Mounce observes that in Rev 4:3 the One sitting upon the throne has the appearance of jasper, and in 21:11 the holy city aglow with the glory of God emits the radiance of crystal-clear jasper.[22] Caird points to the echo of the prophecy of Zech 2:5, that the restored Jerusalem would need no wall because the Lord would be a wall of fire about her. Caird also raises the question as to why the New Jerusalem would need a wall at all, since nothing could threaten it from without. He is probably correct in suggesting that to the ancient mind the possession of a wall was precisely what constitutes a city, and hence John could not dispense with it.[23]

The city's being made of pure gold like clear glass "points to the omnipresent glory."[24] This detail raises an obvious problem, in that no gold is transparent. Morris thinks that in the reference to glass John has in mind the costliness of clear glass, in that glass in the ancient world was characteristically quite impure and pure glass was rare and very expensive.[25] Beasley-Murray asks whether John is trying to convey heavenly realities that transcend any earthly models or whether he has in mind 1 Kgs 6:20–35, which tells of the inner sanctuary and the remainder of the temple being covered completely with gold.[26] Farrer in similar fashion

---

17. Beasley-Murray, *Revelation*, 323–24.
18. Caird, *Commentary on Revelation*, 274.
19. Cf. Morris, *Revelation*, 244–45.
20. Kiddle, *Revelation*, 432.
21. Wilson, *Revelation*, 174.
22. Mounce, *Revelation*, 218.
23. Caird, *Commentary on Revelation*, 274.
24. Ibid.
25. Morris, *Revelation*, 245.
26. Beasley-Murray, *Revelation*, 324.

suggests Solomon's temple as John's model at this point.²⁷ Mounce, on the contrary, suggests Herod's temple as the model. He refers to a passage in Josephus to the effect that the golden front of Herod's temple reflected the early morning sun's rays so brilliantly that those who looked upon it had to turn their eyes away from the "fiery splendor."²⁸ Perhaps nothing of significance is to be gained by trying to determine which—if either—earthly temple served as a model for John's New Jerusalem.

Almost without exception commentators connect the twelve precious stones that are the foundation of the city to the jewels in the breastplate of the Jewish high priest.²⁹ Beasley-Murray thinks there are also overtones of Isa 54:11-12 and the dirge over the king of Tyre in Ezek 28:12-19.³⁰ Caird discusses at some length the various lists of the stones in Scripture and concludes, following Charles, "He must have derived his list not directly from Exodus, but from his knowledge of astrology; and he then deliberately reversed it to indicate his total disavowal of astrological interest."³¹ Kiddle also seems to accept Charles's explanation.³² Farrer, taking an entirely different approach, has noted that nine of the twelve Greek names of the stones end in an "s" sound and the remaining three in an "n" sound; and suggests that euphony dictated the order in which John listed the stones.³³ Morris formerly accepted Charles's position that the Seer has reversed the order of the signs of the zodiac. On that basis he then argued that this reordering indicates that God reverses human judgments. This notion is more in line with allegory than serious exegesis. Morris now claims that Charles's position has been effectively refuted by T. Francis Glasson.³⁴

Since John has told us in 21:18 that the city itself is made of pure gold why, three verses later, does he single out the street(s) as being made of gold? Beasley-Murray has suggested that John is merely trying to emphasize the overwhelming glory of the city. He suggests further that John's

27. Farrer, *Revelation*, 218.
28. Mounce, *Revelation*, 381.
29. See, e.g., Farrer, *Revelation*, 212; Mounce, *Revelation*, 382; Beasley-Murray, *Revelation*, 324; Caird, *Commentary on Revelation*, 274; Wilson, *Revelation*, 174.
30. Beasley-Murray, *Revelation*, 324.
31. Caird, *Commentary on Revelation*, 274-77; cf. Mounce, *Revelation*, 382.
32. Kiddle, *Revelation*, 434.
33. Farrer, *Revelation*, 219.
34. Morris, *Revelation*, 245.

model is the Milky Way, and concludes, "It is not the gods who tread this way, but the multitudes of redeemed humanity who rejoice in God and the Lamb."[35] In his earlier work, *A Rebirth of Images*, Farrer had advocated a similar position, prompting Caird to say, "If astrology were as dominant a source of his imagery as Farrer supposes, we should have to picture it as a golden Milky Way traversing the cosmic chart."[36] In Farrer's later commentary on Revelation, however, there is no trace of an astrological interpretation of the passage under consideration.

Mounce takes yet another approach, noting from 1 Kgs 6:20 that the floors of Solomon's temple were made of gold. He then concludes, "Like the priests of the OT [sic] who ministered in the temple, the servants of God walk upon gold."[37] Given the promise in Exod 19:6 that the covenant people of God will be a kingdom of priests, Mounce's interpretation has much to commend it. Wilson takes a slightly different approach by relating the gold to royal rather than priestly dignity in these words: "The royal dignity of walking upon gold belongs to those who are joint-heirs with Christ." He also notes the stupendous size of the pearls that serve as the gates of the city. "Although we cannot imagine pearls of such a size, the image suggests the transcendent worth of the kingdom, and brings to mind the parable of the merchant who sold all to gain the pearl of greatest price."[38] This last point may be more allegorical than exegetical. Summers notes that the pearl is the only jewel formed through suffering, and suggests that this fact may be related to these exorbitant pearls that form the gates to the New Jerusalem.[39] Again one might question whether this interpretation is allegory or exegesis.

One other verse in Rev 21 claims our attention. In v. 23 we are told that the New Jerusalem has no need of the light of sun or moon because the glory of God illumines it and the Lamb is its lamp. Farrer notes that Isa 60:19 had prophesied this illumination and had also in the same chapter foretold that nations and kings would walk in Zion's light, and would bring wealth and glory through gates which remain open day and

---

35. Beasley-Murray, *Revelation*, 326.
36. Caird, *Commentary on Revelation*, 278.
37. Mounce, *Revelation*, 383.
38. Wilson, *Revelation*, 175.
39. Summers, *Worthy Is the Lamb*, 213.

night.⁴⁰ Mounce likewise refers to the prophecy in Isaiah and also points out the Johannine characterization of Jesus as the light of the world.⁴¹ Beasley-Murray observes that John has both summarized and modified the prophecy in Isaiah, noting that in this prophecy the sun and moon continue to exist. He then quotes Charles's words, "Their splendor is simply put to shame by the glory of God himself."⁴²

Of the passages concerning the holy city which I have chosen to expound, only 22:14 remains. In this verse we find the last of seven beatitudes in this book (cf. 1:3, 14:13, 16:15, 19:9, 20:6, and 22:7). The identity of the speaker of this beatitude is a matter of some difficulty.⁴³ Carrell records five different interpretations of the speaker that various scholars have endorsed.⁴⁴ Perhaps Farrer's approach is the safest one: "We must continue to refuse every temptation to distribute the text among several speakers. One inspired utterance runs on—it is John's, the angel's, Christ's, but fundamentally Christ's."⁴⁵

The beatitude in this passage is pronounced on those who wash their robes. A number of interpretations have attempted to limit these to the martyrs. Caird, for example, is explicit in referring to "those who face martyrdom in the confidence that the Cross [sic] is the sign of God's victory over evil."⁴⁶ Beasley-Murray cites both Lohmeyer and Caird as taking this same position.⁴⁷ He then quotes Swete as giving the "proper" perspective on this beatitude. Swete characterized it as but another version of the beatitude, "Blessed are the pure in heart, for they shall see God" (Matt 5:8).⁴⁸

Mounce is somewhat ambiguous in his comments about this beatitude. He says, "A blessing is pronounced upon those who wash their robes, that is, those who remain undefiled by their steadfast refusal to comply with the demands of the beast." A few sentences later, he quotes Caird's words cited above without either specifically endorsing or reject-

---

40. Farrer. *Revelation*, 221; cf. vss. 24–26.
41. Mounce, *Revelation*, 384.
42. Beasley-Murray, *Revelation*, 327.
43. This difficulty pertains to the entirety of the epilogue (Rev 22:6–21).
44. Carrell, *Jesus and the Angels*, 124–25.
45. Farrer, *Revelation*, 225.
46. Caird, *Commentary on Revelation*, 285.
47. Beasley-Murray, *Revelation*, 340, n. 1.
48. Matt 5:8, Beasley-Murray, *Revelation*, 340, n. 2.

ing Caird's position.[49] Rowland takes essentially the same position as does Beasley-Murray. After quoting Rev 22:14 he says, "That can mean nothing else than identification with the Messiah who offered an 'even better way.'"[50] Rowland's words go far toward an exegesis of the phrase "those who wash their robes." This phrase includes all, the martyrs and those who are not put to death, who participate by faith in the atonement that Christ has made through his death and resurrection. In Beasley-Murray's words, "To participate in the benefit of Christ's atonement is to enter upon renewal of life through entry into the saving sovereignty brought about by the divine action in Christ, and so to share the glory of the divine holiness. It is an apocalyptist's equivalent to the Pauline teaching on the unity of justification, sanctification, and glorification."[51]

Mounce has called attention to a detail that further supports Beasley-Murray's appraisal. He notes that in Rev 7:14 the verb for "washed" is in the aorist tense, which lends itself to interpretation as an action that took place at a particular point in time. In the present passage the present participle *hoi plunontes* ("the ones who are washing") is used. The latter would more naturally be understood as a repeated and ongoing action.[52] Wilson adds the note that the washing must continue throughout the entirety of one's earthly pilgrimage.[53] Kiddle makes the same point in only slightly different language. He says both that those who enter the city must take to themselves the freedom from sin which Christ won through his suffering and death, and also that they must be clothed with the "pure white linen which is the righteous conduct of the saints."[54]

Those who are washing their robes are given the right to the tree of life by so doing. Although I have given the literal translation "authority over the tree of life," most interpreters see this text as the right of access to the tree of life, as an examination of modern translations clearly reveals.

The concept of the tree of life is first mentioned in Revelation in the address to the church at Ephesus in Rev 2:7. There the one conquering is granted permission to eat from the tree of life. This expression is simply

---

49. Mounce, *Revelation*, 393–94.
50. Cf. 1 Cor 12:31; Rowland, *Revelation*, 161.
51. Beasley-Murray, *Revelation*, 340.
52. Mounce, *Revelation*, 393–94; cf. Morris, *Revelation*, 253.
53. Wilson, *Revelation*, 183.
54. Kiddle, *Revelation*, 452–53.

a symbol for participation in the eternal quality of life made available by Christ through his death and resurrection. As Mounce puts it, "Eternal life is the reward of faithfulness in the face of tribulation."[55]

The reference to entering the holy city through its gates is somewhat puzzling. How else would one enter, especially in view of a wall that is something like 216 feet high? Unlike the Fourth Gospel, there is no reference in Revelation to climbing up some other way (John 10:1). We note that the gates bear the names of the twelve tribes of Israel (Rev 21:12). Did John intend to make the point that the believing Christians of his day were in continuity and solidarity with the covenant people of God in the Jewish Scriptures? Or perhaps we have here an echo of Jesus's words that many would come from the east and west and recline at table with Abraham, Isaac, and Jacob in the kingdom (Matt 8:11).

We first encounter the negative use of *city* in Rev 11:8. It is mentioned as the place where the body or bodies of the two witnesses lie after being killed by the beast. As Mounce notes, in Eastern tradition the denial of burial was the height of indignity.[56] This city where the body (or bodies) lay is referred to as one called spiritually Sodom and Egypt and the place where their Lord was crucified. Charles is puzzled by the singular term *body* in this verse. If there are two witnesses it stands to reason there must be two bodies. Charles leaves the matter with the suggestion that Hebrew or Aramaic usage, in which *body* is used collectively, may have influenced John here.[57] This rather weak suggestion would have been unnecessary had he not interpreted the two witnesses as Moses and Elijah instead of the totality of the witnessing church. This verse is simply additional evidence that the two witnesses constitute one entity, the entire witnessing church—although admittedly the plural *ta ptomata* ("the bodies") appears in v. 9b without any dissenting textual evidence. As such it may be taken either as a singular or as a collective plural.

The identification of the city where the body of the witnesses lay is much disputed. Because Charles has identified the two witnesses as Moses and Elijah, he is forced to identify the city as Jerusalem, since Rome did not exist during the lifetime of those two figures; and neither Moses nor Elijah was associated with the area that was to become Rome.

---

55. Mounce, *Revelation*, 394.
56. Ibid., 226.
57. Charles, *Critical and Exegetical Commentary*, 1:286–87.

Though Charles makes this identification, he confesses that the "great city" throughout the rest of the book is Babylon or Rome.[58] Farrer also interprets the "great city" as Jerusalem, based on the phrase "where also their Lord was crucified." He claims that Jerusalem is again referred to in this manner in Rev 16:19.[59] He can only maintain this position at the cost of making the first half of that verse apply to Jerusalem and the second half to "Babylon the great," however. This is highly questionable exegesis. In my judgment the *kai* ("and") is epexegetical, not a mere copulative. Farrer does at least admit that "Babylon the great" depicts Rome.[60]

Moyise may be added to the list of those who interpret the great city here as Jerusalem.[61] Beasley-Murray seems to identify the city neither as Rome nor Jerusalem in any literal sense. He seems to agree with Kiddle's[62] allegorization of the city as Vanity Fair.[63] In a similar vein Caird, after pointing out that John has expressly called the city figurative, adds "The city is heir to the vice of Sodom, the tyranny of Pharaoh's Egypt and the blind disobedience of Jerusalem, but it is not literally to be identified with any of them."[64] Perhaps Kiddle is on the right track in understanding that the witnesses lie dishonored in every location in the world wherever they "hold the word of their testimony."[65] Krodel expresses a similar interpretation.[66] Mounce points out that those who interpret the city as Jerusalem—the majority of commentators, according to him—usually point to Isa 1:9-10 and Ezek 16:46-49 in support of Jerusalem's being called Sodom. He then cites Alford as pointing out that in the Isaiah passage the Jewish people, not the city, are called Sodom; and in Ezekiel Jerusalem is being compared with her "sisters" Samaria and Sodom. He then adds, "In neither place is Jerusalem called Sodom and in the OT [*sic*] it is never designated Egypt."[67] This observation places a strong burden of

---

58. Charles, *Critical and Exegetical Commentary*, 1:281, 286–87.
59. Farrer, *Revelation*, 135; cf. also Wilson, *Revelation*, 97–98.
60. Farrer, *Revelation*, 180.
61. Moyise, *Old Testament in Revelation*, 122.
62. Kiddle, *Revelation*, 135, 199.
63. Beasley-Murray, *Revelation*, 185–86.
64. Caird, *Commentary on Revelation*, 137–38.
65. Kiddle, *Revelation*, 199.
66. Krodel, *Revelation*, 226.
67. Mounce, *Revelation*, 226.

proof upon anyone who would identify the "great city" in this passage as Jerusalem.

Morris, in only slightly different wording, echoes the positions of Beasley-Murray and Krodel cited above. According to him the great city is "every city and no city. It is civilized man in organized community."[68] Mounce cites Kiddle as saying it is "the Earthly City [sic] as opposed to the Heavenly City [sic], 'typified once by Jerusalem, now by all civilization, where the Satanic [sic] power of Rome was dominant.'"[69] Giblin interprets the great city as being the pagan world itself as John saw it, a place that "transcends any geographical location except the earth itself."[70] In a similar fashion Sleeper writes, "The point about the city is, however, not its geographical location, but its spiritual status as the place where evil held sway."[71] I would add my support to those who see the great city as depicting any city with the characteristics of Jerusalem, Sodom, and Egypt.

We next meet the city as a negative image in Rev 16:19, where the "great city" is split into three parts. As noted above, Farrer and others have interpreted the great city of Rev 11:8 as Jerusalem. Farrer advances the same interpretation here. He bases his interpretation in part on an apparent allusion to Zech 14:3–5.[72] I am personally unable to see what Farrer attempts to read out of this passage. As I read Zech 14:3–5, there is one rift extending from east to west that causes sections of the Mount of Olives to move north and south. On any reading of this text, it is difficult if not impossible to obtain the meaning that the city was divided into three parts, as John depicts in this passage of the Revelation. Charles brackets the reference to the division into three parts as "against the usage of our author." Even he, however, interprets the great city in this passage as Babylon or Rome, not Jerusalem.[73] Beasley-Murray also identifies the great city as Rome, and adds the significant note that "Earthquake as an accompaniment of the divine appearing at the end of the age is a standing element of eschatological expectation."[74] Mounce, after stating that

---

68. Morris, *Revelation*, 146.
69. Mounce, *Revelation*, 226, n. 30; Kiddle, *Revelation*, 199.
70. Giblin, "Revelation 11:1–13," 439–40.
71. Sleeper, *Victorious Christ*, 74.
72. Farrer, *Revelation*, 179–80.
73. Charles, *Critical and Exegetical Commentary*, 2:52; cf. Caird, *Commentary on Revelation*, 209.
74. Beasley-Murray, *Revelation*, 247.

"some have interpreted the great city in this passage as Jerusalem," cites Morris, Kiddle, and Bruce as removing it from any geographical location. He then concludes, "For John, at least, the allusion would be to Rome as the center of satanic power and oppression against the fledgling church."[75] For Mounce the division of the city into three parts, rather than being an allusion to Zech 14:3–5, is simply a token of its total destruction. "That all the cities of the nations fall with Rome indicates the dominant role of the great capital in its network of imperial communications."[76] With only slightly different emphasis Beasley-Murray attributes the fall of the "cities of the nations" to their following in the ways of Rome.[77] Farrer seems to simply include Rome as one of the "cities of the nations," having previously identified the "great city" as Jerusalem.[78] Kiddle argues that no distinction is to be made between the terms *city, cities of the nations,* and *Babylon the great*. He sees these three terms as simply expressing the same idea in three ways, and all three as referring to civilization as persecutors of the prophets.[79] Such an approach has much to commend it, in my judgment.

The next occurrence of *city* in a negative sense is again a reference to the great city. The setting is a multifaceted description of the "great prostitute." She is clothed in purple and scarlet, and adorned with gold and precious stones (Rev 17:4). She is said to be drunk with the blood of the saints (17:6). She is to be made desolate and naked, burned with fire, and her flesh eaten (17:16). One can scarcely overlook the allusions to Oholah and Oholibah in Ezek 23:10, 18, 25, and 27. The great prostitute is finally described as the great city who reigns over the kings of the earth (17:18). Commentators are generally agreed on the interpretation that the great city here is Rome. In no sense could Jerusalem at any point in history be said to rule over the kings of the earth. As Beasley-Murray notes, "If verse 9 also be taken into account, there is one city only in the first century to which this description could refer, namely Rome, whose rule reached virtually to the limit of the world of western and mid-orient man." He then proceeds to tackle the issue as to whether John was a false prophet, since no Nero *redivivus* appeared on the scene leading a Parthian host to

---

75. Mounce, *Revelation*, 303–4; cf. Kiddle, *Revelation*, 332.
76. Mounce, *Revelation*, 304; cf. Wilson, *Revelation*, 135.
77. Beasley-Murray, *Revelation*, 247.
78. Farrer, *Revelation*, 180.
79. Kiddle, *Revelation*, 32–33.

destroy Rome suddenly and completely. In fact, Rome was eventually to capitulate to the Lamb. He goes on to point out that all the Biblical prophets thought the word of God's judgment applied to their own day.[80] While there is merit to Beasley-Murray's discussion, he has again stopped short in equating Babylon with Rome. His interpretation needs to be balanced by the insight provided by Mounce. Mounce agrees that for John, the "great prostitute" was Rome, but that she was (is) more than that. "Every great center of power which has prostituted its wealth and influence restores to life the spirit of ancient Babylon. John's words extend beyond his immediate setting in history and sketch the portrait of an eschatological Babylon, which will provide the social, religious, and political base for the last attempt of Antichrist [sic] to establish his kingdom."[81] Although I have previously voiced my rejection of the traditional doctrine of the Antichrist, Mounce's interpretation has the merit of preserving a balance between application to the time in which the Revelation was written and allowing it to speak to later generations as well.

All the remaining negative images of *city* are found in the description of the judgment of the great prostitute in Rev 18. I am dealing only with the passages that explicitly mention the city. In the first passage, Rev 18:9–10, the kings of the earth who are said to have been the "consorts" of the great prostitute lament over her "burning." Kiddle interprets this text as the attack of Antichrist and the Parthian hosts on the civilized world so that the cities of the nations are aflame.[82] The kings make no attempt to come to the prostitute's rescue, however, but instead stand off at a safe distance.[83] Charles interprets these kings as heads of the heathen nations, but in particular those who had some sort of an alliance with Rome.[84] Beasley-Murray advocates a similar interpretation and goes on to discuss the meaning of the phrase "committed fornication and were wanton with her" (v. 9a). "They had not hesitated to adopt Rome's idolatries and her blasphemous emperor-worship, nor resisted her restrictive policies against the people of God."[85] Farrer points to the background of

80. Beasley-Murray, *Revelation*, 260–61.
81. Mounce, *Revelation*, 320; cf. Wilson, *Revelation*, 143–44.
82. Kiddle, *Revelation*, 368.
83. Cf. Mounce, *Revelation*, 329.
84. Charles, *Critical and Exegetical Commentary*, 2:100–1; cf. Mounce, *Revelation*, 328; Wilson, *Revelation*, 148.
85. Beasley-Murray, *Revelation*, 266.

the lamentation over the destruction of the great prostitute in the Jewish Scriptures. The lament over Tyre as found in Ezek 26–27 constitutes perhaps the major source. The phrase "the smoke of her burning" is apparently provided by Isaiah's oracle (Isa 34:10) against Edom.[86] The word *woe* (Greek *ouai*) is an onomatopoetic root. Its very sound bespeaks its origin as a funeral lament. The doubling is probably for emphasis and possibly symbolic of an intensification of the woe.[87] Morris notes the progressing of judgment from the "one day" of v. 8 to "one hour" here.[88] Caird calls attention to the repetition of the phrase "one hour" in 17:12–14: "The one hour of persecution is balanced by the one hour of retribution, because the blood of the martyrs is not only the seed of the church but the ruin of the great whore."[89]

The merchants of the earth then take up the lament in Rev 18:15–16. They too stand off at a distance and cry out, not because of any love for the city, but because their means of becoming wealthy is gone.[90] Caird quotes Kiddle as remarking that this lament contains some "temporal uncertainties." Kiddle goes on to say, "A medley of tenses, present, future, perfect, preterite, testify to John's imaginative journeys from the present into a visionary future and back again."[91] Farrer is less kind to John in his assessment of the language, saying, "The speech contains several linguistic barbarities."[92] Caird notes that John could not seem to make up his mind whether he is talking about a woman or a city. He then goes on to assert that regardless of the visionary elements present, John envisages a real future on the plane of human history. He is not looking at the end of the world, because people could still witness the "burning."[93]

Mounce notes the similarity between the lament of the kings of the earth and the merchants—both stand off at a safe distance because of the fear of her burning—and also an interesting difference: "To the kings, Rome was 'the strong city' (v. 10); to the merchants she was 'lavishly ar-

---

86. Farrer, *Revelation*, 189; cf. Caird, *Commentary on Revelation*, 226.
87. Cf. Morris, *Revelation*, 212.
88. Ibid., 213.
89. Caird, *Commentary on Revelation*, 225–26; cf. Mounce, *Revelation*, 329.
90. Cf. Morris, *Revelation*, 213.
91. Caird, *Commentary on Revelation*, 226; cf. Kiddle, *Revelation*, 361.
92. Farrer, *Revelation*, 190.
93. Caird, *Commentary on Revelation*, 226–27.

rayed and adorned with costly ornaments' (cf. 17:4). Each group sees her fall in terms of its own interests."[94]

The third and final category of people who lament the fall of Babylon are the shipmasters, their passengers, and all who make their living from the sea (18:17a). Like the kings and the merchants, they too are dominated by self-interest and stand off at a safe distance.[95] Their cry of "Who is like the great city?" as Charles notes, seems to be modeled on the lament over Tyre in Ezek 27:32.[96] The act of throwing dust upon their heads (v. 19) is yet another feature held in common with the lament over Tyre. As Beasley-Murray notes, the shipmasters and sailors had no concern even for those perishing in the destruction of the city, but only for their own loss of revenue.[97] Perhaps we should take note along with Caird, that "there was nothing sinful about the commodities which made up Rome's luxury trade until the great whore used them to seduce mankind into utter materialism."[98] Beasley-Murray comments further, "The sin of Babylon was its use of these things to seduce mankind to adopt the kind of gross materialism and mammon-worship which is illustrated in the songs of the merchants and seamen."[99]

While I am in basic agreement with Caird and Beasley-Murray at this point, I think they have missed something quite significant. The last part of v. 13, which concludes the list of cargoes, reads, literally translated, "bodies and souls of men." Admittedly there may be room for discussion as to the exact meaning of this phrase, but I am taking it to mean trafficking in slaves. If that interpretation be valid, we have this one notable exception to the rule that there is nothing inherently sinful in the list of commodities in vss. 12–13. Boesak also interprets the phrase as referring to slaves, and strongly challenges Caird's view that there is nothing inherently sinful about the cargoes.[100]

---

94. Mounce, *Revelation*, 331; cf. Wilson, *Revelation*, 150.

95. 18:17b; cf. Wilson, *Revelation*, 150.

96. Charles, *Critical and Exegetical Commentary*, 2:106; see also Farrer, *Revelation*, 189–90; Mounce, *Revelation*, 332; Kiddle, *Revelation*, 370.

97. Beasley-Murray, *Revelation*, 268.

98. Caird, *Commentary on Revelation*, 227.

99. Beasley-Murray, *Revelation*, 268.

100. Boesak, *Comfort and Protest*, 121; see also Aune, *Revelation 17–22*, 1001-2; Maxwell, *Revelation*, 151; Sweet, *Revelation*, 272; Mounce, *Revelation*, 331; Kealy, *Apocalypse*, 207; Robbins, *Revelation*, 208; Krodel, *Revelation*, 305; Wall, *Revelation*, 216.

Before leaving this passage let me call attention to a literary device that John uses at numerous points in Revelation. He has repeated the phrase "in one hour" three times: "In one hour your judgment came" (v. 10); "In one hour has such great wealth been laid waste" (v. 17); and "In one hour she has been laid waste" (v. 19). This repetition can hardly be accidental, in my judgment. The number three in Jewish-Christian apocalyptic circles had come to signify divinity by the time the Revelation was written. This repetition may be one of several ways in which John keeps his readers or hearers aware that he is describing the outworking of God's judgment.

This stylistic characteristic leads into the final passage that we will consider which refers to the great city Babylon. We find another threefold repetition in the "mighty angel" of v. 21. This phrase appears in Rev 5:2 and 10:1 in connection with the two scrolls. Caird infers from this connection that the appearance of this third mighty angel indicates that we are now seeing the consummation of the contents of both scrolls. He then goes on to note the reminiscence of historical Babylon as contained in Jer 51:60–64, and possibly an echo of Jesus's words in Luke 17:2.[101] As Jeremiah's prophecy proclaimed the sinking of historical Babylon, never to rise again, even so does the Seer prophesy the collapse of the "Babylon" of his day.[102] Charles notes the difficulty of translating *hormēmati*, which describes the manner in which Babylon will be thrown down, in this verse. He notes that Weizsacker and Swete translated it "with a rush." He then opts for the translation "with indignation," then adds "But the matter is uncertain."[103] Kiddle writes, "So sudden, so swift, so spectacular shall be the ruin of Babylon at the hand of God."[104] Perhaps Mounce is on more solid ground in noting that the verb form of this word is used in Mark 5:13 to describe the herd of swine rushing down a steep bank into the sea, and in Acts 19:29 of the rushing of the crowd into the theater at Ephesus. He then concludes, "This [word] stresses how suddenly and spectacularly the judgment of God will be executed not only upon an ancient city but ultimately upon the entire antichristian world in opposition to God."[105]

---

101. Caird, *Commentary on Revelation*, 230–31; cf. Charles, *Critical and Exegetical Commentary*, 2:107; Beasley-Murray, *Revelation*, 268–69; Farrer, *Revelation*, 190; Mounce, *Revelation*, 333; Wilson, *Revelation*, 151.

102. Cf. Kiddle, *Revelation*, 371.

103. Charles, *Critical and Exegetical Commentary*, 2:107–8.

104. Kiddle, *Revelation*, 372.

105. Mounce, *Revelation*, 333–34.

Mounce's interpretation again has the merit of being applicable to the first recipients of Revelation while also allowing it to speak to all future generations as well. This prophecy of the sudden fall of Babylon has been fulfilled several times already, and only God knows how many more times it will be fulfilled before this world ends.[106]

To return to the counterimaging of the two cities and to summarize this section, the Seer has given them almost equal treatment in his writing. As we look at what he says about each, the contrast is rather stark. New Jerusalem is first portrayed as being like a bride fully prepared for her wedding (21:2). John has to be brought "in spirit" to a high mountain in order to view the majestic sight of her descent from Heaven (21:10). The city is "measured" by an angel with a gold measuring rod (21:15). It has the shape of a gigantic cube (like the holy of holies in the temple), measuring some fifteen hundred miles (twelve thousand stadia) on all sides. The city itself is of pure gold, and its walls either made of jasper or in some way adorned with it (21:16-18). The foundation stones of the city are twelve precious stones (21:19-20). The twelve gates each consist of a single pearl (21:21). It has no need of the light of sun or moon because the glory of God and the Lamb provide all the light that is necessary (21:23). The river of the water of life flows from it constantly (22:1). It would appear that John has exhausted human language in trying to express the inexpressible. No detail is spared in portraying the limitless splendor of the New Jerusalem, the Bride of the Lamb.

The other city is first encountered as a place where the body of the two witnesses lies unburied (Rev 11:8). As noted above, a few scholars have interpreted this city as Jerusalem instead of Babylon or Rome. Even those who support this interpretation are compelled to admit that elsewhere in Revelation the "great city" is Babylon or Rome. John is carried "in spirit" to a "great and high mountain" to view the New Jerusalem; he is carried "in spirit" into a wilderness to view the "great prostitute" (17:3). The next reference to this city pictures her as split into three parts and as being

---

106. I cannot resist making an application to the sudden demise of communism that we have seen in the last ten or fifteen years. I was made vividly aware that its collapse was a reality in October 1997, when I was in Moscow. On a Saturday morning we were standing just a few yards off Red Square, when we noticed a small band and communist banners flying. There might have been thirty people at most participating in the rally. As we stood and watched for a few minutes, hundreds of people walked by, totally ignoring the rally. This incident was when I became vividly aware that communism is really dead, at least in Moscow.

"remembered" by God with the cup of the wine of God's wrath (16:19). This woman also has a splendor of her own. She is adorned with purple, scarlet, gold, and precious stones (17:4); but in spite of the beauty of this clothing, it is the attire of a prostitute. For a time she is permitted to rule over the kings of the earth (17:18). Finally, three groups of people—the kings of the earth, the merchants of the earth, and seafarers—lament that "in one hour" she is made desolate (18:9–19). Although she has lived like a queen (18:7) in a sensuous and unbridled fashion, she is destined to be like a great millstone cast into the sea—sinking to rise no more (18:21). Her permanent destruction is starkly contrasted with the eternal establishment of the New Jerusalem (22:5).

There are several details that indicate that John is deliberately counterimaging these cities. We are told that one of the angels who poured out the vials of God's judgment shows each of these cities to John (17:1 and 22:9). Also, as noted above, John is carried "in spirit" to view each city. In this counterimaging John may be portraying the division of all humanity into two groups. Everyone is to be ultimately a part of either the New Jerusalem or of "harlot Babylon." Since the judgment of God is completed with the seven vials (15:1, 16:17), and one of the angels who played a direct role in the execution of that judgment shows the cities to John, the possibility is strengthened that John intends for us to draw the conclusion that every person is either allied with the great prostitute or with the holy city. As Boesak succinctly puts it, "Either we are on our way to the new Jerusalem or we perish with Babylon."[107]

In the interest of completeness I will point out that, in addition to the passages discussed above, the word *city* appears in Rev 3:12, 11:2, 13; 14:20, 20:9, 21:14, 19; and 22:19. Of these, 3:12, 11:2, 20:9, 21:14, 19; and 22:19 refer to "New Jerusalem," "the holy city," or "the beloved city." In 14:20 the ambiguous phrase "the city" appears. I decided that nothing would be added to this study by discussing these passages. The passages that I have discussed contain the essential qualities of the two cities.

---

107. Boesak, *Comfort and Protest*, 38.

20

Rejoice!

Because of this rejoice greatly [euphrainesthe], O heavens, and those who are dwelling in them. Woe to the earth and the sea, because the devil went down to you having great wrath, knowing that he has little opportunity.

(Rev 12:12)

Rejoice greatly [euphrainou], heaven, and the holy ones, the apostles and the prophets; because God judged your sentence of condemnation from her.

(Rev 18:20)

And those dwelling upon the earth rejoice over them and rejoice greatly [euphrainontai]; and they will send gifts to one another because these two prophets tormented those dwelling upon the earth.

(Rev 11:10)

SEVERAL WORDS IN THE Greek language may be translated into English as "rejoice." Therefore, the fact that John has chosen to use the same Greek verb, *euphrainō*, in three passages probably holds some significance. When we note that two of these passages are in the arena of God's actions and one in the arena of the forces of evil, I suggest that we are again dealing with counterimaging.

The context of the first usage of this verb in the arena of God's actions is the war between Michael and his angels on the one hand, and the dragon and his angels on the other. The result is that the dragon and his angels are defeated and cast down to earth (Rev 12:7–12). The heavens and those that dwell in them are exhorted to rejoice greatly because of Michael's victory.

Charles has noted that the plural "heavens" (*ouranoi*) appears nowhere else in the Apocalypse, and that the Septuagint of Isa 44:23 and

49:13 contain this plural form of the noun following the verb *euphrainō*.[1] Since John uses the singular (*ouranos*) in 18:20 and at 49 other points,[2] there is a strong possibility that these passages from Isaiah were his model. As Morris,[3] Charles,[4] and Mounce[5] have noted, the verb *tabernacling* does not imply temporary residence (cf. 7:15, 21:3, where the verb and noun forms of this word respectively are used of God's presence with people), but stands in contrast to the "dwellers upon the earth," for which he uses the verb *katoikeō* (cf. 6:10, 8:13, 11:10 and elsewhere). That the dwellers on the earth are the pagan population contrasted with believers has been noted by Mounce,[6] Charles,[7] Beasley-Murray,[8] and others. The exhortation to the heavens and those dwelling in them to rejoice greatly—and the present tense would imply continuously as well—is countered by a pronouncement of woe upon the earth and sea. The inclusion of *sea* here is probably a reflection of the ancient belief that the sea represents chaos and evil.[9] In the next chapter the first beast arises from the sea, described in such a way as to clearly link him with Satan (13:1, 12:3).

The great wrath of the devil arises from the fact that he has been decisively defeated and that his activities are forever sharply curtailed. As Torrance so colorfully puts it, "If there is a devil of a row, it only means that the dragon is angry and has lost his nerve."[10] In Morris's words, "the troubles of the persecuted righteous arise not because Satan is too strong, but because he is beaten."[11] Charles follows suit by saying, "hence however Satan may rage and his minions . . . this final persecution of the Church is but the last struggle of a beaten foe, whose venom and malignity are all the greater since he knows how short a time he has."[12] His feverish activity is only the death throes of a defeated adversary.

1. Charles, *Critical and Exegetical Commentary*, 1:329.
2. Mounce, *Revelation*, 244, n. 29.
3. Morris, *Revelation*, 158.
4. Charles, *Critical and Exegetical Commentary*, 1:329.
5. Mounce, *Revelation*, 244.
6. Ibid., 244, n 31.
7. Charles, *Critical and Exegetical Commentary*, 1:238.
8. Beasley-Murray, *Revelation*, 159.
9. See A. Collins, *Combat Myth*, 162.
10. Torrance, *Apocalypse Today*, 97.
11. Morris, *Revelation*, 244.
12. Charles, *Critical and Exegetical Commentary*, 1:141, 298; cf. Boesak, *Comfort and*

Most translators and interpreters treat the last part of 12:12 as implying that Satan has but a short time to work (e.g., Charles). Because of this consensus, I perhaps need to explain my translation "little opportunity." To begin with, the Greek language contains no indefinite article; hence the insertion of "a" or "an" is always a judgment call by translators. Second, the word in v. 12 is not the noun used for chronological time *(chronos)* but the word for "opportunity" or "appropriate season" (*kairos*). The former term is used in Revelation, for example, regarding the saints under the altar who are given white robes and told to rest for a little time (6:11); and for the devil's being released for a little time (20:3). I do not wish to deny that the devil does in fact have only a relatively brief time in which to work; I question only whether that limitation is what is being emphasized here. Stating that the devil has only a short time to work and stating that he has little opportunity may boil down to the same thing, but I think there is at least a difference in emphasis. Morris suggests translating *kairos* as "suitable time," and goes on to say, "Not much time remains suitable for the activities of the evil one."[13]

Before leaving this passage we should focus once more on the word *woe*. Its origin as a funeral lament was noted earlier. After the blowing of the fourth trumpet we are told to expect three woes at the blowing of the last three trumpets (8:13). Then, after the blowing of the sixth trumpet, we are told that two woes have now come to pass, and the third woe is to come quickly (11:14). But where do we look for the record of the third woe? As Mounce has noted, some interpreters attempt to make the woe in 12:12 the last of the three woes. He rejects this interpretation, pointing out that the first two woes are unleashed on unbelievers whereas 12:12 depicts the hostile actions of the devil toward Christians.[14] Since the three woes are explicitly connected with the final three trumpets (Rev 8:13), perhaps the final woe should be seen in the seventh trumpet as incorporating within itself the series of the seven vials by which the wrath of God is completed.[15]

The other usage of *euphrainō* in the arena of God's people and actions appears in the lengthy description of the judgment of the "great prostitute"

Protest, 90.

13. Morris, *Revelation*, 158.
14. Mounce, *Revelation*, 244.
15. 16:17; cf. Krodel, *Revelation*, 193.

(18:20). Charles would restore this verse "to its rightful place," which for him means placing it after the dirge over Babylon or Rome in vv. 21–23.[16] Few commentators have supported this rearrangement. In the passage discussed above the rejoicing was on the part of those dwelling in the "heavens." Now the exhortation to rejoice greatly is directed to "heaven" in the singular. We probably should not make any sharp distinction between the singular and plural usage of the word *heaven* because its singular and plural forms seem to be used interchangeably at a number of points in the Christian Testament. See, for example, Mark 14:32, where the singular is used, and Matt 24:36, where the plural is used; Mark 13:27, where the singular is used, and Matt 24:31, where the plural is used. The significant differences lie elsewhere. In 12:12 the rejoicing was related to the defeat of Satan and his being cast down from heaven. Now the rejoicing is exhorted because of the judgment of Satan's agent on earth, the "great prostitute." As Morris notes, some modern interpreters are put off by John's image of the call to rejoice over the destruction of the "great prostitute." Morris rightly notes, however, that no vindictive outcry is found here but only a longing for justice to be done. He then concludes, "Judgment, not vengeance, has been done."[17] In similar words Wilson says, "It is not an expression of vindictive delight in the suffering of the unrighteous, but (in Carpenter's words) 'a summons to all who have fought on the side of their Lord to rejoice at the removal of one of the great obstacles to the manifestation of God's kingdom.'"[18]

In 12:12 the exhortation to rejoice was limited to those dwelling in heaven. Now the holy ones ("saints"), the apostles, and the prophets are invited to join in the celebration. Putting the two passages together, all the living people who belong to God, both in heaven and on earth, are encouraged to rejoice over the defeat of the forces of evil.

The latter part of Rev 18:20 is notoriously difficult to translate and hence to interpret. The most literal translation would be something like "because God judged your judgment from her."[19] The crucial questions are in what sense does the possessive pronoun *your* apply to heaven, the holy ones, the prophets, and the apostles? Who are the holy ones, proph-

---

16. Charles, *Critical and Exegetical Commentary*, 2:111.
17. Morris, *Revelation*, 215–16.
18. Wilson, *Revelation*, 150–51.
19. Cf. Caird, *Commentary on Revelation*, 229.

ets, and apostles? And what is meant by the judgment being judged from her? To deal first with the identification of the holy ones, prophets, and apostles, Mounce takes the position that they represent the glorified church in heaven, not the church on earth. His argument is based upon the fact that in Rev 12:12 only dwellers in heaven are mentioned and that the call to rejoicing in this passage is directed to heaven.[20] Beasley-Murray notes other possibilities. If the saints are the whole people of God in heaven and on earth, then the apostles would represent the saints of the new covenant and the prophets would represent those of the old covenant. On the other hand, if the saints are those who have suffered at the hands of the great prostitute, both apostles and prophets would be representatives of the new covenant.[21] I have already indicated my position that Mounce's view is mistaken—that 12:12 refers to heavenly beings but that this verse includes people on earth. With Beasley-Murray I will leave the matter open as to whether saints of the old covenant, the new covenant, or both are in view.

The questions about the possessive *your* and the phrase *from her* may be taken together. As Charles notes, the word *krima*—"judgment" or "sentence of condemnation"—seems here to have the meaning of "lawsuit" or "case," which it does not have elsewhere in Revelation.[22] Caird points out three possible meanings of *krima*: first, the right to judge; second, the passing of a sentence in a court of law; and third, the actual sentence passed by a judge. He then opts for the third possibility and concludes that the passage means that God has passed upon Babylon or Rome the sentence of condemnation which she had passed upon the saints.[23] Mounce quotes Caird's position approvingly and adds that it fits well with the command in v. 6 to "pay her back even as she has paid" (18:6a, NASB).[24] In a similar vein Beasley-Murray writes, "She had condemned them to death, but God reversed her verdict as he passed judgment upon her."[25] Charles shares the view that *krima* means sentence or judgment but takes the latter to mean the judgment due to the saints as being visited upon her.[26] Charles's view

---

20. Mounce, *Revelation*, 332.
21. Beasley-Murray, *Revelation*, 268.
22. Charles, *Critical and Exegetical Commentary*, 2:11.
23. Caird, *Commentary on Revelation*, 228–30.
24. Mounce, *Revelation*, 332.
25. Beasley-Murray, *Revelation*, 268.
26. Charles, *Critical and Exegetical Commentary*, 2:111.

is not free from ambiguity to say the least. He could be read as agreeing with the positions of Caird and Mounce noted above. He could also be read as saying that the saints determine the judgment to be visited upon the "great prostitute." Both views may have some validity. We are on safe ground to take the position that God's action upon Babylon or Rome is a cause for the saints to rejoice.

The usage of the word *rejoice* in the arena of evil occurs in the context of the death of the two witnesses (11:10). Charles notes that the phrase "those dwelling upon the earth" in this verse is a phrase from the Jewish Scriptures which can mean either dwellers in Palestine or dwellers on the earth, as *gē* can mean either the earth as a whole or a particular region thereof. Since Charles has interpreted the two witnesses as Moses and Elijah and the "great city" as Jerusalem, he is forced to endorse the former reading. He then goes on to point out that the phrase can have a good, bad, or neutral meaning, ethically speaking; and argues for the latter in this verse.[27] Beasley-Murray disagrees and interprets "those dwelling upon the earth" as the enemies of the church.[28] Caird likewise interprets the phrase in its broader sense of inhabitants of the earth and, by implication, as the enemies of the church.[29] Mounce also rejects Charles's position and identifies the "great city" with the whole earth and "those dwelling upon the earth" as its pagan population.[30] I have noted previously a number of scholars who reject Charles's interpretation of the two witnesses as Moses and Elijah and my own reasons for rejecting his interpretation of the great city as Jerusalem. Without these two points his interpretation of 11:10 collapses. In my judgment Mounce, Beasley-Murray, Caird, and others who interpret the "earth-dwellers" as the enemies of the church are correct. Mounce makes the interesting comment that the rejoicing of the "earth-dwellers" and their sending gifts to one another is "a perverse counterpart to the Jewish feast of Purim."[31] Wilson characterizes it simply as a typical Eastern celebration of a festive occasion.[32]

---

27. Charles, *Critical and Exegetical Commentary*, 1:289–90.
28. Beasley-Murray, *Revelation*, 186.
29. Caird, *Commentary on Revelation*, 138.
30. Mounce, *Revelation*, 227.
31. Ibid.; see Esth 9:19, 22.
32. Wilson, *Revelation*, 98.

The rejoicing over the death of the two witnesses is said to take place because they were a source of torment to the "earth-dwellers." In what sense is this true? It is true in the sense that the very presence of good condemns and torments evildoers. Ahab brands Elijah as the troubler of Israel because of the latter's uncompromising proclamation of the word of God (1 Kgs 18:17). Felix quakes and trembles when Paul speaks to him about righteousness, self-control, and the judgment to come (Acts 24:25). The presence of truth is unspeakably painful to those who have chosen to live by the lie. Wherever the witnessing church is faithful to her task, "those dwelling upon the earth" will be tormented by her. As Rowland has said so powerfully, "The life of prophets is not one of niceness and respectability, therefore. They are expected to torment. But that feeling of torment is one that is felt by those who cannot cope with God's justice and prefer not to acknowledge it. It is the torment of the prick of the conscience and the dim realization that what is normally seen as acceptable may not in fact be so."[33] Morris's position is similar, as he points out that "The faithful preaching of the gospel is never soothing to the impenitent, so that the removal of an outstanding preacher is commonly a matter of rejoicing for those whose consciences he has troubled."[34]

To sum up this section, John has presented us with two passages that exhort heaven, saints, apostles, and prophets to rejoice over the defeat of the devil and the judgment of the "great prostitute." Over against these, in sharp contrast, he has depicted the rejoicing of the enemies of the church over its apparent death. His use of the verb *euphrainō* for "rejoice" points to a deliberate counterimaging of the rejoicing.

---

33. Rowland, *Revelation*, 100.
34. Morris, *Revelation*, 146; cf. Wilson, *Revelation*, 98.

21

A Great Sign

And a great sign appeared in heaven, a woman having been clothed (with) the sun, with the moon underneath her feet and a crown of twelve stars upon her head.

(Rev 12:1)

And I saw another sign in heaven, great and marvelous; seven angels having the seven last plagues by which the wrath of God is completed.

(Rev 15:1)

And another sign appeared in heaven, and behold it was a great, fiery-red Dragon having seven heads and ten horns; and upon his heads (were) seven diadems.

(Rev 12:3)

CHARLES, FOLLOWING VISCHER AND Gunkel, has argued that Rev 12 could not have been composed by either a Christian or a Jew. His basic arguments are as follows: first, a Christian would not have left out of consideration the entire earthly life of our Lord. Second, no Christian would have described the birth of our Lord as taking place from a sun goddess. Third, a Christian would not have portrayed the defeat of Satan as accomplished by Michael instead of Christ. Fourth, the chapter contains a number of mythological features that could not have been composed by either a Jew or a Christian. Charles lists these features as:

1. A goddess clothed with the sun and the twelve signs of the zodiac as her crown.

2. A goddess who is with child.

3. A dragon whose tail is capable of throwing down one-third of the stars of heaven.
4. The birth and rapture into heaven of a young sun god.
5. A great eagle transporting the woman into the wilderness.
6. The earth swallowing up the flood by which the dragon attempts to destroy the woman.[1]

No special intelligence is required to see that Charles's arguments contain a number of assumptions. He seems to ignore some of the more obvious allusions to the Jewish Scriptures. I have earlier pointed out the allusions to Joseph's dream in Gen 37:9. Charles has also overlooked the passage in the Jewish Scriptures that speaks of God bearing up Israel on eagles' wings and bringing her up out of Egypt (Exod 19:4, cf. 12:14). How could anyone familiar with the Jewish Scriptures fail to see the parallel that, as God had delivered the original Israel "on eagles' wings" and taken care of her in the wilderness of Sinai, God would now do the same for the new Israel, the church? I support the position of Morris, who argues that the major basis for this passage is Joseph's dream, and cites a similar passage in *Test Naph* 5:3–4. He rightly concludes, "In view of this Old Testament symbolism it is unnecessary to see a reference to pagan mythology."[2]

I am not arguing that extrabiblical mythology has had no influence at all on this chapter of Revelation. Beasley-Murray has an extended discussion in which he mentions several myths whose features seem to be echoed to some degree. He sees the closest parallel in the myth of Python and Leto, in which the latter's child Apollo slays Python. Another possibility is the Babylonian myth of creation in which Tiamat, the seven-headed monster of the deep, flouts the gods of heaven and is killed by Marduk, the young god of light. Persia supplies yet another myth, some of whose features may be seen in Rev 12. "By this myth the brilliant Fire, son of Ahura, fights the evil dragon Azhi Dahaka. Egyptian mythology supplies a similar myth in which Hathor/Isis gives birth to Horus. The dragon Python slays Osiris and pursues the pregnant Hathor who miraculously bears her child and escapes by boat to an island."[3]

---

1. Charles, *Critical and Exegetical Commentary*, 1:299–300.

2. Morris, *Revelation*, 152.

3. See Beasley-Murray, *Revelation*, 191–93, for a complete discussion; cf. also Mounce, *Revelation*, 235; Caird, *Commentary on Revelation*, 147–48.

After discussing the possibility of the influence of pagan myths, Beasley-Murray then turns to possible Biblical influences. Among other things he points out some impressive parallels from Isa 26:16–27. Particularly apt is his citation of Isa 66:7, in which Mother Zion is depicted as bringing forth sons for the age of salvation.[4] Mounce introduces a significant question into the discussion of the Jewish Scriptures versus possible mythological influences on John. "Would a writer who elsewhere in the book displays such a definite antagonism toward paganism draw extensively at this point upon its mythology?"[5] In my judgment this question brings an absolutely necessary perspective to the discussion. Whatever features of pagan mythology may be present in this chapter are overshadowed by the primary influence of the Jewish Scriptures. The conclusion of Beasley-Murray's discussion is instructive. He argues that the real conquest of Satan is the redemptive death and resurrection of Christ, and goes on to say, "By using this vehicle of expression John has at a stroke claimed the fulfillment of pagan hope and Old Testament promise in the Christ of the gospel. There is no other deliverer but Jesus. . . . He is the fulfillment alike of pagan hope and Old Testament prophecy, but the affectations of messianic powers and divine status by the Roman emperors are lies of the Devil."[6]

Whatever positions interpreters may take as to the sources from which John may have drawn, the pivotal nature of Rev 12 is generally acknowledged.[7] Lund has devised a chiastic structure for the entire book, of which chapters 11 and 12 are at the center of the chiasmus.[8] The limitations of this study do not permit the exposition of this entire section; rather we must focus on the woman who is referred to as a great sign appearing in heaven (Rev 12:1). We have met her in a previous section in connection with the counterimaging of the crowns. Some significance may be attributed to John's statement at the beginning of the Apocalypse in which the verb form of the word *sign* (*sēmainō*) is used in reference to God's sending the angel to communicate (*esēmanen*) to his servant John (1:1). Since John uses this verb in relation to the communication

---

4. Beasley-Murray, *Revelation*, 193–94.
5. Mounce, *Revelation*, 235.
6. Beasley-Murray, *Revelation*, 196–97.
7. Cf. Beasley-Murray, *Revelation*, 191; Mounce, *Revelation*, 234.
8. Lund, *Chiasmus*, 325–26.

of the entire Apocalypse, Lund and others who view chapters 11 and 12 as the heart of the book may be on the right track. The woman may be intended as the apex of the "communication by sign" (Rev 1:1) that John received. The details of the crown and the moon beneath her feet suggest sovereignty or dominion. Nothing would have seemed further from the truth at the time John wrote. The people of God seemed to be in anything but a position of dominion, but John demonstrates the conviction throughout the Apocalypse that things are not as they seem—rather, the apparent invincibility of the forces of evil is but a veneer disguising the truly invincible One.

Almost without exception, commentators on this passage in one way or another link the woman's crown of twelve stars to the signs of the zodiac.[9] Since I have already argued that the woman is the messianic community and that the twelve stars allude to the twelve sons of Jacob or Israel, I will conclude the discussion on this passage with the words of Mounce: "The woman is not Mary the mother of Jesus but the messianic community, the ideal Israel. . . . It should cause no trouble that within the same chapter the woman comes to signify the church (vs. 17) [*sic*]. The people of God are one throughout all redemptive history. The early church did not view itself as discontinuous with faithful Israel."[10]

The other positive use of *sign* appears in 15:1. The context is the preparation for the outpouring of the seven vials, which is said to complete the wrath of God (see 16:17). Morris calls attention to the fact that only this sign in Revelation is referred to as *mega kai thaumaston* ("great and marvelous"), but that these adjectives are used of God's own works.[11] Charles argues that this verse is an interpolation which the author could not possibly have written. A part of his argument is that since the seven angels did not come out of the temple until v. 5, John could not possibly have seen them at this point.[12] I cannot resist responding with the question, Why not? It appears that Charles has once again fallen into the trap of literalism in interpretation that blurs his understanding of the present passage. Though Beasley-Murray does not mention Charles at this point, he seems to have Charles's argument in mind as he writes, "The question

9. E.g., Charles, *Critical and Exegetical Commentary*, 1:300; Beasley-Murray, *Revelation*, 197; Farrer, *Revelation*, 141; Caird, *Commentary on Revelation*, 149.

10. Mounce, *Revelation*, 236.

11. Morris, *Revelation*, 182.

12. Charles, *Critical and Exegetical Commentary*, 2:29–32.

is often asked how John can say that he saw this portent at this juncture, when he declares in verses 5ff. [*sic*] that the angels did not appear until after the temple in heaven was opened." He then proceeds to brand the question as an "unreal one."[13] I cannot but agree that such a question has no place in interpreting an apocalyptic vision.

Mounce aptly notes the use of Exodus typology throughout this section and also gives due recognition to the number seven as implying completeness.[14] He is quick to point out, however, that the completing of God's wrath is not the same as to end or finish judgment. As pointed out earlier, the most basic meaning of the verb *teleō* is "to complete"; to bring something to its desired end or fruition.[15] Mounce rightly points out that because the wrath of God is said to be completed with the seven vials "does not mean that the plagues exhaust or bring to an end the wrath of God. The devil, the beast, the false prophet, and all whose names are not written in the book of life are yet to be thrown into the lake of fire."[16]

The use of *sign* as an image in the arena of evil takes us back to Rev 12. There we are told in v. 3 that another sign has appeared. This sign is a great fiery-red dragon with seven heads and ten horns. In 12:1 and 15:1 the word *megas*, ("great") modifies "sign." Here it modifies "dragon," but I do not consider this detail sufficient to reject this passage as a legitimate counterimage to the signs in Rev 12:1 and 15:1. The numerical symbolism of the heads and horns may imply complete knowledge (seven heads) and humanly complete power (ten horns).[17] While scholars may continue to debate the identity of the woman, John leaves us in no doubt as to the dragon's identity. He is the serpent of old, the one called devil and Satan. The English word *devil* is a translation of the Greek *diabolos*, which means "slanderer" or "accuser." *Satan* is the Hebrew word for opponent, brought into English by simply substituting English letters for the Hebrew in transliteration. There is no essential difference in meaning between "devil" and "Satan."

As we have had occasion to note earlier, ancient mythology is replete with dragon imagery. In the Bible this imagery is found in Job 26:12–13,

13. Beasley-Murray, *Revelation*, 234.
14. Mounce, *Revelation*, 285.
15. Cf. Morris, *Revelation*, 182.
16. Mounce, *Revelation*, 285 n. 1.
17. See e.g., Robbins, *Revelation*, 148.

Ps 74:13–14, and Isa 27:1 and 51:9. As Mounce notes, the symbol was frequently used of Israel's enemies in the Old Testament. "In Psalm 74:14 Leviathan is Egypt; in Isa 27:1 he is Assyria and Babylon."[18] Ezekiel wrote of Pharaoh as "the great dragon that lies in the midst of his streams" (Ezek 29:3). Job 40:18 refers to Behemoth, whose bones are tubes of bronze and his limbs like iron bars. Mounce goes on to conclude that "against this background the dragon of John's vision would immediately be understood as the archenemy of God and his people."[19]

In a similar vein, Beasley-Murray identifies the dragon as an allusion to Tiamat, the monster from the watery chaos. Like Mounce, he points out the passages in the Jewish Scriptures which there is some reference to such a monster.[20] Caird notes that the seven heads of the dragon identify him with the monster Leviathan or Lotan (also Tiamat and Rahab) of ancient mythology, and his ten horns with the fourth beast of Dan 7:7.[21] Farrer sees some astrological influence in the description of the dragon and thinks it should be viewed as a seven-headed snake as in the Hercules legend. He does also, however, identify the dragon with the opponent of Eve in Gen 3.[22] Mounce notes that the red color is a symbol of the dragon's murderous character.[23] Morris, on the other hand, appears not to be able to make the connection between the color red and the dragon's murderous character.[24]

Beasley-Murray notes that the diadems on the dragon would have been seen by John as a blasphemous imitation of the royalty and authority of Christ.[25] This point will be explored more fully later.

To bring the counterimaging into focus, John has confronted us with the sign of a majestic woman who gives birth to the Messiah (12:1). He then shows us the seven angels with the seven last plagues that complete the wrath of God as another great sign (15:1). Over against these two signs in the arena of the forces of God he has set the sign of the great fiery-red dragon.

18. Mounce, *Revelation*, 237.
19. Ibid.; cf. Charles, *Critical and Exegetical Commentary*, 1:317–18.
20. Beasley-Murray, *Revelation*, 198–99.
21. Caird, *Commentary on Revelation*, 150.
22. Farrer, *Revelation*, 143–45.
23. Mounce, *Revelation*, 237; cf. Robbins, *Revelation*, 148.
24. Morris, *Revelation*, 153.
25. Beasley-Murray, *Revelation*, 199.

Perhaps I should note here that the phrase "*great* sign" appears only in 12:1. In the other two passages, however, John uses the word *allo*, "another," which normally denotes numerical difference, as opposed to *hetera*, which implies a difference in kind or quality.[26] I am therefore interpreting "another sign" in 12:3 and 15:1 as another *great* sign. Admittedly the distinction between *allos* and *heteros* cannot always be demonstrated unambiguously, but where there is a distinction it is along the lines that I have indicated.

In the interest of completeness I will point out that the plural form of the word "sign" (**sēmeia**) is used in Rev 13:13–14, 16:14, and 19:20; in addition to the passages discussed above; but in an entirely different sense from those passages. In all the latter passages *sēmeion* refers to the counterfeit miracles performed by the "unholy trinity," and will be dealt with later.

---

26. Thayer, *Greek-English Lexicon*, s.v. "*allos*" and "*heteros*."

22

The Woman

And a great sign appeared in heaven, a woman who had been clothed with the sun; and the moon (was) underneath her feet, and upon her head a crown of twelve stars.

(Rev 12:1)

And I saw the holy city, New Jerusalem, coming down out of Heaven from God, having been prepared like a bride having been adorned for her husband.

(Rev 21:2)

And one of the seven angels who held the seven vials filled with the seven last plagues came and spoke to me, saying, Come—I will show you the bride, the wife of the Lamb. And he brought me "in spirit" upon a large and high mountain, and he showed me the holy city, Jerusalem, coming down out of Heaven from God, having the glory of God. Her radiance (was) like a most precious stone, like jasper clear as crystal.

(Rev 21:9–11)

And one of the seven angels who held the seven vials came and spoke to me, saying, Come—I will show you the judgment of the great prostitute who is sitting upon many waters.

(Rev 17:1)

And he brought me into a desert "in spirit." And I saw a woman sitting upon a scarlet beast full of names of blasphemy, having seven heads and ten horns; And the woman had been clothed (in) purple and scarlet, and had been adorned with gold and precious stone and pearls.

(Rev 17:3–4c)

IN THE PASSAGES THAT I have translated above I have made no attempt to include all the passages dealing with some particular woman. For the most part I have limited my exegesis to those passages that most obviously reflect the Seer's use of counterimaging. This limitation means placing the focus on the woman of Rev 12:1 and the bride of the Lamb or New Jerusalem over against the "great prostitute," Babylon or Rome. Schüssler Fiorenza has taken note of what we might call a double parody in her comment that "the great harlot is a contrast image to the woman in chap. 12 [sic] as well as to the bride of the Lamb, the New Jerusalem."[1] I have not attempted to deal with the complete description of these two women but only those passages that describe their essence and hence their antithesis. Obviously this selectivity involves some arbitrariness or subjective judgment, for which I take full responsibility. I will call attention to the other passages that I have omitted from my discussion and leave the matter there. I have omitted the reference to Jezebel in Rev 2:20 because she is not described in language in any way reminiscent of any of the other three women in the passages above. Seven singular usages of *gynē* ("woman") appear in Rev 12:4, 6, and 13–17. All of these refer to the woman of 12:1 discussed below. Four singular usages also appear in Rev 17:6-7, 9, and 18; all in reference to the "great prostitute." Plural occurrences may be found in Rev 9:8 and 14:4. The demonic locusts are described in the former as having hair like women, among other things. In the latter passage, the one hundred forty-four thousand with the Lamb on Mount Zion are described as those who had not been defiled by women.

We have had occasion to consider the first positive usage of "woman" (Rev 12:1) above in the chapter on mystery. I noted there the tendency of several scholars to make this woman an astrological figure and my dissenting opinion that Joseph's dream is the primary background of the text.[2] Farrer supports this position and also makes an important connection between this woman and the bride of Christ or the New Jerusalem. He admits that the mother of the Messiah in the present passage is not the bride of Christ but argues that they point to the same reality, "the congregation of God."[3] I will defer further discussion at this point and move on to the imagery of the New Jerusalem in Rev 21:2.

---

1. Schüssler Fiorenza, *Justice and Judgment*, 171; cf. also Coggan, *Five Makers*, 81–82; Barnett, "Polemical Parallelism," 112; Kiddle, *Revelation*, 225–26.

2. Cf. Morris, *Revelation*, 152.

3. Farrer, *Revelation*, 215.

In typical fashion John has drawn from a wide background of imagery for this description. Morris has noted the reminiscence of Isa 61:10.[4] In addition, in Isa 54 the prophet pictures Yahweh as the husband of his people—an image further developed in Hos 2, Ezek 23, and elsewhere—and then proceeds to describe the restored city of Jerusalem. No doubt the prophetic writings are a primary source of imagery for the present passage. As Beasley-Murray points out, Jerusalem's glorification is found in the writings from Qumran and in *Tob* 13:16–18. He also notes 2 Esd 10:25–27, in which a woman who addresses that seer is transformed before his eyes into a city; and adds, "She too is Zion, not the earthly Jerusalem but a heavenly city, pre-existing and hidden with God."[5]

Has John used these images as his sources used them? We have found on other occasions that he has freely adapted his imagery, and so we have grounds for suspecting that he may have done so in Rev 21 as well. He has prefaced the present passage with a brief picture of a new heaven and a new earth in which there is no more sea (v. 1). Are we to understand a new creation *ex nihilo* ("out of nothing") or is there some relationship to the present heaven, earth, and Jerusalem? We have linguistic grounds for suggesting that John is thinking of a "gloriously rejuvenated" present heaven and earth.[6] In both verses he has used the word *kainos* ("new") which, in contrast with *neos*, implies something new in quality rather than new in time.[7] John's vision may be therefore the counterpart to Paul's redeemed creation. In Rom 8:19–22 Paul pictures the entire created order as being like a woman in childbirth awaiting redemption. Paul never expounded or explained this image in any of his surviving writings, but he makes very clear the fact that not only people but the created order itself is to be ultimately redeemed.

It would appear that John's new heaven and new earth are brought into the picture only as a place for the New Jerusalem, since the latter dominates the former almost to oblivion. Mounce has said in a classic understatement, "Some difference of opinion exists as to whether the New Jerusalem in John's vision should be taken as an actual city or as a symbol of the church in its perfected and eternal state." He further notes

4. Morris, *Revelation*, 237.
5. Beasley-Murray, *Revelation*, 309.
6. Cf. Robbins, *Revelation*, 232.
7. G. Abbott-Smith, *Manual Greek Lexicon*, s.v. *kainos* and *neos*; cf. Charles, *Critical and Exegetical Commentary*, 1:146, 2:158.

that Walvoord interprets it as an actual city while Ladd argues that it is the dwelling place of departed saints between death and resurrection; and that Lilje interprets it as the church universal. Mounce also quotes without endorsing or rejecting Kiddle's position that "It is a city which is a family. The ideal of perfect community, unrealizable on earth because of the curse of sin which vitiated the first creation, is now embodied in the redeemed from all nations."[8] Given the disparity of this small sampling of scholarly opinion, one ought not to expect a consensus in the foreseeable future. Once more we are seeking to portray timeless realities by and for creatures of time and place. This difficulty meets us at every turn when we attempt in any fashion to speak of the eternal purposes of God. I will suggest that John's New Jerusalem is an attempt to portray the eternal felicity of the people of God in their permanent and complete communion with God—and that neither time nor place is significant any longer in this setting.

The detail that it is one of the angels who poured out the vials of God's judgment who shows John the celestial city is in some ways perplexing. Caird makes the somewhat humorous comment, "Perhaps John believed that the demolition squad had also an interest in the reconstruction for which they had cleared the ground!"[9] Perhaps it is the Seer's way of expressing the truth that God's love and his wrath, salvation and judgment, are two sides of the same coin. The same heavenly messengers participate in both.

John is brought in spirit to a great high mountain in order to view the city. Caird translates *en pneuma* as "in a trance" instead of "in spirit," as I have done. He offers no justification for this unusual translation. He further argues that the mountain is not merely an exalted viewpoint but, as in Ezek 40:2, the actual site of the city.[10] Regarding John's being carried away "in spirit," Mounce argues that "the reference is to that state of ecstasy in which John experienced the entire visionary experience recorded in the Apocalypse."[11] While this inference may very well be correct, it goes beyond anything that the text will support in any specific way.

Mounce contends that the mountain is neither a literal mountain nor merely that elevation of spirit necessary to see the heavenly vision,

---

8. Mounce, *Revelation*, 370.
9. Caird, *Commentary on Revelation*, 269.
10. Ibid., 269–70.
11. Mounce, *Revelation*, 208.

as Swete had claimed. "The mountain 'existed' in John's vision of eternal realities."[12] Caird suggests a double ancestry of this vision of a heavenly city built upon a mountain: an ancient myth about a high mountain that reaches into heaven and is the home of the gods, and the idealized picture of Mount Zion in the Jewish Scriptures.[13] Once more the difficulty of location arises, which has spawned a variety of interpretations of both the mountain and the city. The range of interpretations may give some small support to my contention above that both time and place are irrelevant to the celestial city.

The fact that John sees the city "coming down" in both 21:2 and 21:10 does not mean, as some have suggested, either two different cities or two descents. Caird notes the extreme difficulty with any sort of literal interpretation of this city. He specifically challenges Charles's argument that the present passage has been displaced and should be transposed to a point before the millennium—and that we should understand one descent as the holy city of the millennial kingdom and another as the eternal New Jerusalem. Caird then aptly concludes, "But all this is unnecessary when we recognize that the descent from heaven is not a single nor even a double event, but a permanent characteristic of the city.... to the crack of doom Jerusalem can never appear otherwise than coming down out of heaven, for it owes its existence to the condescension of God and not to the building of men."[14] In Beasley-Murray's words, "The heavenly city accordingly is the dwelling of God, made accessible to men through Christ the Redeemer."[15]

The city is further described as having the glory of God. In the Jewish Scriptures the glory of God can scarcely be separated from the actual divine presence. See, for example, Exod 24:16 and 40:34-38; 1 Kgs 8:10-12; Ezek 43:5, and elsewhere.[16] In Mounce's words we find here "the eternal fulfillment of God's promise to captive Israel that in the

---

12. Ibid., 377-78.

13. Caird, *Commentary on Revelation*, 270; cf. Beasley-Murray, *Revelation*, 319.

14. Caird, *Commentary on Revelation*, 170-71; cf. Charles, *Critical and Exegetical Commentary*, 2:205; Morris, *Revelation*, 242.

15. Beasley-Murray, *Revelation*, 319.

16. See Beasley-Murray, *Revelation*, 311 for an excellent discussion of the roots of the glory of God in the Jewish Scriptures.

restoration the glory of God will be upon them and he will be their everlasting light" (Isa 60:1, 2, 19).[17]

Verse 11 presents several difficulties of interpretation. First of all, what is meant by the *phoster* ("radiance")? Second, what is meant by "jasper clear as crystal"? Caird,[18] along with Beasley-Murray, interprets the *phoster* as the light with which the city glows. Beasley-Murray's comment is, "The whole city, therefore, is conceived of as glowing with the glory of God, reflecting the divine nature in its every part."[19] Mounce also interprets *phoster* as depicting "a shimmering radiance which manifests the presence and glory of God," although in a footnote he acknowledges that *phoster* properly means a light-giving body rather than emitted radiance.[20] Mounce also notes that in Philippians 2:15, the only other place in the Christian Testament where this word appears, Paul seems to be using *phoster* in its proper sense.

Farrer will have none of the interpretation of *phoster* as luminosity or radiance. He says quite dogmatically, "Although our dictionaries allege that the sense 'luminosity' is found, the cases they quote do not bear them out; they are at best ambiguous; [sic] the sense 'luminary' can be read everywhere and therefore should be." He goes on to argue that "we do not yet know that the jewel-like quality of the city's *phoster* is to be extended to herself and reflected in her walls." He then proceeds to interpret the *phoster* as the sun or moon of the holy city.[21] We have noted at other points Farrer's affinity for astral interpretation. The fact that Revelation 21:23 says explicitly that the New Jerusalem has no need of the light of either sun or moon calls Farrer's interpretation into serious question.

What then about the second issue, the comparison of the *phoster* of the city to "a jasper clear as crystal"? Since no form of jasper as we know it can in any sense be described in this fashion, a variety of explanations has been offered. Beasley-Murray[22] relates this description to the divine appearance of the One on the throne in 4:3, as does Caird.[23] Mounce claims

---

17. Mounce, *Revelation*, 378.
18. Caird, *Commentary on Revelation*, 271.
19. Beasley-Murray, *Revelation*, 319.
20. Mounce, *Revelation*, 378.
21. Farrer, *Revelation*, 216.
22. Beasley-Murray, *Revelation*, 319.
23. Caird, *Commentary on Revelation*, 271.

that in antiquity any opaque precious stone was called jasper, and "The point of comparison is the brilliance and sparkle of the gem. The reference could be to the diamond."[24] In the same passage Mounce refers in a footnote to yet another suggestion. In the Bauer-Arndt-Gingrich lexicon, an older usage of *krystallos*, or "crystal," as meaning "ice" is mentioned, and the question asked whether this might not be the preferable translation in the present passage. The lexicon notes that "a precious stone would shimmer like a sheet of ice."[25]

When we come to Rev 17:3, we see John transported "in spirit" again, but this time into an *erēmos*, a "desert" or "wilderness." Again it is one of the angels who held the seven vials of God's wrath who invites John to come and see something. This time the vision is of the "great prostitute" who sits upon many waters (v. 1). Boesak, in commenting on the two women, says, "We are again in the wilderness, and we are again faced with a woman. But this time the woman is the exact opposite of the woman we met in chapter 12. They are both women, they are both called 'mother,' but the differences cannot be more fundamental. In chapter 12 we met the Messianic mother, the giver of life. Here we are confronted with the mother of whores, the very personification of the evil she is associated with [sic]."[26]

Numerous scholars have noted the juxtaposition of these two women. Beasley-Murray speaks of the two being "compared" but goes on to say "Both represent communities, the former possessing a heavenly calling, the latter being an agent of hell."[27] In my judgment this assessment depicts a contrast more than a comparison. In similar language Barnett speaks of the woman of Rev 12 being "paralleled" by the "great prostitute."[28] His further discussion also points more in the direction of a contrast than a parallel. I prefer Morris's terminology at this point: "The 'woman clothed with the sun'. . . is to be understood in contrast to 'the great prostitute.'"[29]

I have dealt with the prostitute to some degree in the chapter on mystery. She sits upon a beast having seven heads and ten horns, full of blasphemous names that identify him with the beast from the sea of Rev

---

24. Mounce, *Revelation*, 378; cf. Morris, *Revelation*, 242.
25. Ibid., 378 n. 29.
26. Boesak, *Comfort and Protest*, 110.
27. Beasley-Murray, *Revelation*, 197.
28. Barnett, "Polemical Parallelism," 112.
29. Morris, *Revelation*, 151.

13:1. The woman herself is clothed with purple and scarlet, the colors of wealth and royalty. Beasley-Murray has suggested a common origin for the woman and the beast, noting that in Babylonian mythology the monster Tiamat was female; and that the transformation of a beast into a woman is a common development in pagan mythology. He then explicitly identifies the woman with the city of Rome and the beast as the "antichristian empire." He also notes the difference of details in describing the beast. In 13:1 the names of blasphemy appear only on the heads of the beast; here, however, he is covered with them. Beasley-Murray interprets this new detail as meaning that "the empire embraced a multitude of forms of idolatry, not the least of which was Rome's own claims to be divine."[30] Charles in similar fashion writes, "Here they cover the entire body, and may refer to the innumerable deities of her own and subject countries which Rome recognized.[31]

In summary, the Seer has set the woman clothed with the sun of 12:1 and the bride or New Jerusalem of 21:2–4 over against the "great prostitute," Babylon or Rome. The specific details do not establish the woman of Rev 12 as the counterimage of the prostitute to any great degree, but nevertheless quite a few scholars have noted the contrast. Charles cautiously suggests only the possibility that we have an indirect contrast with the woman of 12:1.[32] Caird, after noting the colors of royalty which the prostitute wears, suggests that her splendid clothing "is meant to seem a tawdry parody of the heavenly splendor of the other woman who was clothed with the sun." He also views her jewels as "a poor contrast with the richness of the heavenly Jerusalem."[33] Farrer approaches the contrast in slightly different wording: "There is no symbolical identity, indeed, between the wilderness into which the woman flew on eagles' pinions, to be nourished in a place prepared, and the wilderness where St. John, carried by his angel, sees the woman's opposite."[34] Beasley-Murray notes the common reference to the wilderness and comments, "In chapter 12 the mother of the Messiah escapes from the dragon into the wilderness, there to be cared for in safety by God. When the mother of harlots is represented as

---

30. Beasley-Murray, *Revelation*, 252; cf. Boesak, *Comfort and Protest*, 110.
31. Charles, *Critical and Exegetical Commentary*, 2:64; cf. Mounce, *Revelation*, 309.
32. Charles, *Critical and Exegetical Commentary*, 2:64.
33. Caird, *Commentary on Revelation*, 213.
34. Farrer, *Revelation*, 182.

residing in the wilderness, it is then conceived as the dwelling place of the Devil and evil spirits (cf. Tob 8:3, Luke 11:24) [sic]."[35]

If the contrast of the harlot with the woman of 12:1 is indirect and somewhat nonspecific, the contrast with the New Jerusalem is clearly explicit and intentional. One has only to look at the corresponding language used in order to see this contrast. The parallels are as follows:

1. One of the angels who held the seven vials of God's wrath shows John both women.
2. The language by which John is summoned to view both women is identical: *deuro deixō soi* ("Come, I will show to you" [17:1, 21:9]).
3. John is brought "in spirit" to view both women.
4. The harlot is decked out in purple and scarlet and is adorned with gold, precious stones, and pearls; the New Jerusalem is like a bride adorned for her husband, she reflects the glory of God, and her *phoster* ("radiance") is like a most precious stone.
5. The phrase *kai eidon* ("and I saw") is used of both women (17:3, 21:2).

These correspondences in language can scarcely be accidental. John is clearly inviting the reader or hearer to contrast the two women. This contrast, as I have pointed out above, has been noted by a number of interpreters. Mounce gives a slightly new focus to the contrast from that of other interpreters. After noting that the same angel showed John both women, he says, "The connection is not accidental. When the great harlot with all her seductive allurements is exposed and destroyed, then the Bride of Christ will be seen in all her beauty and true worth."[36] Garrow, in commenting on the statement that the "ten horns" will destroy the harlot says, "This image of the faithless woman destroyed by her faithless partner sits in direct opposition to that of Christ's faithful bride made secure by the one who is Faithful and True."[37]

---

35. Beasley-Murray, *Revelation*, 251–52.
36. Mounce, *Revelation*, 307.
37. Garrow, *Revelation*, 99.

23

The Diadems

And his eyes were like a flame of fire, and upon his head (were) many diadems, (and he was) having a written name which no one knows except him.

(Rev 19:12)

And another sign appeared in heaven, and behold (it was) a great, fiery-red dragon having seven heads and ten horns; and upon his heads (were) seven diadems.

(Rev 12:3)

And I saw a beast coming up out of the sea, having ten horns and seven heads; and upon his horns ten diadems and upon his head names of blasphemy.

(Rev 13:1)

THE ONLY MENTION OF diadems in the arena of God's operation is in connection with the appearance of the conquering Christ arriving on a white horse (19:12). The counterimaging of the white horse itself has been dealt with in a previous chapter. The eyes like a flame of fire connect the victorious Christ with the "one like a son of man" in John's inaugural vision (1:14). In the present passage Christ appears suddenly and without any preparation for the readers or hearers (19:11). Farrer has called this scene an act of "naked omnipotence."[1] Although we are given a vivid picture of armies preparing for battle, however, no actual battle scene is included in the vision. As Beasley-Murray has noted, "The 'battle'

---

1. Farrer, *Revelation*, 197.

resolves itself into a judgment uttered by the Word of God."² Schlatter, as cited by Mounce, also speaks of the metaphor being transformed from one of battle into one of judgment. "God triumphantly clears the battle field and swallows up his enemies in death."³ The wearing of many diadems depicts the transfer of sovereignty over the world to the victorious Christ.⁴ Morris notes that both majesty and dominion are attributed to Christ in this reference to his wearing many diadems.⁵ At the last mention of Christ, however, the diadems were not in view. Are we to assume that they have been won in the interim? Caird thinks so. He then raises the question as to how the diadems were won and answers that Christ has done so through the Conquerors [sic]. Caird notes the promise in Rev 3:21 that the one conquering will be given a place on God's throne just as Christ shares that throne. "He is in fact the representative figure, incorporating his faithful followers in his own inclusive person; for they died 'in the Lord'" (14:13).⁶ I suggest that this interpretation expresses one side of a paradox. The other side is that Christ wins dominion through his own suffering and death.

Charles argues that the phrase "having a name written which no one knows except him," while being Johannine in diction, is an interpolation. He gives three basic reasons: first, the phrase breaks the thought of the passage; second, the phrase is "flatly contradicted" in the next verse; and third, omission of this clause restores the parallelism with v. 13.⁷ Charles has again developed tunnel vision at this point. He has failed to consider the issue of the many names the triumphant Christ may bear. The late Ray Robbins has demonstrated that no fewer than 173 different designations of Christ appear in the Christian Testament.⁸

Charles's other two arguments are likewise weak. He fails to explain why we should not expect a reference to the name in the midst of a discussion of the person and his appearance. One could with equal or stronger force argue that the name is the climax to which the description

---

2. Beasley-Murray, *Revelation*, 278.
3. Mounce, *Revelation*, 343.
4. Cf. Wilson, *Revelation*, 157.
5. Morris, *Revelation*, 223.
6. Caird, *Commentary on Revelation*, 241–42.
7. Charles, *Critical and Exegetical Commentary*, 2:132.
8. Robbins, *Revelation*, 166–70.

of the person and his attire has been building. As for parallelism, by what sort of reasoning are we to assume that the author here intended a parallelism with v. 13? Charles has been caught in the counterfeit dilemma of either/or, i.e., that the name of Christ must be either known or unknown. When we take into account the ancient belief that a name is inseparable from the person who bears it, it should be rather obvious that human beings can know some of the names of Christ but that knowing him in any complete sense lies beyond human knowledge.[9] Wilson's quotation of Swete's words that "only the Son of God can understand the mystery of His own Being [sic]" are appropriate here.[10] One might also invoke Paul's words: "For who knows the things belonging to humanity except the spirit of humanity which (is) in him; so also no one knows the things of God except the Spirit of God" (1 Cor 2:11).

Morris notes that for modern Westerners, a name is no more than a label by which we are identified, but that in antiquity (as I noted above) the name was inseparable from the person. He further notes the ancient belief, prominent among practitioners of magic, that to know someone's name gives one a certain amount of control over that person. John may well be saying, among other things, that no one has power over Christ.[11] The inseparability of the name from the person is clearly reflected in Revelation in the reference to a few "names" in Sardis who had not defiled their garments (Rev 3:4). Obviously persons are in view in that passage, not labels.

Mounce discusses a number of specific interpretations of the unknowable name. He notes the attempt of some scholars to equate it with the tetragrammaton, YHWH, the personal name of God in the Jewish Scriptures, which was considered to be too sacred for human beings to pronounce. Associated with this belief was the companion notion noted above that to know the name of someone is to have some degree of power over that person. The reader may consider Mark 5:8–9, in which Jesus seems unable to cast out a demon until he secures the demon's name. In English, "Yahweh" and "Jehovah" represent two educated guesses as to the way in which this sacred name of God should be pronounced, in view of the fact that originally the Hebrew language had no written vowels.

---

9. Cf. Carrell, *Jesus and the Angels*, 202.
10. Wilson, *Revelation*, 157.
11. Morris, *Revelation*, 68–69, 223.

Mounce cites Farrer's position that the name is mentioned after the diadems because the Jewish high priests wore the sacred tetragrammaton on their foreheads; and Lilje as suggesting that the name is the one on Christ's thigh which could not be seen at first because of the radiance of the vision. He then cites as the "most common interpretation" that the name expresses the mystery of Christ's person and hence is veiled from all created beings. Mounce then notes the relationship to the divine visitors in the Old Testament who refused to give their names (Gen 32:29, Judg 13:18). Surprisingly, he then concludes, "It is highly questionable that the returning Messiah would share such a reluctance."[12] This comment misses the point. The issue is not the willingness or lack thereof on the part of Christ to reveal his name(s), but human inability to know that name in any complete sense. As Caird has put it succinctly, "When they have joined all the glorious names that adoring wonder can ascribe to him, he still confronts them with an ultimate mystery."[13] As Morris puts it, "Here we are reminded that there are hidden depths; Christ's person can never be completely understood by his creation."[14]

The first use of the word *diadem* in the arena of evil takes us back into the vision of the great fiery-red dragon of Rev 12:3. The use of the word *sign* in this verse was discussed in a previous chapter. There I also suggested that the seven heads and ten horns possibly symbolize complete knowledge and humanly complete power. To follow through with the numerical symbolism in this fashion admittedly leads to a difficulty. The obvious conclusion would be that the dragon's seven diadems would indicate his complete sovereignty.[15] In Revelation, however, John will often parody aspects of God's nature in his descriptions of the powers of evil, and this is the manner in which I am taking the seven diadems here.[16] Wilson approximates this interpretation when he speaks of the diadems as symbolizing the "usurped dominion" of the dragon.[17]

The second and final passage in which diadems appear in the arena of evil occurs with the emergence of the dragon's primary ally, the beast

12. Mounce, *Revelation*, 344–45; cf. also Beasley-Murray, *Revelation*, 279–80.
13. Caird, *Commentary on Revelation*, 242.
14. Morris, *Revelation*, 223.
15. Cf. Ibid., 154.
16. The literary device of parody will be discussed more fully in the later chapters of this study.
17. Wilson, *Revelation*, 104.

from the sea (13:1). Like the dragon, the beast is described as having seven heads and ten horns. As most commentators have noted, this beast has characteristics of the four beasts of Dan 7. He is the same beast that was noted in Rev 11:7. Caird refers to the Jewish belief that God had created the sea-monster Leviathan and the earth-monster Behemoth; and also observes that this beast from the sea resembles Leviathan. If there should be any question regarding the fact that in 11:7 the beast comes up out of the abyss, whereas in the present passage he comes up out of the sea, Caird also notes that the word *abyssos* ("abyss") is used for the primeval ocean in the Greek version of the creation story (Gen 1) and of the sea in general in Job 28:14 and 38:16.[18]

John's imagery taxes the limit of our ability to visualize. How does one locate ten horns upon seven heads on a creature with only one mouth (v. 5)? Such questions miss the point, as Beasley-Murray [19] and Mounce[20] have noted. The composite figure echoing the four beasts of Dan 7 and its alliance with the dragon seem to dominate John's thinking here. Caird notes that there may be some literal kernel of meaning here in that the beast represented Roman imperial power which literally came up out of the sea every year with the arrival of the proconsul at Ephesus.[21] Charles likewise identifies the beast as the Roman Empire.[22] Mounce concurs that for John the beast was the Roman Empire, specifically in its function as the enemy of the church, but does not stop with this identification. He again leaves room for the application of the image to times and situations other than the first century c.e. by identifying the beast more broadly as deified secular authority.[23]

I have accepted the reading "names" in 13:11, with Codex Alexandrinus and several minuscule manuscripts. Admittedly, however, the textual evidence is rather evenly balanced between the singular and the plural, as Charles and Morris[24] have noted. Charles further argues that if the singular reading be accepted, the "name of blasphemy" would be the name

---

18. Caird, *Commentary on Revelation*, 161.
19. Beasley-Murray, *Revelation*, 209.
20. Mounce, *Revelation*, 250.
21. Caird, *Commentary on Revelation*, 162.
22. Charles, *Critical and Exegetical Commentary*, 1:345.
23. Mounce, *Revelation*, 251.
24. Morris, *Revelation*, 161.

Sebastos ("divine") as applied to Augustus. If the plural be accepted, the names would be those of the Caesars.[25] Wilson accepts the plural reading also, and identifies the names of blasphemy with the divine honors assumed by the various emperors of Rome.[26] Mounce in similar fashion says that the names of blasphemy referred to the increasing tendency of the emperors to accept the appellation "divine," though, as noted above, he does not limit the "beast" to the Roman Empire.[27] Morris makes the additional point that if the singular "name" be correct, each head of the beast would be depicted as having the same name, whereas if the plural be correct each head would have one or more different names.[28]

I return to the question of the diadems. We would expect diadems to crown the heads, but instead John places them on the horns. Many different suggestions have been made concerning this conundrum. Mounce is probably on the right track in arguing "the most plausible suggestion is that [the beast's] claim to authority rests on brute force."[29] This interpretation accords well with the commonly accepted view that horns are a symbol of power in apocalyptic writings.

In these passages John has confronted us with the dragon possessing seven diadems, and his primary ally, the beast from the sea, as possessing ten diadems. The diadem suggests royalty and sovereignty, and the numbers incline us to think in terms of completeness. But, as Beasley-Murray[30] and Mounce[31] have observed, John has presented us with the counterimage of the victorious Christ as wearing *many* diadems. Charles, in a similar vein, has commented that the conception of sovereignty signified by the diadems is appropriate to the dragon, because he "is in many respects a caricature of Christ."[32] If there be any sense in which the sovereignty of the dragon and the beast from the sea may be termed complete, that of the victorious Christ surpasses both.

---

25. Charles, *Critical and Exegetical Commentary*, 1:347–48.
26. Wilson, *Revelation*, 110.
27. Mounce, *Revelation*, 250–51.
28. Morris, *Revelation*, 161.
29. Mounce, *Revelation*, 250; cf. Morris, *Revelation*, 161.
30. Beasley-Murray, *Revelation*, 209.
31. Mounce, *Revelation*, 344.
32. Charles, *Critical and Exegetical Commentary*, 1:347.

24

Who Is Like . . . ?

> *And there became war in heaven, with Michael and his angels fighting with the dragon.*
>
> (REV 12:7)
>
> *And the earth marveled after the beast and they worshiped the dragon because he gave authority to the beast; they also worshiped the beast, saying, "Who is like the beast and who is able to fight with him?".*
>
> (REV 13:3c–4)
>
> *And they were crying out while seeing the smoke of her burning, saying, "Who is like the great city?"*
>
> (REV 18:18)

THE COUNTERIMAGING IN THIS case is a bit more subtle than any discussed thus far. Some readers may even accuse me of reading a subtlety into the passage that the author of Revelation did not intend and that the readers or hearers would not have understood. In my defense, however, I adduce the name *Michael*, which in Hebrew means, "Who is like God?" I am suggesting that John is counterimaging this question over against the questions "Who is like the beast?" in Rev 13:3c–4 and "Who is like the great city?" in 18:18. Aside from the name of Michael, there is a further connection between 12:7 and 13:4. The infinitive *polemēsai*, "to fight," or "to do battle," is used in both passages. The infinitive is the natural form for a writer to use in 13:4, but not so in 12:7. I therefore conclude that John has deliberately given this clue that the two passages should be looked at together.

If the meaning of Michael's name be considered too subtle for John's readers or hearers, another sort of counterimaging may be considered. The question, "Who is like thee among the gods, O Lord?" appears in the Jewish Scriptures at Exod 15:11, and similar questions are found in Ps 89:6, Isa 40:25, and Micah 7:18. And, as Lohmeyer has noted, "The gist of verse four is a parody of an ancient saying [for example, Exod 15:11: Who is like you among gods, Lord?], and a contrast to the call of the angels in 5:2ff [sic]."[1] Regarding the first passage mentioned above, Bauckham has also interpreted the question "Who is like the beast?" as a parody of these words from the song of Moses.[2] Swete speaks of the same parody.[3] Morris is one interpreter who has detected the counterimaging I am suggesting for this passage, although he does not use the term. "*Who is like the beast?* [sic] may be meant as a parody of a similar Old Testament expression (Exod. 15:11; Pss 35:10) [sic]. Also, in view of the activities of the angel Michael, it is possible that we should also detect a reference to the meaning of his name, 'Who is like God?'"[4] Bauckham, Swete, and Morris appear to be using the term *parody* in the sense in which I use *counterimaging*.

The passage under consideration depicts war in heaven between Michael and his (subordinate) angels fighting against the dragon and his angels. The result is the defeat of the dragon and his angels, and their being cast down to earth (12:9). Echoes of an ancient but un-Biblical tradition appear here. Popular theologians have expounded the idea of Satan as a fallen angel who was expelled from heaven as though the idea were taught in the Bible. No unambiguous evidence exists in the Bible for this teaching. The primary source of the notion in popular thought is John Milton's epic poem *Paradise Lost*.[5] In that writing Milton erroneously equated the "Lucifer" of Isa 14:12 with Satan. This equation is one of the greatest ironies of all time in that the name *Lucifer* is a combination of the Latin noun *lux, lucis* and the verb *ferro*, and means "light-bearer." Modern translators thus commonly translate *Lucifer* as "morning star" or "day star." In context, Isa 14:4 clearly indicates that the "Lucifer" is the king of Babylon. His "falling

---

1. Der Zug in 4 ist eine Parodie auf altliche Wendungen (z. B. Ex 15.11: tis homois soi en theois, kurie) und ein Kontrast zu dem Ruf des Engels in 5.2ff.

2. Bauckham, *Climax*, 301; see also Charles, *Critical and Exegetical Commentary*, 1:351; Mounce, *Revelation*, 252–53, C. Scott, *Revelation*, 237.

3. Swete, *Apocalypse*, 164–65.

4. Morris, *Revelation*, 163.

5. Cf. Mounce, *Revelation*, 240; Caird, *Commentary on Revelation*, 153.

from heaven" is beyond reasonable doubt the fall described in Dan 4:28–33. Nebuchadnezzar fell from the highest place a human being could occupy to the lowest—eating grass with the beasts of the field.

A passage in the Christian Testament that has been used to support the idea of Satan as being an angel expelled from heaven is Luke 10:18. If people had not on other grounds been predisposed to the idea, probably no one would ever have thought of it at this point, however. In the Lukan context, Jesus's disciples have just returned from their mission and are rejoicing that even the demons are subject to them in the name of Jesus (Luke 10:17). Jesus replies, "I was seeing Satan, like lightning from heaven, falling." Translation and punctuation often obscure the meaning of Jesus's words. The imperfect tense of the verb *seeing* indicates an ongoing or repetitive action. In other words, each time a human being was freed from the clutches of demonic power, Satan "fell." To refer this image to Satan being ejected from heaven at some indeterminate time in the ancient past leaves it with no connection at all to its immediate context. In Luke 10:18 the Greek text makes rather clear the fact that it is the lightning, not Satan, which falls from heaven in that passage. With the suddenness in which lightning falls from heaven, so Satan "fell" every time Jesus's disciples cast out a demon.

Another primary source for the idea that Satan was an angel who was expelled from heaven is the intertestamental literature. Several of these noncanonical writings relate this incident. *De vita Adam et Eva* ("The Life of Adam and Eve") is among the most explicit, describing in some detail the confrontation with Michael that led to Satan's being cast out of heaven.[6]

What then about Rev 12? If we follow the sequence of events from 12:1 onward, the woman has given birth to the Messiah. The dragon has attempted to destroy the child when it was born, presumably on earth. The child is caught up to the throne of God (v. 6). Then follows the battle in which Satan and his angels are defeated and cast down to earth. There is no necessity for understanding this text as meaning that Satan ever was *in*

---

6. See Charlesworth, *Old Testament Pseudepigrapha*, 2:249-65. As I discussed this point in one of my classes at Georgetown College in 1983 or 1984, one of my brighter students commented that what bothered her about this idea was that, if an angel could be kicked out of Heaven permanently, what assurance could she have that the same thing might not happen to her? I am not sure that many who have tacitly accepted this idea of Satan as an angel who was kicked out of heaven have thought about it in that light!

heaven.⁷ Taken in the overall context, Satan attempts to destroy Jesus when he is born but is unable to do so. He then follows him on up to heaven, still trying to destroy him, but is repelled by Michael and his angels.

Mounce, on the contrary, denies that there is any basis in the text for interpreting the battle as resulting from Satan's pursuit of Christ at his ascension.⁸ As is true in most cases, that depends on how one reads the evidence. The interpretation I am suggesting would require, instead of reading *oude eti* as saying there was "no longer" a place for him in heaven, to render it "not even yet" was there a place for him in Heaven. I readily concede that John does not characteristically use *eti* in this manner but it is a grammatical possibility.

Many commentators have noticed the apparent incongruity of Michael's fighting the dragon instead of the Messiah. Beasley-Murray is very emphatic in saying, "This feature of the story can hardly have been instigated by a Christian writer, for whom there is but one mediator between God and man."⁹ Caird is less explicit but refers to the detail of Michael and his angels fighting the battle as an "unexpected twist."¹⁰ As Mounce¹¹ and Beasley-Murray¹² both note, however, numerous passages in the intertestamental literature assign to Michael the role of mediator and angelic intercessor who will bring victory against Satan and his hosts. Obviously John could have been influenced by these intertestamental writings. Furthermore, there is nothing at all incompatible in the light of the overall theology of Revelation in Michael's being the instrument by which God and Christ carry out their sovereign purpose. As Wilson puts it, Michael was able to conquer in heaven only because of the decisive conquest of Christ on earth.¹³ The same argument of Beasley-Murray noted above could be made regarding the pouring-out of the seven vials. The fact that seven angels pour out the vials of God's wrath does not make the vials any less the judgment of God or the Messiah.

---

7. Cf. Summers, *Worthy Is the Lamb*, 172–73.
8. Mounce, *Revelation*, 241.
9. Beasley-Murray, *Revelation*, 201.
10. Caird, *Commentary on Revelation*, 153.
11. Mounce, *Revelation*, 241.
12. Beasley-Murray, *Revelation*, 201.
13. Wilson, *Revelation*, 106.

After the dragon calls his "lieutenant," the beast from the sea, John reports that all the earth marveled at the beast and worshiped the dragon who gave authority to the beast (13:3c–4). Furthermore, they worshiped the beast himself and asked, "Who is like the beast?" and "Who is able to fight against him?" The phrase *kai ethaumasthē holē hē gē opisō tou theriou* ("and the whole world marveled after the beast") does not conform to any known Greek usage, sacred or profane. Blass[14] attempted to solve the problem by inserting *kai eporeuthē* ("and they went") before *opisō* ("after"), hence making the phrase read "and the whole earth marveled and went after the beast." Charles thinks the problem could be solved by translating the phrase back into Hebrew. He argues that the phrase should run *kai ethaumase holē hē gē idousa* (or *blepousa*) *to thērion* ("and the whole earth marveled when they saw the beast"). He then concludes, "The meaning therefore of this clause is exactly the same as in 17:8. The world was astonished at the marvelous return of Nero *redivivus*."[15] The restricted nature of Charles's interpretation of the beast has been previously noted, so I will leave it at this point.

Although many interpreters see the stricken head of the beast (13:3a) as referring to the death of Nero, Mounce,[16] Barr,[17] and others have noted a serious problem with this interpretation. It is not the wounded head of the beast but the beast itself that recovers, according to 13:14. This problem is also reflected in 13:3a in that the masculine (or neuter) pronoun *autou* appears; but if the head were the referent, it would call for the feminine *autēs*, since the word *kephalē*, or "head," in Greek is feminine in gender. Mounce suggests further, although with a noticeable lack of conviction, that the recovery of the wounded beast could refer to the reestablishment of order in the empire after the death of Nero and the bloody turmoil in which Galba, Otho, and Vitellius each reigned for only a few months in 69 C.E.[18] Mounce then suggests an alternative view that "perhaps no historical allusion is intended and the purpose of the figure is to underscore the tremendous vitality of the beast."[19]

---

14. Cited in Charles, *Critical and Exegetical Commentary*, 1:351.
15. Ibid.
16. Mounce, *Revelation*, 252–53.
17. Barr, *New Testament Story*, 405.
18. Cf. Wilson, *Revelation*, 111.
19. Mounce, *Revelation*, 253.

Beasley-Murray notes that the reference in 13:3a to the head of the beast, most literally translated, means "as though it has been slaughtered unto death." He then notes that v. 14 indicates that the beast really had been dead but came back to life. In his further arguments, however, he fails to note that it was the beast itself that came back to life, not the stricken head. He says very dogmatically, "There is one person only whom this description can fit, and that is Nero."[20] Morris is on much safer ground, in my judgment, in his interpretation that an evil which has its source in the dragon lies in the heart of both individuals and communities and apparently cannot be slain. Each time it seems to have received a mortal wound, it recovers, and each time people marvel over the beast's vitality.[21]

Caird is yet another commentator who identifies the smitten head of the beast as Nero. He notes that Nero's suicide in 68 C.E. might have been seen as a deadly wound to the monster as a whole, not just to one of its heads. He then discusses those who pretended to be Nero *redivivus*—three imposters are mentioned by the Roman historians Tacitus and Suetonius—and the turmoil that they caused. He concludes his discussion (a conclusion that Beasley-Murray supports[22]) with these words: "Nero will indeed return, but reincarnated in a new persecuting emperor who is one of the seven (17:11)."[23]

Mounce notes the apparent echo of Exod 15:11 and others in the question, "Who is like the beast?" Wilson refers to the worship of the beast as a parody of the true worship of God as reflected in that passage.[24] Mounce also aptly points out that the worship of the beast is not a result of its greatness but purely because of its awesome power.[25] Charles quotes approvingly a similar remark by Swete that "it was not moral greatness but brute force which commanded the homage of the provinces." He also notes that in this verse we find the major reason for the composition of the book as a whole: "the worship of the Beast, the imperial cultus."[26] Farrer's comments on this passage are also worth noting: "Men worship

---

20. Beasley-Murray, *Revelation*, 210.
21. Morris, *Revelation*, 162–63.
22. Beasley-Murray, *Revelation*, 211.
23. Caird, *Commentary on Revelation*, 164-65.
24. Wilson, *Revelation*, 112.
25. Mounce, *Revelation*, 253–54; cf. Charles, *Critical and Exegetical Commentary*, 1:351.
26. Ibid.

the dragon because he has conferred authority on the beast. This is the epitome of political religion; gods are worshiped as the support of established power. It is also a parody of Christianity."[27]

The second and final occurrence of *tis homoios/a* ("Who is like?") appears in Rev 18:18. This time the adulation is directed to the "great city" at the time she is being destroyed. As noted previously, some interpreters argue that the "great city" in 11:8 is Jerusalem, not Rome. With regard to the present passage almost no dissenting voices are heard arguing that the "great city" is any other than Babylon or Rome. Mounce notes the similarity of the question to Ezek 27:32, "Who was ever destroyed like Tyre?"[28] Morris also refers to Ezek 27:32, noting the similarity in the Hebrew text but also observing that the Septuagint reads differently.[29] Rowland notes that despite the exhortation to the heavens, saints, apostles and prophets to rejoice over her destruction (v. 20) "there is some real sadness expressed at the passing of Babylon."[30] John himself seems to have had a grudging admiration for the city. When he first saw her he said, "I marveled a great marvel (17:6)." Admittedly not all interpreters agree on the meaning of *ethaumasa thauma mega* ("I marveled a great marvel") in this verse. Mounce suggests that John's response to "the revolting and gory spectacle" was totally negative.[31] Farrer, on the other hand, takes the words of the angel in 17:7 as suggesting superstitious awe or genuine admiration on John's part.[32] Beasley-Murray thinks there is no reason to seek hidden motives or causes beyond that of actual admiration.[33] Caird argues, "We cannot escape the impression that he was sensitive to the grandeur that was Rome." He then comments, regarding the temptation of the churches to be taken in by Rome's splendor, counterfeit though it was, "If he has to steel himself against the intoxicating draughts of the golden cup she holds, how easy it must have been for the people of Thyatira to make themselves drunk with the influence of their local Jezebel."[34] Charles reflects only a

---

27. Farrer, *Revelation*, 152.
28. Mounce, *Revelation*, 332.
29. Morris, *Revelation*, 215.
30. Rowland, *Revelation*, 143.
31. Mounce, *Revelation*, 311.
32. Farrer, *Revelation*, 184.
33. Beasley-Murray, *Revelation*, 253.
34. Caird, *Commentary on Revelation*, 213–14.

slightly different understanding when he speaks of John's astonishment at the "fearful vision he has just seen."[35]

To sum up this section, the Seer has counterimaged the questions, "Who is like the beast?" and "Who is like the great city?" over against the name *Michael*, "Who is like God?" He may have also intended for his readers or hearers to be reminded of the questions regarding resemblances to God in the Jewish Scriptures. John has placed the question concerning the beast in very close proximity to the passage in which Michael is the chief character. He has also used the infinitive *polemēsai* very awkwardly, after he had used it correctly in 13:4. We observe an example of the black-and-white perspective of the Seer emerging from this mass of material. One segment of humanity marvels over the beast and the harlot Babylon, and makes them the objects of worship. The other segment of humanity marvels over the greatness of God and worships God.[36] For John there is no middle ground. One is either a Jew or part of the synagogue of Satan (cf. Rev 2:9, 3:9). One is either a true apostle or a false one (cf. Rev 2:3). One is either a citizen of the New Jerusalem (cf. Rev 21:1–2) or a citizen of the harlot Babylon (cf. Rev 18:4). Boesak has said it well: "He (John) confronts us with stark choices: obedience to God and God's word or subjection to Caesar, the living God or the one who calls himself God, the Lord or the dragon, the Messiah king or the beast. The church must choose. Either we are on our way to the New Jerusalem or we perish with Babylon."[37]

---

35. Charles, *Critical and Exegetical Commentary*, 2:66.
36. Mounce, *Revelation*, 253–54.
37. Boesak, *Comfort and Protest*, 38.

25

Wrath and Passion

If anyone worships the beast and his image, and receives (the beast's) mark upon his forehead or his hand, he also drinks from the wine of the wrath of God which has been mixed full strength in the cup of his anger; and he shall be tormented by fire and sulfur in the presence of the holy angels and the Lamb.

(Rev 14:9b–10)

And the angel cast his sickle into the earth and harvested the vineyard of the earth; and he cast (the grapes) into the great wine-vat of the wrath of God.

(Rev 14:19)

And I saw another sign in heaven, great and marvelous; seven angels having the seven last plagues by which the wrath of God is completed.

(Rev 15:1)

And one of the four living creatures gave to the seven angels seven golden vials full of the wrath of the God who lives forever and ever.

(Rev 15:7)

And I heard a loud voice out of the inner sanctuary saying to the seven angels, "Go and pour out the seven vials of the wrath of God into the earth".

(Rev 16:1)

And the great city was split into three parts; the cities of the nations also fell. And Babylon the Great was remembered before God who gave to her the cup of the wrath of his anger.

(Rev 16:19)

And a sharp sword is coming out of his mouth in order that by it he might smite the nations; and he will shepherd them with an iron rod, and he will tread the wine-vat of the wine of the wrath of the anger of God the Almighty.

(REV 19:15)

Because of this rejoice continually, heavens, and the ones dwelling in them; woe (to) the earth and the sea because the devil went down to you having great wrath, knowing that he has little opportunity.

(REV 12:12)

And another angel, a second, followed, saying, "It fell!" "It fell!" Babylon the Great, who has given all the nations to drink from the wine of the passion [thymos] of her fornication (fell)

(REV 14:8)

Because from the wine of the passion [thymos] of her fornication she has given all the nations to drink, and the kings of the earth committed fornication, and the merchants of the earth became wealthy from the strength of her eager desire.

(REV 18:3)

JOHN'S USE OF COUNTERIMAGING escapes notice in many English translations because the Greek word *thymos* is variously translated as "wrath," "anger," "passion," "raging wine," or "fury." Where it refers to the harlot Babylon, the word *passion* is more often used. Hence the English reader would have no way of knowing that the same word lies behind these different translations. In one case, as I will note below, only one verse separates the usage of *thymos* where it refers to harlot Babylon from a text that refers to God.

In Rev 14:9b–10 we find the warning that anyone who receives the mark of the beast must face the wrath of God, which has been mixed full strength. This wrath is further described as eternal torment by fire and sulfur ("brimstone") in the presence of the Lamb and the holy angels. As both Charles[1] and Mounce[2] have noted, this passage counters the proclamation in 13:17 that only people who had received the mark of the beast

---

1. Charles, *Critical and Exegetical Commentary*, 2:15.
2. Mounce, *Revelation*, 274–75.

could engage in any kind of commerce.³ Now those who *do* receive that mark are threatened with a much more severe penalty.

God's wrath as a cup of wine is rooted in the teachings of the Jewish Scriptures in such passages as Job 21:20, Ps 75:8, Isa 51:17, and Jer 25:15–38.⁴ The phrase I have translated as "mixed full strength" literally means "mixed unmixed."⁵ Two different words are used in the Greek text. Charles is probably correct in arguing that the first word implies a mixing of wine with spices which, rather than weakening the wine, would make it stronger or even poisonous. The second refers to the common practice in the first century of mixing water with wine to weaken it.⁶ Beasley-Murray reflects the appropriate emphasis of the passage when he remarks simply, "God's wine is strong stuff."⁷

The intertestamental literature is replete with images of the torment of the damned being increased by their ability to view the bliss of the righteous. Prominent examples are 2 Esd 7:35–38; *2 Bar* 30:4; and *1 Enoch* 27:3–4, 48:9, and 90:20–27.⁸ Does the Seer share such a vindictive understanding of the punishment of the damned? A partial answer is provided by Mounce, who points out that in Revelation, there is no picture of the damned being tormented in the presence of the redeemed—only in the presence of God and the angels.⁹ Beasley-Murray suggests the possibility that even the angels should be removed from the picture. He suggests that the "holy angels" may be a periphrasis for God, in which case the judgment is executed only in the presence of God and the Lamb. Bousset had earlier made the same suggestion, according to Charles.¹⁰ Whether or not this suggestion has any merit, Beasley-Murray is correct to point out that this picture is very different from that in the noncanonical writings mentioned above.¹¹ Morris suggests that the Seer may have had in mind

---

3. Cf. Beasley-Murray, *Revelation*, 225.

4. Cf. Mounce, *Revelation*, 275; Caird, *Commentary on Revelation*, 16.

5. Cf. Morris, *Revelation*, 175–76.

6. Charles, *Critical and Exegetical Commentary*, 2:16; cf. Beasley-Murray, *Revelation*, 226; Wilson, *Revelation*, 121–22.

7. Beasley-Murray, *Revelation*, 226.

8. Cited in Beasley-Murray, *Revelation*, 226, and Mounce, *Revelation*, 276; cf. also Charles, *Critical and Exegetical Commentary*, 2:17.

9. Mounce, *Revelation*, 276.

10. Charles, *Critical and Exegetical Commentary*, 2:117.

11. Beasley-Murray, *Revelation*, 226.

an ironic reversal—Christians persecuted by the Romans were made to suffer with thousands of people looking on. The picture of the redeemed as viewing the suffering of their tormentors would therefore be only just recompense.[12] Morris seems not to note, however, the vast difference between temporal suffering and watching that suffering, and suffering for eternity.

In commenting on this passage Mounce indicates very dogmatically, "God's wrath is not the outworking of impersonal laws of retribution which are built into the structure of reality, but the response of a righteous God to man's adamant refusal to accept his love. The Greek word refers to anger that is passionate and vehement."[13] Morris similarly notes that *thymos* usually denotes a more passionate sort of wrath, and that elsewhere in the Christian Testament it is used only once of the wrath of God. I must agree that this is the most characteristic usage of *thymos*, but I will argue that the language Mounce uses is unworthy of the God revealed in Jesus Christ. Hanson takes a different view and argues rather cogently that the present passage should be referred to the historical disaster which was to befall Rome. He adds further that "we can claim that *thymos* is always a sign of the wrath process worked out in history."[14] This position is in accord with Paul's teachings on the wrath of God in Rom 1:18–32.[15] Worth noting is the fact that in two of the passages under discussion (Rev 16:19 and 19:15) we find the phrase "the *thymos* of the *orgē*," which weakens any argument based on the fact that Paul uses *orgē* instead of *thymos*. Farrer, after using the phrase "the wine of God's fury," says parenthetically, "The translation we have offered verges on blasphemy: we ought not to speak of the fury of God. The divine heart is not subject to negative passions."[16]

The reference to being tormented with fire and sulfur would have reminded anyone familiar with the Jewish Scriptures of the fate of Sodom and Gomorrah. Though this passage seems to speak of individual destiny, Caird argues that "it is the doomed city from which smoke . . . will rise forever, leaving no prospect of restoration."[17] Beasley-Murray appears to

---

12. Morris, *Revelation*, 176.
13. Mounce, *Revelation*, 275.
14. Hanson, *Wrath of the Lamb*, 161–64.
15. To be sure, Paul uses *orgē* for "wrath" in that passage rather than *thymos*.
16. Farrer, *Revelation*, 163.
17. Caird, *Commentary on Revelation*, 186.

be thinking along the same lines when he says, "The immediate thought appears to be that the worshipers of the beast will share the fate of the city of the beast. Babylon will become as Sodom and Gomorrah, and so will her supporters, wherever they may be."[18] Even Mounce agrees that the symbolism here should not be taken literally. After noting the background of God's judgment upon Sodom and Gomorrah, he goes on to say, "That we are dealing with a rather obvious apocalyptic symbol should not lead us to take it lightly."[19] I would not wish to argue the point. I would add, however, that neither should we allow it to encourage assertions about God which are crudely anthropomorphic and misleading as to the character of God as revealed in Jesus Christ.

The next passage in which *thymos* is attributed to God is the great harvest scene in Rev 14. "One like a son of man" appears on a cloud with a sharp sickle and harvests the grain of the earth (14:14–16). Following this event, "another angel" comes out of the heavenly temple, also with a sharp sickle; and reaps the vintage of the earth. He then casts them into the "winepress of the wrath of God" (14:19).

Commentators are divided in their interpretation of this passage. The primary dividing point is whether there is a first harvest of the righteous performed by Christ followed by a harvest of the unrighteous performed by an angel, or whether we are dealing with only one harvest. Morris represents one side of the current debate. He argues that the passage depicts only one harvest under two different symbols. In order to maintain this position, he has to equate the "one like a son of man" with the "other angel" of v. 17. He argues that the phrase "another angel" means that the first angel is the "one like a son of man."[20] This reading seems highly unlikely for at least three reasons:

1. The phrase "one like a son of man" is identical with that in 1:13. The description in that passage seems clearly to identify him as the exalted Christ.
2. The phrase "another angel" is used elsewhere without any specific reference to a previous angel, e.g., in Rev 14:6. If the phrase does have an antecedent in the present passage, it would have to be the

---

18. Beasley-Murray, *Revelation*, 226.
19. Mounce, *Revelation*, 275.
20. Morris, *Revelation*, 178–79.

angel who gives the signal to put in the sickle and reap, not the "one like a son of man."

3. Nowhere else in Revelation is Jesus referred to as an angel.

Carrell has also rejected Morris's conclusions concerning the "one like a son of man" in 14:14. He argues that "there is no need to suppose, on the basis of Apocalypse 14:15, that the human-like figure in 14:14 is an angel, and the expression *allos angelos* in 14:15 may be plausibly explained in terms of the angel in 14:19."[21]

Contra Morris, Mounce says the "one like a son of man" is the Messiah and argues for two judgment scenes instead of one. After noting that Charles attempts to expunge vv. 15–17 as an interpolation, he responds, "Such textual surgery is not only unnecessary, but forfeits the dramatic parallelism of the two judgment scenes."[22] Maxwell is another recent interpreter who understands the grain harvest as a harvest of the righteous performed by Christ and the vintage as a gathering of the wicked for judgment performed by an angel.[23]

Beasley-Murray reflects most explicitly the division among scholars on the passage. He cites Swete, Lohmeyer, Behm, Farrer, and Rissi as supporting the idea that the first harvest gathers the righteous into the kingdom, while the second depicts the gathering of the unrighteous for judgment. For the other view he cites Bousset, Charles, Kiddle, and Lohse. He then argues that the echoes of Joel 3:13 and the parallelism of imagery argue against this view, and goes on to say "most therefore consider that the two visions depict a single event of judgment executed upon the unrighteous."[24] The latter comment is most interesting, in view of the fact that Beasley-Murray cites only four scholars as supporting this view, while citing five for the view he opposes!

Beasley-Murray and those who follow the interpretation that the passage refers to one harvest depicted in a double symbolism fail to answer a very obvious question. Why bother with two portrayals of the same event one after the other? Further, why attribute the harvest in the one case to "one like a son of man" and the other to an angel? The weakness of the argument that the "one like a son of man" is an angel has already been

21. Carrell, *Jesus and the Angels*, 177–79 and 225–26.
22. Mounce, *Revelation*, 281.
23. Maxwell, *Revelation*, 124–25.
24. Beasley-Murray, *Revelation*, 228.

pointed out. Perhaps some echoes of the Gospel traditions have been overlooked. In the Synoptic tradition, the function of reaping is at some points attributed to Christ and at other points to angels. In the explanation of the parable of the wheat and tares, the reapers are the angels (Matt 13:39). In that passage the angels are depicted as "harvesting" both righteous and unrighteous—they are to gather up the tares and burn them as well as gather the wheat into the barn. In the same chapter, however, Jesus says that the angels will come at the end of the age and take out the wicked from among the righteous (13:49). In Mark 13:27, the Son of man is said to gather his elect from the four corners of the earth. To be sure, the passage says that he will send out his angels, but that *he* will gather (*episunaxei*) his elect. Admittedly the Synoptic evidence is not clear-cut, but these texts at least leave room for the image of Christ gathering his elect while leaving the harvest of the unrighteous to angels. I will also have to admit that at one point in Revelation, at least, Christ is said to tread the wine vat of God's judgment (19:15). In 14:20, however, the passive verb would seem to attribute that function to God. A distinction between gathering people *for* judgment and actually carrying out the judgment may be in order.

Perhaps the Fourth Gospel may shed some light on the harvest metaphor. In John 4:35 Jesus invites his disciples to look up and see that the fields are white for harvest. In the next verse he says, "Already he who reaps is receiving wages, and is *gathering fruit for life eternal*."[25] Here is a precedent for viewing the grain harvest as referring to the gathering of the righteous. Joel provides the precedent for the vintage as the gathering of the unrighteous. As for Beasley-Murray's claim that Joel provides the background imagery for both the harvest of grain and the reaping of the vintage, there is no necessity for reading Joel as referring to anything but the harvest of grapes. In fact, as Farrer argues, "Joel's oracle probably speaks of vintage only; if a 'harvest' is mentioned it is the harvest of grapes."[26] Worth noting also is the fact that the wrath of God is mentioned only in relation to the gathering of the grapes. I take my stand with those who see the grain harvest as the gathering of the elect people of God and the grape harvest as the gathering of the unrighteous. I am not convinced that the Christian Testament gives warrant at any point for seeing the

---

25. Emphasis mine.
26. Farrer, *Revelation*, 164.

wicked as being harvested at one time and the righteous at some later time, as Beasley-Murray's interpretation would require.

God's wrath appears for the second time in relation to the seven vials (15:7). In this verse one of the four living creatures gives the angels the vials full of the wrath of the eternal God. Morris notes that the word *phialas* ("vial" or "bowl") depicts the same container as the one which held the prayers of the saints (5:8), and comments that the Seer may have intended for us to be reminded of that passage at this point. If I have appropriately interpreted the four living creatures as symbolizing the created order, this reading means that the destructive plagues arise from the creation itself and comports with the view mentioned earlier that evil is self-destructive. God does not so much punish from heaven, i.e., from outside the created order, as allow people to suffer the effects of their misuse of that created order. God's wrath is perhaps *both* the allowing of the outworking of sin's natural consequences in a moral universe *and* a specific action on God's part. I am not comfortable with an either/or approach to this issue.

I have commented earlier on the completing of the wrath of God by the outpouring of the seven vials in the chapter on the great signs. Mounce notes the numerical symbolism of the passage in these words: "That there are seven angels having seven plagues speaks of the certainty and completeness of divine wrath against all unrighteousness."[27]

The use of Exodus typology in the seven vials has been noted by most commentators. As elements from the Exodus experience of the Israelites, Caird has noted that "the plagues, the crossing of the sea, the engulfing of the pursuers, the song of Moses, the giving of the law amid the smoke of Sinai, and the erection of the Tent of Testimony—all these have their place in the vision; and, because the great city is figuratively called Sodom as well as Egypt, the fire that fell on Sodom is added to the picture."[28] I have dealt previously with the notion of the wrath of God being finished or ended with the seven vials. Instead of the translation "with them the wrath of God is finished," Caird more appropriately translates "with them the wrath of God is accomplished."[29] Morris, on the other

---

27. Mounce, *Revelation*, 285.
28. Caird, *Commentary on Revelation*, 197.
29. Ibid., 196.

hand, interprets *etelesthē* as meaning "termination," saying, "These plagues are the last earth will know."[30]

In the opening verse of Rev 16 a voice from the temple commands the angels to pour out the vials of God's wrath. Mounce notes the reminiscence of Isa 66:6, in which another voice from the temple speaks of recompense to God's enemies. He also says that because 15:8 tells us that no one could enter the temple until the plagues were completed, the voice must be that of God.[31] Noting the similarities to the Egyptian plagues in both the trumpet and vial visions, Caird comments, "These plagues follow the Exodus and are part of the doom, corresponding to the submersion of the Egyptians in the sea."[32] This observation leads naturally to the conclusion that the bowls represent the outworking of the judgment of God on the plane of history rather than a cataclysmic intervention bringing history to a close. This reading is further confirmed after the outpouring of the seventh vial, in that Babylon or Rome is said to receive the cup of the wine of the wrath (*thymos*) of the anger (*orgē*) of God (16:19). The NASB translates this phrase "the cup of the wine of his fierce wrath," taking *tou thymou tēs orgēs* as implying the intensity of God's wrath. This interpretation may well be legitimate, but whether it can be said to translate the phrase accurately is an open question. Mounce cites Lenski as translating the phrase "the wrath that is hot with anger."[33] This rendering again leads into that dangerous area of attributing human passions to God, the legitimacy of which I am very skeptical.

I have dealt with the identity of the great city at some length earlier. As Mounce notes, some interpreters would see a distinction between the great city and Babylon, i.e., they would argue that two cities are in view, not one.[34] This reading strains the text almost to a breaking point. I will restate my earlier conclusion that the "great city" is Babylon or Rome *and* any succeeding city which manifests the same characteristics of deifying human wealth and power in a way similar to those ancient cities.

---

30. Morris, *Revelation*, 182.

31. Mounce, *Revelation*, 293; cf. also Beasley-Murray, *Revelation*, 241; Wilson, *Revelation*, 130; Morris, *Revelation*, 186.

32. Caird, *Commentary on Revelation*, 201.

33. Mounce, *Revelation*, 304 n. 39.

34. Ibid., 303.

Charles has bracketed the phrase referring to the great city being split into three parts as "against the use of our author."[35] And, as I noted earlier, Farrer identified the great city as Jerusalem and attempted to relate this passage to Zech 14:4–8. He is among those who interpret the great city as Jerusalem and Babylon as Rome. Mounce, on the other hand, argues plausibly that *for John* the great city and Babylon both refer to Rome; and that the division into three parts, rather than reflecting Zechariah's prophecy, simply depicts the completeness of the destruction.[36] Noting that nothing is said about any earthquake in the extended account of the fall of Babylon in the next two chapters, Farrer aptly remarks that "the language of earthquake need express no more than the belief, [sic] that the Creator's vengeance lies behind the wrath of man."[37]

With the downfall of Babylon or Rome comes also the downfall of the "cities of the nations." Although the word translated as *nations* is also the word for Gentiles, no ethnic connotation is to be understood. Probably the best explanation is that the intimate relationship of the "great city" to the other cities of the Empire is such that they stand or fall together.[38] Morris argues along the same lines. After noting the complete destruction of Babylon and the fall of the "cities of the nations" he comments, "The one implies the other."[39]

That the great city was remembered is probably a "divine passive," meaning that God remembered her. In the Jewish Scriptures, "to remember" means not merely to recall to mind but to act appropriately in view of what is remembered (cf. Exod 13:3, Deut 15:15, 1 Kgs 17:18, Jer 31:34, and elsewhere). God's wrath is appropriate in view of the character that Babylon or Rome had developed. As Mounce notes, "If God were not to punish unrighteousness, the concept of a moral universe would have to be discarded."[40]

The phrase that I have translated "wine of the wrath of his anger" appears once more, in Rev 19:15. Here it is connected with the treading of the wine vat. This passage was dealt with at some length in the section

---

35. Charles, *Critical and Exegetical Commentary*, 2:52.
36. Mounce, *Revelation*, 303–4; cf. Morris, *Revelation*, 195.
37. Farrer, *Revelation*, 180.
38. Cf. Mounce, *Revelation*, 304.
39. Morris, *Revelation*, 195.
40. Mounce, *Revelation*, 304.

on the chapter on the sword. As both Mounce[41] and Beasley-Murray[42] have noted, the execution of God's judgment by the conquering Christ is depicted under three figures drawn from the Jewish Scriptures: the sharp sword of his mouth; his ruling with an iron rod: and his treading the wine press of God's wrath.[43] Morris interprets the treading of the wine vat in terms of Isa 63:1–6 but seems not to take any notice of the present tense of *patei*, "he treads," which implies that the treading is already in progress, not just an act to occur at the end of the world. He correctly notes that this passage refers to "the complete overthrow of those who resist God."[44]

When we turn our attention to the use of *thymos* in the arena of evil, we first meet the term in connection with the defeat of the devil and his angels by Michael and his angels (12:12). Part of this verse I have dealt with in the chapter on rejoicing. The heavens and those dwelling in them are to rejoice because of the devil's defeat, but a woe is pronounced on the earth and sea because of the devil's great wrath (*thymon megan*) over his defeat. In this context I gladly accept Caird's translation of *thymos* as "fury." Caird also appropriately points out that the great attack on the church in the next two chapters should be viewed as "the death throes of the Devil."[45] He has been decisively defeated once and for all through the cross of Christ. Nevertheless his evil power must still be "absorbed by innocent suffering and neutralized by forgiving love."[46] Even though the victory is being celebrated in heaven, believers will still undergo grievous troubles on earth.[47] As long as the world stands, Satan's furious activity is fostered by the knowledge that he has little opportunity. I have previously defended my translation of *oligon kairon* as "little opportunity." I will add only the fact that when John wants to express a short period of time, he uses the phrase *mikron chronon*, as in Rev 6:11 and 20:3. The fact that in the latter passage the reference is to the activity of Satan strengthens the argument that John means something different here. The issue here is not chronological time but limitation of what Satan is allowed to do.

41. Ibid., 346–47.
42. Beasley-Murray, *Revelation*, 281.
43. Cf. Caird, *Commentary on Revelation*, 245; Wilson, *Revelation*, 158.
44. Morris, *Revelation*, 225.
45. Caird, *Commentary on Revelation*, 156.
46. Ibid., 157.
47. Cf. Morris, *Revelation*, 158.

We next see *thymos* used in the arena of evil in the context of the fall of Babylon (14:8). An unspecified angel announces that fall. I am not sure why translators have so universally treated *epesen* as though it were a participle and rendered it "fallen" instead of "It fell!" There may be no essential difference in meaning, but the latter is much more vivid. Babylon is further described as the one who has given the nations to drink from the wine of the passion (*thymos*) of her fornication. Both Caird[48] and Beasley-Murray[49] have pointed to the reminiscences of Isa 21:8–9 and other passages in the Jewish Scriptures relating to historical Babylon. These same scholars wrestle at some length with the phrase "the wine of the *thymos* of her fornication," and cite various translations of that phrase. They both miss the point in my judgment by attempting to treat it as a parallel to the "wine of the *thymos* of God" in v. 10 instead of seeing the obvious. It is not a parallel but a counterimage. Charles, in dealing with the difficulty of translating this phrase, resorts to his usual expedient of excising *tou thymou* as an interpolation.[50]

Those who drink from the wine of the *thymos* of Babylon's fornication must also drink the wine of the *thymos* of God. As Mounce well expresses the matter, "By joining the two symbols (harlot Rome and the cup of God's wrath) the angel may be pointing out that the heady potion of Rome's seductive practices inevitably involves the wrath of God."[51]

The same troublesome phrase appears in 18:3, again as a reference to Babylon. In the preceding verse the fall of Babylon is announced in the same words as in 14:8. Added to the announcement of Babylon's fall are the consequences of that fall: she becomes a dwelling place for demons and a prison of every unclean spirit and of every unclean fowl and of every unclean and hated beast.[52] Unlike 14:8, that fall is then related to the fact that all the nations have drunk from the wine of the *thymos* of her fornication, the kings of the earth have committed fornication with her, and the merchants of the earth have become wealthy from the strength of her eager desire.

---

48. Caird, *Commentary on Revelation*, 184.
49. Beasley-Murray, *Revelation*, 225.
50. Charles, *Critical and Exegetical Commentary*, 2:14–15.
51. Mounce, *Revelation*, 274.
52. 18:2; cf. Farrer, *Revelation*, 187–88.

Though admitting that *tou thymou* has the support of the best manuscripts, Charles again brackets the phrase as an interpolation. He offers the feeble excuse that "the extraordinary diversity among the authorities points to some corruption in the above text."[53] Beasley-Murray takes *thymos* here as "impure passion" and notes the reminiscences of historical Babylon in Jer 51:37 and of Edom in Isa 34:11–15.[54] Caird leaves the translation in a literal fashion as "the wine of the wrath of her fornication," and concentrates his discussion on John's amplification of the reason for "Babylon's" fall. He interprets John, probably correctly, as giving the reason people might think it a reasonable action to worship the beast and as explaining the nature of her "fornication." "Rome has given peace and security to the world, thus making possible the growth of a vast luxury trade and bringing widespread prosperity . . . the kings of the earth were guilty of an economic dalliance, which involved the idolatrous worship of Mammon."[55] In a similar vein Mounce notes the widespread use of fornication in the Old Testament as a metaphor for apostasy from God, and comments, "It is used here to denote the unclean and illicit relationships between the capital of the empire and all the nations of the earth."[56]

In summation, we have looked at seven passages in which *thymos* is used of the wrath of God. In two of those the expression is "the wine of the *thymos* of God" (14:9b–10 and 16:19). Two involve the use of the wine vat as a metaphor for God's judgment (14:19 and 19:15). Three are related to the pouring-out of the seven vials by which the *thymos* of God is said to be completed (15:1, 7; 16:1). Over against these usages we have noted one passage in which *thymos* expresses the raging fury of the devil following his being cast down to earth (12:12). Then we looked at two passages in which *thymos* is used of the passion of "Babylon's" fornication. In the latter the counterimaging is most obvious and undeniable. The similarity of the expression "the wine of the *thymos*" and its being applied to both God and Babylon can scarcely be deemed accidental.

---

53. Charles, *Critical and Exegetical Commentary*, 2:56.
54. Beasley-Murray, *Revelation*, 264.
55. Caird, *Commentary on Revelation*, 223.
56. Mounce, *Revelation*, 324.

26

The Mountain

And I looked and behold the Lamb had taken his stand upon Mount Zion, and with him (were the) one hundred forty-four thousand having his name and the name of his Father written upon their foreheads.

(Rev 14:1)

And he brought me in spirit unto a mountain great and high, and he showed me the holy city, Jerusalem, coming down out of Heaven from God.

(Rev 21:10)

And he gathered them together in the place which is called in Hebrew Armageddon.

(Rev 16:16)

THE FIRST POSITIVE USAGE of *mountain* in the Apocalypse is in 14:1. Let me at this point make a small clarification of my translation, based on my understanding that the one hundred forty-four thousand here are the same as the one hundred forty-four thousand we saw in Rev 7. Admittedly the definite article is not in the Greek text here, and scholars are by no means agreed that the one hundred forty-four thousand here are the same as those in the earlier passage. Charles represents those who, while identifying the one hundred forty-four thousand in Rev 14 as the same ones met in Chapter 7, limits them to the martyrs. He does indicate that they are not only Jewish martyrs, but "the spiritual Israel, the entire Christian community."[1] Implicit in Charles's interpretation is the position that John believed the whole church would suffer martyrdom, a position I am unable to accept. For example, in the addresses to the seven churches,

---

1. Charles, *Critical and Exegetical Commentary*, 2:4–5.

why is the exhortation to be faithful unto death found explicitly only in the address to the church at Smyrna, if all the churches were expected to face martyrdom? Charles's identification of the "great multitude which no man could number" in 7:9–17 with the one hundred forty-four thousand is also questionable in my judgment.[2] The one hundred forty-four thousand are being sealed *on earth*, whereas the great multitude consists of those who are coming out of the "great tribulation" and are already with God, as 7:15–17 clearly shows.

As both Charles[3] and Mounce[4] have noted, 2 Ezra 13 reflects a Jewish expectation of the appearance of the Messiah on Mount Zion with a large number of followers. Over the centuries the term *Zion* had evolved from designating the original hill on which Jerusalem was built to the entire city of Jerusalem to the entire Jewish nation. As Mounce notes, Mount Zion had a long history as a place of deliverance, and the prophet Joel (2:52) prophesied that those on Mount Zion would escape the great and terrible day of the Lord.[5] As Caird notes, the mention of Mount Zion also reminds us that the Seer is expounding Ps 2. But instead of the fierce warrior king whom the Psalmist expected, the Lamb appears on Mount Zion.[6]

At this point a major division occurs among interpreters. Is the Lamb pictured as standing on the earthly Mount Zion, or do we interpret this passage as referring to the heavenly Zion? Mounce cites Walvoord as arguing for the earthly Zion during the millennial reign but claims that the entire scene is one of praise before the throne of heaven.[7] Charles claims the vision is proleptic of the risen martyrs during the millennial reign.[8] Farrer says, "St. John transfers the figure of the Lamb to the earthly scene, and in doing so continues the exposition of Psalm 2 which has given form to the whole complex of seventh-trumpet visions."[9] Beasley-Murray, after taking note of the views presented above, says, "Probably it is right not to think of a location, though it is the triumph of the saints in the kingdom of

---

2. Ibid., 2:5.
3. Ibid., 2:4–5.
4. Mounce, *Revelation*, 267 n. 2.
5. Ibid., 267.
6. Caird, *Commentary on Revelation*, 178.
7. Mounce, *Revelation*, 267.
8. Charles, *Critical and Exegetical Commentary*, 2:4.
9. Farrer, *Revelation*, 160.

Christ rather than in this age which is in view."[10] He has undercut his own interpretation, however, by saying, "Every feature of the opening sentence of the first oracle stands in contrast to what is written in chapter 13."[11] The emergence of the two beasts and the marking of the followers of the beast take place on earth. Since John has not signaled any change of location it seems most reasonable to assume that the scene is still on earth. When John talks about the heavenly city, he does not speak of Mount Zion but of the New Jerusalem (21:1-2). Admittedly the one hundred forty-four thousand are depicted as singing a new song before the throne, the elders, and the living creatures (v. 3), but where is the location that cannot be said to be "before the throne of God?" And if, as argued earlier, the twenty-four elders symbolize the people of God in heaven and on earth, and the four living creatures represent the created order, no necessity exists for seeing the hundred forty-four thousand as being in heaven.

Rowland,[12] along with Giblin[13] and others, has called attention to the overtones of holy war in the reference to the hundred forty-four thousand being sexually pure—*parthenoi* ("virgins"). If this scene is correctly placed in heaven, the warfare is over. Charles, in arguing that the hundred forty-four thousand have already been "sacrificed," points out the sacrificial overtones of the word *amomoi* ("blameless") in this passage. The point is well taken—but is irrelevant to the issue of whether the reference is to past or future sacrifice. One could argue that the epithet *amomoi* is one that would normally be applied to an animal *before* it was sacrificed.

The detail of the names written on the foreheads of the one hundred forty-four thousand will be dealt with in greater detail in a later chapter. I want to focus here on the Lamb as having taken his stand on the mount of deliverance—Zion—along with those who have received the seal of God.

The second positive usage of *mountain* occurs in Rev 21:10. John is brought "in spirit" (cf. 1:10, 4:2, and 17:3) to a great and high mountain where he receives the vision of the New Jerusalem. Charles calls attention to the reminiscences of the vision of Ezekiel recorded in Ezek 40:2. The major difference is that Ezekiel was brought to the high mountain

---

10. Beasley-Murray, *Revelation*, 222.
11. Ibid., 221; cf. Mounce, *Revelation*, 267.
12. Rowland, *Revelation*, 120-21.
13. Giblin, *Open Book of Prophecy*, 222-31.

"by the visions of God," whereas John is brought "in spirit."[14] On Ezekiel's mountain stood something like the structure of a city and he was met by a man with a measuring rod who proceeded to measure the (nonexistent) temple.[15]

The contrast between John's being carried into a wilderness to view the "great prostitute" and his being carried to a great high mountain to view the New Jerusalem has been noted by a number of interpreters.[16] In pointing out the significant role that mountains had played for centuries, Mounce mentions Sinai, Ezekiel's vision noted above, and a passage from *1 Enoch* (24–25), which portrayed one of seven magnificent mountains that excelled all others as being the throne of God.[17] Beasley-Murray notes that John has combined two ancient religious traditions: one from Babylonia referring to a heavenly Garden of Eden or paradise (cf. Ezek 28:13–14) where the gods lived, and the other the prophetic picture contained in Isa 2:1–3 of a "mountain of the house of the Lord" to which all people would flow to worship the Lord of hosts. "In this way he relates the fulfillment of God's purpose in history to both pagan aspirations and the prophetic word of the Old Testament."[18]

The negative use of *mountain* is not one the English-speaking reader would notice, but one that anyone familiar with the Jewish Scriptures would not be likely to miss. It is found in Rev 16:16. We again have a textual problem, with some manuscripts reading "he gathered" and others reading "they gathered." I have again followed the Nestle-Aland text, which supports the third-person singular reading instead of the third-person plural. The difference in the Greek text is between *sunēgagon* and *sunēgagen*. Little is at stake in the two readings as far as interpretation goes. The dragon, the beast, and the false prophet are mentioned in v. 13. The third-person singular reading would make the verb refer to the dragon, whereas the third-person plural reading would refer to all three persons of the "unholy trinity." These demonic powers are in the process

---

14. Charles, *Critical and Exegetical Commentary*, 2:156; cf. Beasley-Murray, *Revelation*, 319; Mounce, *Revelation*, 378.

15. Ezek 40; cf. Charles, *Critical and Exegetical Commentary*, 2:156–57.

16. E.g., Farrer, *Revelation*, 214; Caird, *Commentary on Revelation*, 269; Mounce, *Revelation*, 378; Morris, *Revelation*, 242.

17. Mounce, *Revelation*, 378; cf. Farrer, *Revelation*, 214–25; Caird, *Commentary on Revelation*, 270.

18. Beasley-Murray, *Revelation*, 319; cf. Caird, *Commentary on Revelation*, 270.

of gathering people from the whole world to the war of the great day of almighty God (v. 14). The place in which they are gathered is Armageddon. The first syllable of this word is Hebrew for "mountain," and the rest of the word is probably a variant form of the name of Megiddo, although admittedly no consensus on this issue has been achieved by Biblical scholars. Even less consensus exists as to the meaning of Armageddon. Charles says pointedly, "No convincing interpretation has yet been given to the phrase (Armageddon), which should probably be translated "the mountains of Megiddo." He notes that no evidence for this phrase can be found, and hence accepts Hilgenfeld's suggestion of a slight change to the Hebrew which would make it read "city of Megiddo." Charles also mentions Volter's suggestion of a different change that would make the word read "land of Megiddo." Since *har* ("mountain") is singular, Charles had to explain in some way the translation suggested above. His justification is that in Ezek 38:8, 21 and 39:2, 14, and 17 the final conflict is said to take place on "the mountains of Israel."[19] He also notes several other conjectures suggested by various scholars in this section of his commentary.

Most of the interpreters of whom I am aware point out that no Mount Megiddo ever existed. While in the strict sense this is true, if we read *Armageddon* as mountain *of* Megiddo another possibility arises. In the area of Megiddo to the northwest lies a mountain very famous in the Jewish Scriptures as the place where Elijah defeated and slaughtered the prophets of Baal, namely Mount Carmel. Farrer supports this understanding, saying, "Ar-mageddon, i.e. Mount Megiddo, is not a name ever used in fact, but if it were, it would presumably describe the Carmel-range; and it was to Carmel that Elijah persuaded Ahab to gather all the prophets of Baal (I Kings XVIII, 10) [*sic*]; and there they contested with God, and met their doom."[20] Mounce[21] and Farrer[22] may be on the right track in suggesting that perhaps John wanted to bring together in the same reference the plain of Megiddo and Mount Carmel. The area of Megiddo had been the site of significant battles all the way back to the period of the Judges. When Deborah and Barak fought against the Canaanites under Sisera, "the stars in their courses fought against Sisera." He was decisively

---

19. Charles, *Critical and Exegetical Commentary*, 2:50–51.
20. Farrer, *Revelation*, 286–87.
21. Mounce, *Revelation*, 301.
22. Farrer, *Revelation*, 178.

defeated and later killed by Jael (Judg 5:20, 4:21–22). Ahaziah, king of Judah, died there, and his brother Joram (Jehoram) was killed by Jehu in the same general area. Jezebel was thrown to her death and eaten by dogs from the palace at nearby Jezreel. Finally, Josiah, the last king of Judah about which anything good is said in the Jewish Scriptures, died at Megiddo in an abortive attempt to stop Pharaoh Necho from coming to the aid of the Assyrians at Carchemish. These are the associations that "mountain of Megiddo" would have brought to the mind of anyone familiar with the Jewish Scriptures.[23] Caird makes the significant point that "whatever may have been the source or sources of the word Armageddon, this much at least is clear, that, like John's other names it is a symbol. He was not expecting a battle in northern Palestine, but at Rome."[24] Morris suggests that in John's mind Armageddon may have been a symbol of decisive conflict, in which case "it will stand as a symbol for the final overthrow of all the forces of evil by Almighty God."[25] Wilson may be on the right track in suggesting that Armageddon refers to an *event* as opposed to a recognizable geographical location.[26] Robbins has suggested that Armageddon would have had something of the connotations of Waterloo in more recent times.[27]

In summation, we have seen the positive use of *mountain* in the assembly of the Lamb with the one hundred forty-four thousand upon Mount Zion, and in the unnamed "great and high mountain" to which the Seer is summoned to view the New Jerusalem. Over against this is set the "mountain of Megiddo." Garrow has noted the contrast of these mountains and comments, "Mount Zion is the place where the Lamb musters his army of martyrs for the final battle against the beast and the false prophet, which they join in 19:14. Harmagedon [sic], by contrast, is the mountain where the dragon, beast, and false prophet muster their armies for this same battle."[28] As I have noted earlier, I do not agree with limiting

---

23. Cf. Summers, *Worthy Is the Lamb*, 189. For an exhaustive treatment of the battles fought in the area of Megiddo, see Cline, *Battles of Armageddon*.

24. Caird, *Commentary on Revelation*, 207.

25. Morris, *Revelation*, 194.

26. Wilson, *Revelation*, 134–35.

27. Robbins, *Revelation*, 191. For other conjectures regarding the meaning of Armageddon, see Mounce, *Revelation*, 301–2, Charles, *Critical and Exegetical Commentary*, 2:50–51.

28. Garrow, *Revelation*, 94–95.

the one hundred forty-four thousand on Mount Zion to the martyrs, but Garrow's expression of the contrast of the two mountains is well taken.

However one interprets Armageddon, it depicts the location of the great eschatological battle that is to be followed by the gory "great supper of God" (Rev 19:17). Its negative connotations are more than obvious.

To complete the picture of the use of *oros* ("mountain") in the Apocalypse, two other singular usages occur and four plural. In 6:14 it is used in an indefinite sense—"every mountain." In 8:8 it is used symbolically in the phrase "(something) like a great mountain burning with fire" following the sounding of the second trumpet. In 6:15–16 and 16:20 the plural form occurs in the indefinite sense of "the mountains." Finally, in 17:9 a reference is made to the seven mountains upon which the "great prostitute" sits. I have discussed above only the passages referring to a specific mountain.

27

The Cup

If anyone worships the beast and his image, and receives (the beast's) mark upon his forehead or his hand, he also drinks from the wine of the wrath of God which has been mixed full strength in the cup of his anger; and he shall be tormented by fire and sulfur in the presence of the holy angels and the Lamb.

(Rev 14:9b–10)

And the great city became (divided) into three parts and the cities of the nations fell. And Babylon the Great was remembered before God to give to her the cup of the wine of the wrath of his anger.

(Rev 16:19)

And the woman was clothed (in) purple and scarlet and was adorned with gold and precious stone and pearls, having a golden cup in her hand full of abominations and the unclean things of her fornication.

(Rev 17:4)

Give to her as she also gave and double the double (measure) according to her works; in the cup which she mixed, mix to her double.

(Rev 18:6)

The first passage (Rev. 14:9b–10) has been discussed above. We need only note here that the "cup" is in the hands of God, rather than belonging to any of the characterizations of evil mentioned in the Apocalypse.

The second appearance of the word *cup* in the arena of divine operations is in Rev 16:19. I have also dealt with this verse in the chapter on wrath and passion. For present purposes I will point out only that, as in 14:9b–10, the cup in v. 19 is in the hands of God.

The cup in the arena of evil is first mentioned in 17:4. The setting is the description of the "great prostitute." As Charles notes, the purple and scarlet the prostitute wears are symbols of the luxury and splendor of imperial Rome.[1] Dyes of both colors were difficult to extract and hence were very expensive. Purple was the color of royalty, which provides another clue that the "woman" depicts imperial power.[2] Her attire is reminiscent of the way in which the father of Bathshua is said to have adorned her in order to seduce Judah in *Test Jud* 13:5, as Charles has noted.[3] The woman has a golden cup in her hand filled with the *bdelygma* ("abominations") and unclean things of her fornication. Morris notes that such an expensive cup would lead one to expect a very satisfying drink, but "The attractive cup is revealed as no more than an enticement to people to join the glittering harlot in her evil ways. It is her method of seducing them from God."[4]

From 1 Macc 1:54 we know that the altar which Antiochus Epiphanes had placed over the golden altar at Jerusalem and offered swine flesh to Zeus upon was called the *bdelygma tēs erēmōseōs*, the "abomination of desolation."[5] This phrase also appears in Dan 11:31 and 12:11, and in Mark 13:14 = Matt 24:15.[6] The golden cup echoes Jer 51:7, although in that passage Babylon herself is a golden cup in the hand of the Lord.[7] Beasley-Murray has appropriately noted that the term *bdelygma* did not so much suggest immoral actions—though they are not excluded—as idolatry. "Abomination was a characteristic Jewish term for an idol. A cup which implicates those who drink it in abominations and fornication is therefore a consistent idea, for idolatry is spiritual fornication."[8] In Caird's words, "The two counts which John has against Rome are the idolatry she diffuses throughout the world and her persecution of those who refuse to participate in it."[9]

1. Charles, *Critical and Exegetical Commentary*, 2:64; cf. Beasley-Murray, *Revelation*, 252; Morris, *Revelation*, 199.
2. Cf. Mounce, *Revelation*, 309.
3. Charles, *Critical and Exegetical Commentary*, 2:64–65.
4. Morris, *Revelation*, 200.
5. Cf. Josephus, *Ant.* 12:5:4.
6. Cf. Beasley-Murray, *Revelation*, 252 n. 2.
7. Cf. Charles, *Critical and Exegetical Commentary*, 2:64–65; Caird, *Commentary on Revelation*, 214; Beasley-Murray, *Revelation*, 252.
8. Beasley-Murray, *Revelation*, 252–53.
9. Caird, *Commentary on Revelation*, 214.

The only other usage of *cup* in the arena of evil is also found in connection with the great prostitute (18:6). This verse spells out the retribution to which the prostitute will be subjected. According to the first part of the verse, the principle of *lex talionis* ("law of retaliation") is to be applied to the prostitute. She is to be given what she gave. The remainder of the verse seems to say she is to receive double that which she gave. This part of the verse must be interpreted in the light of the Jewish Scriptures and Jewish tradition instead of in a literal fashion, however. In that tradition the number two was the number of strengthening, going back to the Jewish requirement of two witnesses to validate a testimony.[10]

Isaiah 40:2 is instructive in interpreting the present passage. There Jerusalem is said to have received double for all her sins. Jeremiah also prophesied a double repayment for the sins of Judah (Jer 16:18). The doubling in this verse of the Apocalypse should therefore be read in terms of a *strong* repayment of "Babylon" in kind.[11] Wilson quotes the apt words of Carpenter, "The cup of her luxuriousness becomes the cup of vengeance."[12] Mounce seems to be correct in stating, "Not divine revenge but just requital is the issue." He also appropriately notes the connection with the cry of the martyrs in 6:10.[13] Caird offers a different insight by saying, "The punishment is simply the crime allowed to take its destructive course."[14] Hanson, arguing along the same lines, points out that the working-out of God's wrath in history does in fact bring compound interest.[15]

John's functional dualism again makes difficult the decision as to the arena in which this cup belongs. Hanson is probably right in saying, "There is only one cup, God's, but he allows Babylon to use it for a period."[16] Nevertheless, since the cup is depicted in 16:19 as belonging to God and in the other two passages as belonging to "Babylon," it appears to be another example of the Seer's use of counterimaging.

---

10. Deut 17:6 and 19:15; cf. 1 Tim 5:19; also the difficulty of finding two witnesses to make the same charge against Jesus as reflected in Mark 14:56 and Matt 26:60–61.

11. Cf. Morris, *Revelation*, 211.

12. Wilson, *Revelation*, 147.

13. Mounce, *Revelation*, 325; cf. Beasley-Murray, *Revelation*, 265.

14. Caird, *Commentary on Revelation*, 224.

15. Hanson, *Wrath of the Lamb*, 164.

16. Ibid.

28

In One Hour

> *And the ten horns which you saw are ten kings who did not yet receive a kingdom, but they receive authority as kings (for) one hour along with the beast.*
>
> (REV 17:12)

> *And the kings of the earth who committed fornication and lived sensuously with her will weep and beat their breasts over her when they see the smoke of her burning, while having taken their stand from afar because of the fear of her torment, saying Alas! Alas! the great city—Babylon the strong city—because in one hour your judgment came.*
>
> (REV 18:9–10)

> *The merchants selling these things who became wealthy from her will stand from afar because of the fear of her torment, weeping and morning, saying, Alas! Alas! the great city—the one who has been clothed (with) fine linen and purple and scarlet; and has been adorned with gold and precious stone and pearl—because in one hour such wealth was made desolate.*
>
> (REV 18:15–17A)

> *And they threw dust upon their heads and kept crying out, weeping and mourning, saying, Alas! Alas! the great city—by which all those having boats in the sea were made wealthy from her riches—because in one hour she was made desolate.*
>
> (REV 18:19)

THE FIRST PASSAGE (17:12) further explains the beast on which the "great prostitute" rides (cf. v. 3). This is the same "beast from the sea" first encountered at 13:1 (and perhaps the beast from the abyss in 11:7), and who is the "lieutenant" of the dragon, Satan.[1] While it is commonplace for interpreters to identify the beast with the Roman Empire or a particular emperor,[2] such interpretations are too limited in that they confine the meaning to the original recipients of Revelation. Beale's interpretation of the beast as a "transtemporal force opposing the Lamb"[3] has more to commend it. In a similar vein Mounce, while conceding that for John the beast from the sea was Rome, identifies it further as "the deification of secular authority."[4] For Sweet the beast "personifies all opposition to God and his people from the beginning."[5] Kealy likewise notes the modern tendency to interpret the beast in terms of the Roman Empire but suggests that the reality of the beast is present in every age.[6] Wall, in similar fashion, suggests that "it is best to recognize it as a universal symbol for secular power and cultural idols, with historical counterparts in every age."[7] Maxwell also, while conceding that John's original readers would have recognized Rome as the beast, goes on to say that the beast is "the machinery of worldly power: armies and politicians, oppression, injustice and cruelty."[8] Robbins has summarized the matter well: "In the light of John's apocalyptic method, it seems that he intended this beast to represent world power. It is the aggregation of powers expressing themselves in opposition to God in Christ.... Rome was only one in the successive forms of the same God-defying world power."[9]

Who then are the "ten horns" of the beast? The same pattern of interpretation that we have examined in the interpretation of the beast is

1. Cf. Jeske, *Revelation for Today*, 82.

2. E.g. Summers, *Worthy Is the Lamb*, 175; Jeske, *Revelation for Today*, 89–90; Boring, *Revelation*, 160; Metzger, *Breaking the Code*, 75; Krodel, *Revelation*, 249; Aune, *Revelation 17–22*, 733. In fairness to Jeske and Boring, they both later give a broader interpretation. Jeske says on p. 104 that "it should not be limited to any one point of reference but may be applied to any human institution which devastates people by prostituting its wealth, influence and power." Boring likewise says on p. 184, "It is arrogant human empire that is condemned here, not just its embodiment in Rome in John's time."

3. Beale, *Book of Revelation*, 878.

4. Mounce, *Revelation*, 251.

5. Sweet, *Revelation*, 208.

6. Kealy, *Apocalypse*, 174.

7. Wall, *Revelation*, 168.

8. Maxwell, *Revelation*, 108.

9. Robbins, *Revelation*, 156.

present here as well. Those who interpret the beast as Rome tend to interpret the ten horns as vassals of Rome.[10] Such interpretation overlooks the phrase "who did not yet receive a kingdom." Robbins, on the other hand, fully takes this phrase into account by interpreting the ten kings as the completeness of nations subservient to world power, including both the present and the future.[11] Beale has given a similar interpretation by reading the number ten in a symbolic fashion and interpreting the ten horns as "the completeness of oppressive power and its worldwide effect."[12] He later says, "The number 'ten' does not likely refer to ten literal kings but is figurative for the great power of these future kings. . . . Just as the beast is a transtemporal force opposing the eternal Lamb, so the ten kings span the ages, since they are the direct opposite of the 'called and elect and faithful.'"[13] Boring takes his interpretation in a similar direction. While he does not deny the text's applicability to the Roman Empire of John's day, he goes beyond this setting to speak of the ten kings as the cohorts of the beast in the last days.[14] Caird, while interpreting the number ten symbolically, makes the opposite error of Summers *et al.* by identifying the ten kings as belonging wholly to the future at the time of the *parousia*, the second coming of Jesus.[15] Krodel essentially agrees with Caird that these are future kings, "vassals of the Antichrist who is to come," although he seems to take the number ten literally rather than symbolically.[16] Jeske, as noted earlier, has issued an appropriate warning against limiting John's message to any one point of reference.[17] We must, as I have stated in the Introduction, leave room for application to Rome in John's day and also for any future age. When we recognize that the beast is deified human power, we can easily recognize that it is present in every age of history and that the "beast" always has its subordinate authorities—the "ten kings." The power of the ten kings is always for "one hour," i.e., a brief but indefinite

---

10. E.g., Summers, *Worthy Is the Lamb*, 192; Krodel, *Revelation*, 299; Aune, *Revelation 17–22*, 951.
11. Robbins, *Revelation*, 199–200.
12. Beale, *Book of Revelation*, 684.
13. Ibid., 878.
14. Boring, *Revelation*, 184–85.
15. Caird, *Commentary on Revelation*, 219.
16. Krodel, *Revelation*, 298; cf. Mounce, *Revelation*, 317.
17. Jeske, *Revelation for Today*, 104–5.

time.[18] The reason is that, as many interpreters have pointed out, evil is inherently self-destructive.[19]

As we approach Rev 18:9–10, the reader should note that the "kings of the earth" and the nature of their "fornication" with the "great prostitute" have been discussed in an earlier chapter. Here in Rev 18 the kings stand at a distance out of fear and lament their loss, not the fate of the city. As Aune has noted, the nominative "city" should probably be understood as a vocative—a direct address to the city.[20] A part of the kings' lament, as Beale has suggested, is probably the sense that because of their complicity in "Babylon's" crimes they deserve the same punishment.[21] Beale also notes the overtones of the Septuagint version of Dan 4:17a, 19 in the phrase "one hour." There it refers to a period of punishment in which Nebuchadnezzar, then king of Babylon, ate grass with the beasts of the field because of his refusal to acknowledge God's sovereignty or to show mercy to the poor. The "Babylon" of John's day was guilty of the same misdeeds and hence must suffer a like punishment. This parallel is admittedly inexact, in that in Daniel it is the king of Babylon who is punished rather than the city itself, but to the Hebrew mindset of a writer like John the two would have been considered inseparable.

Aune adds another possible dimension to the meaning of "one hour" by citing Josephus's use of this phrase for the Jews' burning of the Roman siege machines and for the residents of Caesarea slaughtering the Jews in that city. In Josephus the phrase signifies "an unexpectedly quick destruction."[22] John quite possibly included this aspect of "one hour" as he used the phrase.

The next passage (18:15–17a) follows a list of some twenty-nine items of commerce between merchants and "Babylon," by which the merchants have become wealthy. Some interpreters have taken this list in a primarily historical fashion as reflecting actual commodities commonly bought

---

18. Cf. Bauckham, *Climax*, 308; Sweet, *Revelation*, 261; Aune, *Revelation 17–22*, 997; Robbins, *Revelation*, 207.

19. E.g., Jeske, *Revelation for Today*, 105; Kealy, *Apocalypse*, 203; Krodel, *Revelation*, 299; Wall, *Revelation*, 209; Robbins, *Revelation*, 201; Boring, *Revelation*, 185; Beale, *Commentary on Revelation*, 887; Rowland, *Revelation*, 132; Caird, *Commentary on Revelation*, 221; Maxwell, *Revelation*, 148.

20. Aune, *Revelation 17–22*, 997.

21. Beale, *Book of Revelation*, 907.

22. Aune, *Revelation 17–22*, 998.

and sold in first-century Rome.[23] I have no doubt that this view contains a significant element of truth. A casual look at the list of items reveals the dominance of luxury goods for which Rome was famous.[24] Krodel,[25] Kealy,[26] and Mounce[27] refer to a passage in the Talmud that implied that Rome consumed ninety percent of the world's riches, leaving only ten percent for the rest of the world.

Many modern scholars have noted, in addition to the historical reference, an allusion to the lament over Tyre in Ezekiel 27.[28] Beale has noted that of the twenty-nine items mentioned in vv. 12–13, Ezekiel 27 contains fifteen.[29] He goes on to suggest that the items not in Ezekiel's list represented actual trade items in first-century Rome[30] and that those appearing in both lists were also part of the Roman trade system.

Mounce has appropriately commented on this passage, "To the kings, Rome was 'the strong city' (vs. 10) [sic]; to the merchants she was 'lavishly arrayed and adorned with costly ornaments' (cf. 17:4). *Each group sees her fall in terms of its own interests.*"[31] Just as in the lament of the kings her judgment came "in one hour" so in the lament of the merchants such wealth is made desolate "in one hour." The word *erēmoō* is the verb form of a word meaning "desolate" or "uninhabited." The primary connotation of the word is the absence of human life.[32] As Beale has noted, the present passage is a rather clear allusion to Ezek 26:19, further underscoring the fact that Ezek 26–27 forms the background of Rev 18.[33] The connotations

---

23. E.g., Mounce, *Revelation*, 329–30; Barclay, "Great Themes," 207–10; Bauckham, *Climax*, 351; Caird, *Commentary on Revelation*, 226–27. Ashcraft, "Revelation," 337.

24. Cf. Bauckham, *Climax*, 329.

25. Krodel, *Revelation*, 305.

26. Kealy, *Apocalypse*, 207.

27. Mounce, *Revelation*, 329.

28. E.g., Kealy, *Apocalypse*, 207; Beale, *Book of Revelation*, 909; Sweet, *Revelation*, 270–71; Caird, *Commentary on Revelation*, 226; Barclay, "Great Themes," 205; Wall, *Revelation*, 216; Robbins, *Revelation*, 207; Mounce, *Revelation*, 329.

29. Beale, *Book of Revelation*, 909; cf. Bauckham, *Climax*, 350–51, in which he claims that John largely formulated his list independently of Ezekiel.

30. Cf. Royalty, *Streets of Heaven*, 206.

31. Mounce, *Revelation*, 331; emphasis mine.

32. G. Abbott-Smith, *Manual Greek Lexicon*, s.v. *erēmos*.

33. Beale, *Book of Revelation*, 913; cf. Sweet, *Revelation*, 270–71.

of brevity and suddenness of the phrase "in one hour" should be understood just as in the lament of the kings.

Revelation 18:19 is the final passage that contains the phrase "in one hour." We are still in the general context of the lamentations over "Babylon's" fall. As attested both in the Jewish Scriptures and extrabiblical writings, throwing dust on the head was a sign of mourning or, when combined with prayer, of contrition.[34] No hint of contrition or prayer is to be found in the present context but, just as in the two prior laments, self-interest dominates. In the lament of the merchants the *wealth* of the "great prostitute" is made desolate (*ērēmōthē*). Now the same word describes the "great prostitute" herself.

In summation, the phrase "in one hour" is used first of the period of time in which the "ten kings" share authority with the beast (17:12). This usage is countered by the "one hour" in which the "great prostitute," Babylon or Rome, and her lavish wealth are devastated. As Wall comments concerning the threefold lament, "God's power will quickly overwhelm the evil city to judge it justly for its 'one hour's authority' (17:12) during which its ruling elite persecuted the Lamb."[35] In a similar vein Caird comments, "The one hour of persecution is balanced by the one hour of retribution, because the blood of the martyrs is not only the seed of the church but the ruin of the great whore."[36]

---

34. Cf. Aune, *Revelation 17–22*, 1006; Kealy, *Apocalypse*, 208; Barclay, "Great Themes," 212; Robbins, *Revelation*, 208.

35. Wall, *Revelation*, 216.

36. Caird, *Commentary on Revelation*, 226.

29

One Purpose

For God gave into their hearts to accomplish his purpose,
both to accomplish (his) one purpose and to give their kingdom
to the beast until the words of God should be completed.

(Rev 17:17)

These have one purpose, which is
to give their power and authority to the beast.

(Rev 17:13)

Because we have only two passages in which *gnōmē* ("purpose") is used, both in the same chapter, and since the usage in the arena of evil comes first, I am reversing my usual procedure of beginning with the positive use of the term. In the immediate context of Rev 17:13 the seven heads of the beast have been identified as seven mountains on which the "woman" sits (v. 9), and as seven kings (v. 10). The ten horns of the beast are then identified as ten kings who have not yet received a kingdom (v. 12). Charles has identified the beast as Nero *redivivus* and the ten kings as the Parthian armies.[1] This historical reference may have been the meaning of the beast in the original context, but it does not allow the passage to speak meaningfully to future generations. Each historical beast, whether Nero or, for example, Stalin, will always have its puppet "kings" who give their full support to the beast.

At the opposite pole of interpretation from Charles is Beckwith, who sees the ten kings as "purely eschatological figures representing the

---

1. Charles, *Critical and Exegetical Commentary*, 2:71–73; cf. Hanson, *Wrath of the Lamb*, 199.

totality of the powers of all nations on the earth which are to be made subservient to Antichrist [sic]."[2]

Yet another approach is that which sees the ten kings as the Roman governors of the senatorial provinces who ruled for only one year.[3] The reference to their ruling for "one hour" with the beast should probably be more directly compared with the "one hour" of Babylon or Rome's destruction (18:19) rather than to any literal period of one year, however.

However one identifies the ten kings, their sole purpose is to give their *dynamis* ("power") and *exousia* ("authority") to the beast. Morris brings out the fact that these kings are not independent thinkers; rather, all willingly give their authority to the beast. "They are willing collaborators, not men forced into an unwelcome association."[4] The terms *power* and *authority* can be used of moral and spiritual power and authority as well as of military force. Swete—probably correctly—interprets this passage to mean that the ten kings not only put their military forces at the disposition of the beast but their moral force as well.[5]

The counterimage to the one *gnōmē* of the ten kings to give their allegiance to the beast whose ultimate fate is the lake of fire and sulfur (Rev 19:20) appears just four verses later, in 17:17. Charles brackets as an interpolation the phrase *kai poiēsai mian gnōmēn*, which can be translated as "and to accomplish one purpose."[6] Equally if not more plausible is the interpretation that this phrase is John's deliberate echo of v. 13. God also has one purpose, but it is very different from that of the ten kings. God uses their "one purpose" to accomplish the divine purpose. As Morris expresses it, God sees to it that the ten kings have the necessary unity to carry out their act of destruction.[7] The Seer, while being keenly aware of the struggle against evil in this world, did not believe in any ultimate ontological dualism. As Mounce expresses it, "In the final analysis the powers of evil serve the purposes of God."[8] Beasley-Murray echoes the same understanding, saying, "That the agents of the Devil execute the will of God

---

2. Cited in Mounce, *Revelation*, 317.
3. Ibid.
4. Morris, *Revelation*, 205–6.
5. Swete, *Apocalypse*, 223.
6. Charles, *Critical and Exegetical Commentary*, 2:73.
7. Morris, *Revelation*, 206–7.
8. Mounce, *Revelation*, 319–20.

vividly illustrates that there is no real dualism in the Revelation. The beast and his allies remain in the hand of the God they defy, and by the impulse of the Devil they unitedly fulfil the words of God."[9] Caird's conclusion is along the same lines: "God put it into their heads to carry out his purpose, the purpose mentioned in the opening sentence of the book, that every power which sets itself up against God shall in the end break itself upon the Cross of his Son and the martyr witness of his saints."[10]

Thus we are driven to conclude that in one sense, two very different purposes are depicted in these verses. In another sense both purposes become one under the ultimate sovereignty of God. The goal of the ten kings is anything but a desire to participate in the purpose of God. They collaborate with the beast for the sole purpose of sharing the beast's power and wealth. Their one purpose is self-aggrandizement. God's one purpose, on the other hand, is the ultimate defeat of evil and the triumph of righteousness, and he uses the self-destructive tendencies of evil to accomplish that end. Charles argues that the phrase "until the words of God should be completed" in the present context must relate to the destruction of Rome by Nero and his Parthian allies, but would also have in view "the overthrow of the power of the beast and his Parthian allies."[11] The limitations of this view have been noted previously. The phrase must be left open to be applied to each and every personification of the "beast" throughout human history.

---

9. Beasley-Murray, *Revelation*, 260; cf. Charles, *Critical and Exegetical Commentary*, 2:73.

10. Caird, *Commentary on Revelation*, 221.

11. Charles, *Critical and Exegetical Commentary*, 2:73.

30

The Supper

And he says to me, "Write: Blessed are the ones who have been invited to the supper of the marriage of the Lamb." Then he says to me, "These words are true (words) of God."

(Rev 19:9)

And I saw one angel who had taken his stand in the sun; and he cried out in a loud voice, saying to all the birds flying in mid-heaven, "Come, be gathered for the great supper of God."

(Rev 19:17)

THE POSITIVE USAGE OF the word *supper* appears as one of two figures of speech for the eschatological people of God. In 19:7 John refers to this people as the bride of the Lamb; then, in v. 9 he changes the designation to those invited to the marriage supper of the Lamb. Wilson comments appropriately that "This beatitude makes apparent the fluidity of biblical metaphors, for the saints are not only the bride, but are also the guests at the wedding!"[1] The latter is prefigured in Isa 25:6–8. In that passage *Yahweh Sabaoth* ("the Lord of Hosts") is depicted as preparing a lavish banquet for his people on "this mountain"—possibly Zion—swallowing up death for all time and cleansing all the reproaches of his people. This text is but one indication and expression of the idea of the messianic banquet that is deeply rooted in the traditions of Israel. As Mounce notes, *3 Enoch* locates this banquet at Jerusalem. Mounce also calls attention to this tradition in the *Apocalypse of Elijah*.[2]

---

1. Wilson, *Revelation*, 156.
2. Mounce, *Revelation*, 341.

Charles notes the ambiguity in the word *keklēmenoi*, or "invited." It leaves open the question not only of the identity of those invited but also the meaning of the term itself. Charles "solves" the problem by making Rev 19:5-9 refer only to the martyrs and the supper refer to the climax of the millennium.³ Beasley-Murray sharply criticizes Charles's view, arguing that the "invited" are simply believers in Christ who have responded to the Lamb's invitation to repentance and faith. He then says explicitly of Charles's interpretation, "This interpretation can scarcely be reconciled with the intention of the text, namely that the Church will be united with its Lord when he is revealed in glory and will share with him in the joy of the kingdom. That is salvation as John understands it."⁴

Charles takes the phrase "these are the true words of God" as "rather inept" at this point, but as "full of significance" in Rev 22:6. His stated reason is that the words referred to are the words of the martyrs and angels in heaven.⁵ That depends totally on the antecedent of the pronoun *these*. I would argue that no necessity exists for making that antecedent anything other than the words of invitation to the marriage supper of the Lamb that precede this pronoun.

Since the explicit command to write appears only five times in Revelation outside the addresses to the seven churches (1:11, 19; 14:13, 19:9, and 21:5), some have raised the question as to why these words merit an explicit command. From a modern vantage point these words do not stand out as possessing extraordinary significance. If we put ourselves in the place of the first recipients, however, the matter looks entirely different. The content of what the Seer was instructed to write here would have been extremely important. As Morris correctly notes, the assurance that the struggling Christians, not their persecutors, were really the blessed ones would have been of key importance.⁶

The negative usage of *supper* occurs in Rev 19:17. In the Seer's vision an angel who is standing in the sun invites the birds of prey flying in midheaven to come together for the "great supper of God." Charles appropriately notes that this passage, in part at least, has been modeled on Ezek

---

3. Charles, *Critical and Exegetical Commentary*, 2:129.
4. Beasley-Murray, *Revelation*, 275.
5. Charles, *Critical and Exegetical Commentary*, 2:128.
6. Morris, *Revelation*, 221.

39:17-18.[7] Caird notes the relation of the phrase "flying in midheaven" to the eagle of 8:13, who announces three woes to follow the three last trumpets. Since the Seer never explicitly presents the third woe, Caird thinks the present passage should be seen in that light.[8]

That the "great supper of God" is the counterimage of the wedding banquet of the Lamb has been widely recognized. Beasley-Murray writes, "What for Ezekiel is a sacrificial feast, prepared by the Lord on the mountains of Israel . . . in the Revelation becomes a terrible counterpart to the marriage supper of the Lamb."[9] In similar language Mounce says, "The supper of God presents a grim contrast to the marriage feast of the Lamb."[10] Regarding this passage Farrer concludes, "The shocking comparison between the two invitations to the great supper (19:9 and 17) must be deliberate on St. John's part."[11]

I would quarrel with Beasley-Murray's use of "counterpart" and even more strongly with Farrer's use of "comparison." There is no true counterpart or comparison. We have one *deipnon* ("supper") that is a celebration of the eternal union of the Lamb with his followers. We have another *deipnon* that is a gory, grisly picture of a feast in which human beings are the menu for birds of prey. One is not a part of the other in any sense, neither is there any comparison between the two. All that the two have in common is the word *deipnon*. What we are confronted with here is a mind-jarring counterimage.

---

7. Charles, *Critical and Exegetical Commentary*, 2:138; cf. Farrer, *Revelation*, 200-1; Caird, *Commentary on Revelation*, 247.

8. Ibid.

9. Beasley-Murray, *Revelation*, 282.

10. Mounce, *Revelation*, 349; cf. Wilson, *Revelation*, 159; Morris, *Revelation*, 226.

11. Farrer, *Revelation*, 201.

Part Two
Parody

31

Threefold Designations

*John to the seven churches in Asia: grace and peace to you
from the One who is, and who was, and who is coming;
and from the seven Spirits which (are) before his throne.*

(Rev 1:4)

*I am the alpha and the omega, says the Lord God; the One who is,
and who was, and who is coming: the Almighty.*

(Rev 1:8)

*. . . and the four living creatures, each one of them having six wings and
being full of eyes outside and inside; and they have no rest day and night,
saying, Holy, Holy, Holy Lord, God, the Almighty; the One who was,
and who is, and who is coming.*

(Rev 4:8)

*And I heard the angel of the waters saying, You are righteous,
the One who is and who was, the holy One.*

(Rev 16:5)

*And the beast which I saw was like a leopard and his feet like (feet)
of a bear and his mouth was like the mouth of a lion.
And the dragon gave to him his power
and his throne and great authority.*

(Rev 13:2)

> *The beast which you saw was, and is not, and is about to come up out of the abyss; also he goes away into destruction. And those dwelling upon the earth will be astonished, (those) whose names have not been written in the book of life (which existed) from the foundation of the world, when they see that the beast was, and is not, and will come.*
>
> (REV 17:8)

I HAVE NOTED EARLIER that in Jewish-Christian apocalyptic circles, the number three connoted divinity. Just how many times John is giving a threefold grouping of terms with the explicit intent of conveying the idea of divinity is an open question. In choosing the verses above, I have limited my selection to four passages in which there is an undisputed threefold designation of God, and two passages in which we find a similar threefold designation of the beast, in one case, and a threefold designation of the dragon in the other. The threefold designation of the dragon contains three terms that are repeatedly applied to God in Revelation.

Looking first at Rev 1:4, we find John identifying himself for the first time and addressing the seven churches in Asia, although he does not name the churches until v. 11. As Charles notes, with the transfer of the kingdom of Attalus III to Rome, the proconsular province of Asia was formed and was coterminous with that kingdom. He also notes that the references to Asia in the New Testament, with a few exceptions, refer to proconsular Asia.[1] This province was located on the western side of ancient Asia Minor in what is modern-day Turkey.

It is well known that far more than seven churches existed in Asia at the time John wrote. Colossae and Hierapolis were located less than ten miles from Laodicea, yet they are not mentioned in Revelation. Other known churches in the province were established at Magnesia, Tralles, and Troas, just to name a few. Various reasons have been given for John's selectivity. Sir William Ramsey argued that the seven churches John names lay on the route of a Roman postal system;[2] more recent scholars, however, have found evidence of any organized postal system to be lacking.[3] Summers suggests that the seven churches lay along the main cir-

---

1. Charles, *Critical and Exegetical Commentary*, 1:9; cf. Beasley-Murray, *Revelation*, 53.
2. Ramsey, *Letters*, 133–41.
3. See Aune, *Revelation 1–5*, 131 for a discussion of this issue.

cular road that bound together the west-central section of the province.[4] Charles relates the choice to the fact that seven was "a sacred number not only in Jewish Apocalyptic and Judaism generally, but particularly in our Author [*sic*]."[5] But what does its being a "sacred number" tell us? Caird is more explicit, saying, "John uses the number seven as a symbol for completeness or wholeness."[6] Mounce mentions this view without endorsing it, and suggests that "these particular seven were chosen because of some special relationship to emperor worship."[7] Farrer, after discussing the seven spirits of God, writes, "Similarly the seven churches on whom the seven blessings are invoked will appear as organically one, and typical of the perfect unity or wholeness which embraces all Christian congregations."[8] Morris, after noting the suggestion that John may have had pastoral responsibility for these seven churches along with the existence of other churches in the area, notes that seven is the number of perfection and that John is fond of this number. He then concludes, "For one so fond of symbolism this can scarcely be without significance."[9] The major difficulty with Morris's comments is that he, like Charles, neglects to tell us the significance of the number. Boesak is more explicit in saying that the seven churches signify the whole church.[10]

Beasley-Murray suggests three possibilities for the choosing of these seven churches:

1. They may have been the congregations for which John was personally responsible.
2. The number seven may be simply an anticipation of v. 11.
3. John may have chosen them because of the sanctity and completeness associated with the number seven.

Beasley-Murray then opts for the position that John is writing to a group of churches for which he had pastoral responsibility.[11] His expla-

4. Summers, *Worthy Is the Lamb*, 86.
5. Charles, *Critical and Exegetical Commentary*, 1:8–9.
6. Caird, *Commentary on Revelation*, 14; see also Robbins, *Revelation*, 32–33; McDowell, *Meaning and Message*, 15.
7. Mounce, *Revelation*, 68.
8. Farrer, *Revelation*, 61–62.
9. Morris, *Revelation*, 48.
10. Boesak, *Comfort and Protest*, 26.
11. Beasley-Murray, *Revelation*, 53.

nation is rendered questionable by the aforementioned proximity of the churches at Colossae and Hierapolis. That John might be responsible for the church at Laodicea and not the other two congregations is not impossible but is rather implausible. One could also raise the question as to whether Beasley-Murray and others who support this interpretation may not be reading a much later development into the first-century situation. That clear lines of pastoral supervision of churches had developed by the time John wrote is anything but clear.

Before leaving this issue, I will point out that as early as the Muratorian Canon (c. 180 C.E.), Victorinus, John Chrysostom, and Augustine, the number seven in the Apocalypse was interpreted as the symbol of the complete church. A long and impressive list of modern scholars have followed suit. Let me be very clear at this point that I am not denying the historicity of the seven churches to which John wrote. The either/or pitfall is to be avoided here as elsewhere. I am suggesting that John wrote *both* to seven actual historical churches with which he may have had a special relationship *and* to the church as a whole.

John invokes a twofold blessing upon his recipients in the literary fashion typical of the day. The terms *charis* ("grace") and *eirēnē* ("peace") were loaded with theological implications. At one level they represented the typical Jewish greeting. *Shalom* is the Hebrew counterpart of *eirēnē* and the customary Hellenistic greeting *charis* (the verb form of which was often used simply in the sense of "greetings" or "hello"), but the meaning goes much deeper in a Christian context.[12] As Beasley-Murray appropriately notes, these two words combine the typical gift of the new age—grace—with the typical blessing of the old—peace. "The latter had become the embodiment of the Old Testament hope, the peace of the age to come, and so a comprehensive term for the salvation of the kingdom of God."[13] As Mounce concisely expresses it, "Grace is the divine favor showed to man [sic], and peace is that state of spiritual well-being which follows as a result."[14] Charles similarly comments that grace "here is the favor of God and of Jesus Christ," and that peace is "the harmony restored between God and man [sic] through Christ."[15]

---

12. Cf. Mounce, *Revelation*, 68.
13. Beasley-Murray, *Revelation*, 53–54.
14. Mounce, *Revelation*, 68.
15. Charles, *Critical and Exegetical Commentary*, 1:9.

This greeting brings us to the threefold designation of God as "the One who is, who was, and is coming," with which this study is particularly concerned. As is often the case with John's symbolism, it has both a Biblical and a non-Biblical precedent. For the latter, Mounce cites a reference from Pausanias to Zeus who was, Zeus who is, and Zeus who will be. He also notes an inscription from the shrine of Minerva that reads, "I am all that hath been and is and shall be."[16]

The Biblical background of the designation has been widely recognized as Exod 3:14–15. The Septuagint represents God as saying "*egō eimi ho ōn*," which can be translated as "I am the one who [continually] is." Caird speaks of the current title *ho ōn kai ho ēn kai ho erchomenos*—"he who is, and was, and is coming"—as a "Christian elaboration" of this title. The breaches of Greek grammar in this phrase have been widely discussed.[17] No consensus among scholars for explaining this phenomenon seems to lie on any near horizon. Perhaps the most profitable course lies in setting aside the grammatical issues and focusing instead on John's theological intention. Mounce's approach is instructive: "Since the finite cannot conceive of the eternal in other than temporal terms, John paraphrases the divine name in such a way as to remind his readers that God is eternally existent, without beginning or end."[18] Caird's remarks are also to the point: "It sets the church's coming ordeal against a background of God's eternity, but it also brings God down into the arena of history. He is Lord of past, present, and future."[19]

Charles brackets the remainder of v. 4 as an interpolation but also deals with the interpretations of those who take it otherwise. He lists the ancient commentators Victorinus, Primasius, Apringius, and Beatus; and the modern commentators Alford and Swete as interpreting the "seven spirits" as "the sevenfold energies of God or the Holy Spirit." He also refers to the rather common interpretation that they are the seven archangels of Jewish tradition.[20] Mounce surveys the other three loci in Revelation where this phrase occurs and concludes that sufficient information for certain understanding of this "enigmatic phrase" is lacking. He then offers

---

16. Mounce, *Revelation*, 68; cf. Charles, *Critical and Exegetical Commentary*, 1:10.

17. See Farrer, *Revelation*, 61; Mounce, *Revelation*, 68 n. 13; Caird, *Commentary on Revelation*, 16; Charles, *Critical and Exegetical Commentary*, 1:10.

18. Mounce, *Revelation*, 68.

19. Caird, *Commentary on Revelation*, 160; see also Farrer, *Revelation*, 61.

20. Charles, *Critical and Exegetical Commentary*, 1:11.

the conjecture "that they are perhaps part of a heavenly entourage that has a special ministry in connection with the Lamb."[21]

To Charles's list of modern interpreters who take the seven spirits to be the Holy Spirit may be added Bauckham,[22] Moyise,[23] Rowland,[24] Mulholland,[25] Caird,[26] Farrer,[27] Beasley-Murray,[28] Robbins,[29] McDowell,[30] Summers,[31] and Morris;[32] and, if the reader has not surmised as much by now, I agree with them.

The next appearance of the threefold designation of God occurs in Rev 1:8. It is prefaced by the divine claim to be the alpha and the omega. Charles comments, "This is a natural symbol for the first and last among all things." He further notes that this type of expression was known among the Romans, and that among the Jews aleph and tau (the first and last letters of the Hebrew alphabet, as alpha and omega are the first and last of the Greek alphabet) were often used similarly of the entire extent of a thing.[33] Mounce notes that only here and in Rev 21:5–8 does God speak directly, and in the latter passage the parallel phrase, "the beginning and the end" is added.[34] And although the speaker appears to be Christ in 22:13, the formula there has yet another parallel phrase, "the first and the last."

The phrase "the One who is, and who was, and who is coming" is identical with that in v. 4 and hence requires no further discussion. The term *pantokratōr*, or "almighty," is new, however. Mounce notes that of the ten times this word appears in the New Testament, nine are in Revelation (1:8, 4:8, 11:17, 15:3, 16:7, 14; 19:6, 15; and 21:22). He thinks the title refers

---

21. Mounce, *Revelation*, 69–70.
22. Bauckham, *Climax*, 110.
23. Moyise, *Old Testament in Revelation*, 33.
24. Rowland, *Revelation*, 58.
25. Mulholland, *Holy Living*, 71.
26. Caird, *Commentary on Revelation*, 15.
27. Farrer, *Revelation*, 61.
28. Beasley-Murray, *Revelation*, 55.
29. Robbins, *Revelation*, 34.
30. McDowell, *Meaning and Message*, 25.
31. Summers, *Worthy Is the Lamb*, 101.
32. Morris, *Revelation*, 49.
33. Charles, *Critical and Exegetical Commentary*, 1:20; see also Beasley-Murray, *Revelation*, 59.
34. Mounce, *Revelation*, 73.

more to God's supremacy over all things than to the theological idea of divine omnipotence.[35] Morris echoes a similar interpretation in saying that *almighty* "denotes not so much the exercise of naked power as the all-embracing sovereignty that God exercises."[36]

Beasley-Murray notes that "Lord God Almighty" renders the phrase *Yahweh Sabaoth* ("Lord of hosts") in the Greek version of the Jewish Scriptures. He comments further that this locution reflects John's appreciation of the idea in the Jewish Scriptures that God is in control of all nations, not just the Israelites.[37] Caird also notes the relationship to "Lord of hosts," then comments that "like all other terms from the Jewish Scriptures John uses it with a difference; for he has learned from Christ that the omnipotence of God is not the power of unlimited coercion but the power of invincible love."[38]

The third time this threefold designation appears—and is it mere coincidence that we find in the present passage a threefold repetition of the term *holy*?—is in Rev 4:8. I have dealt with most of this verse in the chapter titled "They Have No Rest." As at 1:8 we have the threefold designation with "the Almighty" added, but with two differences: *almighty* is moved to a position before the threefold designation; and the first and second terms of the designation are reversed. Farrer argues that the rearrangement of the terms is based on the unbroken praise of the four living creatures. It was designed to give the chronological sequence of past, present, and future.[39] Charles, Caird, and Beasley-Murray take no notice of the rearrangement, nor have I found anyone else as yet who has noticed it. This arrangement is John's way of emphasizing the paramount importance of the threefold designation over and beyond the idea that God is the Lord of past, present, and future. As I have noted earlier, he does the same thing with the fourfold designation of people, tribes, tongues, and nations. In the next passage we consider (16:5) he has similarly replaced the third element with *ho hosios* ("the holy One").

Charles has bracketed the phrase "and I heard the angel of the waters saying" as an interpolation, and "restores" the remainder of the verse to

---

35. Ibid.; cf. Charles, *Critical and Exegetical Commentary*, 1:20.
36. Morris, *Revelation*, 51.
37. Beasley-Murray, *Revelation*, 59–60.
38. Caird, *Commentary on Revelation*, 19.
39. Farrer, *Revelation*, 92.

what he considers to be its original place after 19:4. He also argues that if *ho hosios* be the correct reading, this nominative should be taken as a vocative.[40] As attractive as this interpretation is to me—without it we would have three repetitions of the threefold title of God—I think the evidence is against it. Admittedly the textual evidence is divided, but the support for the reading *ho hosios* is fairly strong. The threefold repetition of the definite article also argues against Charles' position. If John had intended for *hosios* to be a vocative, to have left off the article before *hosios* would have been very simple. Since he repeats the article three times I am assuming that he intended another threefold designation for God. Morris argues that the article before *hosios* is equivalent to a vocative.[41] Why is this article "equivalent to a vocative" and not the two preceding? Has Morris been swayed by Charles's position? This argument is rather weak, in my judgment.

Caird notes the widespread belief that all of the elements of nature had their guardian angels.[42] Mounce notes that we have two possibilities: either a guardian angel who is in charge of the waters or, as Lenski has suggested, the reference may be simply to the angel of v. 4 who poured out the vial on the waters.[43] Taking it in the former sense would mean that even the angel who was thought to protect the waters is compelled to admit that God's judgment is fully justified.[44] Morris notes a reference in *1 Enoch* 66:2 to angels being in charge of the waters but rightly notes that no passage in the canonical Scriptures refers to this belief.[45]

Boring also notes that most modern translators take *ho hosios* as a vocative in this verse. This is true; however, they also regularly translate *teleios* as "perfect" in such passages as Phil 3:15 and Heb 5:9, but that does not change the fact that this is a *mis*translation in these passages. What we have here is another threefold designation of God in which John has in typical fashion changed one of the elements.

Without detailed exegesis, I will mention the occurrence of another threefold designation of God. Three times (other than the one discussed

---

40. Charles, *Critical and Exegetical Commentary*, 2:44, 122-23.

41. Morris, *Revelation*, 188.

42. Caird, *Commentary on Revelation*, 202; cf. Beasley-Murray, *Revelation*, 241–42; Mounce, *Revelation*, 294.

43. Cited in Mounce, *Revelation*, 294–95.

44. Cf. Krodel, *Revelation*, 283; Robbins, *Revelation*, 185.

45. Morris, *Revelation*, 188.

above at 4:8) the title "Lord God Almighty" appears in Revelation, at 15:3, 16:7, and 21:22. It is possible that John intended this title to be considered alongside "the One who is, who was and who is coming." Since no one of the three elements corresponds with the latter, I have chosen not to deal with these passages in detail.

Before moving on to the parody of the threefold designation in the arena of evil, let us take a brief look at one passage in which we have a twofold designation of God that uses two of the three terms discussed above (11:17). In this passage we also find the threefold designation "Lord, God, the Almighty" as in 1:8 and 4:8. Another similarity to 4:8 is the worship of God by the four living creatures. "Almighty" also precedes "the One who is," as in 4:8. The order is restored to that in verses 1:4 and 1:8, *ho ōn kai ho ēn* ("the One who is and who was"). Clearly the Seer intends for us to remember the passages in which the threefold designation was used. Why then does he omit *ho erchomenos*, "the One who is coming"? Krodel's answer is that God is no longer coming—God has come at this point.[46] Mounce agrees that God's coming is no longer seen as a future event—God has come and entered upon his reign. Mounce also notes that the AV, following a few inferior manuscripts, adds the third element, "the One who is coming."[47] Caird makes the similar argument that "now futurity is caught up in the eternal present, and the choirs of heaven address him as **Lord God Omnipotent, who are and were**."[48] Beasley-Murray also concurs, arguing, "No longer can it be said 'and who is to come (1:4),' for he has come."[49] This interpretation echoes Farrer's earlier words, "Equally pointed is the description of God as the Almighty who is and who was—no longer 'and who is to come,' for he *has* come—he has taken his great dominion, and begun his reign."[50] Morris also says very dogmatically, "There is no 'who is to come' this time for the coming is now present; this is the time of consummation."[51] I have previously called attention to the predominance of the present tense of the word *coming* in the Apocalypse. In my judgment the use of this tense calls into question

---

46. Krodel, *Revelation*, 230.
47. Mounce, *Revelation*, 231.
48. Caird, *Commentary on Revelation*, 141; emphasis in the original.
49. Beasley-Murray, *Revelation*, 189.
50. Farrer, *Revelation*, 138.
51. Morris, *Revelation*, 149.

the interpretation that what is in view here is the final eschatological coming of Jesus. God is by nature and purpose the "coming One" at all points in history.

The first threefold designation that parodies the threefold title of God appears in Rev 13:2. The beast from the sea is described there as being like a leopard with feet like a bear and a mouth like that of a lion. That the writer has combined features of Daniel's individual beasts (Dan 7) has been widely recognized.[52] The prophet Hosea mentioned the same three beasts in an oracle of judgment upon Israel (Hos 13:7–8). In that passage it is Yahweh who is compared with the three beasts, unlike the present passage. Rev 13 may again have overtones of the idea that the forces of evil are ultimately made to accomplish God's purpose of judgment.

Although the dragon was defeated in the previous chapter, he still has power wherever people acknowledge him. The adjective *great* in this verse may imply that many people acknowledge the dragon and hence are under his power. The words *throne, power,* and *authority* are something of a double parody of the divine. Not only do we have the threefold designation, but all three words are repeatedly used of God in the Apocalypse.

We encounter the threefold title that most obviously parodies the divine in Rev 17:8. The context is the description of the "great prostitute" and the beast on which she rides. The identity of this beast as the "beast from the sea" of 13:1 has, I think, been sufficiently established. The phrase "he was, and is not, and is about to come up out of the abyss" seems to be an obvious parody of the God who is, and who was, and who is coming. But if one should miss it at this point, John repeats the parody in more unmistakable language at the end of the verse, "the beast who was, and is not, and will come." Morris refers to this as "probably an intentional contrast" with Rev 1:4.[53] As Mounce notes, "This is an obvious parody of the Lamb, who was put to death yet came back to life and now is alive forevermore (1:18, 2:8). The description is also an intentional antithesis to the One 'who is and who was and who is to come (1:4, 4:8).'"[54]

Beasley-Murray has noted something of an anomaly here in that in v. 3 the beast is the antichristian empire, whereas in v. 11 he is one of the kings of the empire. Where does the transformation from empire to king

---

52. E.g., Mounce, *Revelation*, 251; Charles, *Critical and Exegetical Commentary*, 1:348; Beasley-Murray, *Revelation*, 208.

53. Morris, *Revelation*, 202.

54. Mounce, *Revelation*, 312; cf. Wilson, *Revelation*, 140.

take place? If such a transformation has taken place, then v. 8 must mean that "he will arrogate to himself divine claims, but they are the reverse of true divinity, for unlike Him who is, and was, and is to come the beast was, but is not and is to ascend from the pit but go to destruction."[55]

Charles argues that the original identity of the beast as indicated by comparing 17:3 with 13:1 has been altered to accommodate the Nero *redivivus* myth. "The beast now means the demonic Nero returning from the abyss, and it is clearly the intention of our author that 11 should be taken in this sense." He goes on to say that the "Neronic Antichrist" [*sic*] is "the hellish antitype of Christ." He also notes the parody of the divine name.[56] Caird also notes the parody of the divine name and points out that the third verb *parestai* ("he will come") is the one from which the noun *parousia* ("coming" or "presence"), the typical term for the future advent of Christ, is derived.[57] Caird argues further, quite cogently in my judgment, that the beast's "coming up out of the abyss" and "going away to destruction" are not episodic events in the life of one "beast," but are permanent attributes of the beast that are constantly manifest in human history.[58] Farrer refers to the beast's threefold title as a "defective parody" of God's being and argues that the "exact comparison" is "between the beast as a falsification of the divine image, and the Lamb as a true offprint of it." He then goes on to say, "It is in parody of Christ that the beast has his first and second advents; but they are separated by a period of non-existence, and the second leads to perdition, not immortal life."[59] Niles seems to have a similar interpretation in mind when he speaks of the beast as a caricature of the Lamb.[60]

Almost without exception commentators connect the beast who was and is not and will come with the Nero *redivivus* myth. I have no quarrel with this interpretation so long as it is not allowed to eclipse the parody of the threefold name of God and the parody of the death and resurrection of Christ. As Lohmeyer puts it, "This difference is explainable simply out of a different tradition [see excursus on 13:10], but not out of any legend

55. Beasley-Murray, *Revelation*, 253–54.

56. Charles, *Critical and Exegetical Commentary*, 2:67–68; cf. Sleeper, *Victorious Christ*, 113.

57. Caird, *Commentary on Revelation*, 215–16; see also Mounce, *Revelation*, 313.

58. Caird, *Commentary on Revelation*, 215–16.

59. Farrer, *Revelation*, 184.

60. Niles, *Seeing the Invisible*, 77.

of Nero *redivivus*. Therefore the phrase 'he was and is not and will come' is neither a historical nor a legendary designation, but doubtless a contrasting idea to 'the One who is and who was, and who is coming [1:4],' while the [contrast] in 13:3 is to the attributes of Christ."[61]

In summation, we have examined three passages in which there is a threefold designation of God as the One who was, who is, and who is coming. The only variation is the reversal of the first two elements in Rev 4:8. We then looked at one passage containing the twofold title "the One who is and who was" but without the phrase "who is coming." The general consensus seems to be that the third element was omitted because God was viewed as already having come. Whether this be the correct understanding, or whether the Seer has simply shifted to a twofold designation because of the symbolism of the number two (strengthening) may be debated.

Over against these, John has placed the threefold designation of the beast as "the one who was, and is not, and will come" as a rather obvious parody of God. In addition, John has depicted the dragon as giving to the beast his power and throne and authority. The threefold designation may be merely coincidental, but I think it more probable that it is a deliberate parody of the threefold designation of God.

---

61. "Diese Verschiedenheiten erklaren sich nur aus einer anderen Tradition (s. Exk. Nach 13:10), aber nicht aus einer Ueberlieferung von Nero redivivus. Denn das en kai ouk estin kai parestai ist keine historische oder legendare Bestimmung, sondern deutliche Kontrastbildung zu ho on kai ho en kai ho erchomenos (1.4), wahrend die in 13:3 eine solche zu den Attributen Christi ist." Lohmeyer, *Offenbarung*, 139.

32

The Holy Trinity and the Unholy Trinity

John to the seven churches in Asia: grace and peace to you from the One who is, and who was, and who is coming; and from the seven spirits which (are) before his throne, and from Jesus Christ the faithful witness, the firstborn from the dead ones, and the ruler of the kings of the earth.

(Rev 1:4–5a)

And I was weeping greatly because no one was found worthy to open the scroll or to see it. And one of the elders says to me, Stop weeping. Look, the Lion of the tribe of Judah, the Root of David, overcame (so as) to open the scroll, even its seven seals. And I saw in the midst of the throne and the four living creatures and in the midst of the elders a Lamb, having taken his stand as one that had been slain, having seven horns and seven eyes; which are the seven spirits of God having been sent out into all the earth. And he came and took (it) out of the right hand of the One sitting upon the throne.

(Rev 5:4–7)

And another sign was seen in heaven; behold a great, fiery-red dragon having seven heads and ten horns, with seven diadems upon his heads (appeared).

(Rev 12:3)

And I saw a beast coming up out of the sea, having ten horns and seven heads; and upon his horns (were) ten diadems, and upon his heads names of blasphemy. And the beast which I saw was like a leopard, and his feet like (feet of) a bear, and his mouth like a lion; and the dragon gave him his power and his throne and great authority. And one of his heads (looked) like it had been slain unto death; and the wound of its death was healed. And

> *the whole earth marveled after the beast. And they worshiped the dragon because he gave authority to the beast, and they worshiped the beast, saying, "Who is like the beast and who is able to do battle with him?"*
>
> (Rev 13:1–4)
>
> *And I saw another beast coming up out of the earth. It had two horns like a lamb, but was speaking like a dragon. And he exercises all the authority of the first beast before him; and he causes the earth and those dwelling in it to worship the first beast, whose wound of death was healed.*
>
> (Rev 13:11–12)
>
> *And it was given to him to give breath to the image of the beast in order that the image of the beast might speak, and also however many would not worship the beast might be killed.*
>
> (Rev 13:15)

I recognize that I am leaving myself open to the charge of anachronism here. I do not mean in any sense to suggest that the theological formulations of Nicaea and Chalcedon had already been made by the late first century C.E. I will argue, however, that the Apocalypse contains at least an incipient trinitarian view of God. Whether John himself could have verbalized such a view may be questionable; however, I believe the materials for a trinitarian view are present in the Apocalypse.

In order to keep the study manageable I have opted to focus on just a few passages that I regard as implying a trinitarian view of God and a few others that parody that view. I have chosen to look first at Rev 1:4, which has been dealt with in part in earlier chapters. The reference to the seven spirits of God will be the focus at this point. Though I have previously taken the position that the seven spirits represent the Holy Spirit, I will elaborate on this point a bit more. This reference to the seven spirits appears between the reference to God as "the One who is, and who was, and who is coming" and the reference to Jesus Christ. That the Seer would have framed a reference to angels or other spiritual beings between a reference to God and to Jesus I consider highly unlikely. Mounce admits that the interpretation of the seven spirits as the Holy Spirit is "tempting," but finally rejects it. Referring to the point I have made above, he claims that this argument loses its force in view of such passages as Luke 9:26

and 1 Tim 5:21, in which God, Christ, and then angels are mentioned.[1] This argument misses the point. In the passages Mounce cites, the reference to angels comes after the references to God and Jesus, not between them. As noted earlier, Mounce ends by saying that there is insufficient evidence from the other usages of the phrase in Revelation to make a solid judgment.

Beasley-Murray believes that the phase under discussion has a pagan as well as a Biblical history. He suggests that Zechariah 4 is the latter, and the ancient worship of the planets is the former. He notes that John might have been able to find a Jewish writing with the reference to God and the seven spirits in conjunction. He adds that if this were the case, John has added the reference to Jesus, producing a sort of "trinitarian formula" that a non-Christian Jew could not have voiced. He then concludes, "The seven spirits of God represent the Holy Spirit in his fullness of life and blessing."[2] Morris likewise advocates taking the number seven in the sense of completeness and hence the seven spirits as a reference to the Holy Spirit, although he rightly notes that John nowhere uses that term specifically.[3]

The only other passage I have selected for exegesis related to the Holy Trinity is Rev 5:4–6. Since passages dealing with God as creator and the Lamb as redeemer are numerous, I chose this one because of its reference to the seven spirits of God. In the immediate context, the One on the throne is depicted as holding a scroll sealed with seven seals that no one in heaven, on earth, or under the earth can open. John begins to weep because no one can open the scroll. One of the elders tells him to stop weeping because there is one who can open the scroll—the Lion of the tribe of Judah. When John turns to see the Lion, he sees instead a Lamb that has been slain but now is standing.

The vision is one in which the ultimate purposes of God are completely sealed (seven seals) to the entire created order. Whether John's weeping is a matter of personal disappointment, as some have suggested, an indefinite delay in the revelation and execution of the purposes of God, or some other reason is a question that need not detain us here. He is told to stop weeping (*mē* with present imperative) and informed that someone can open the scroll. That someone is the Lion of the tribe of Judah, the

---

1. Mounce, *Revelation*, 69.
2. Beasley-Murray, *Revelation*, 55–56.
3. Morris, *Revelation*, 49.

Root of David. The symbolism of the lion appears to be a reflection of Gen 49:9 in which Judah is said to be a lion's whelp. The phrase "root of David" no doubt relies upon Isa 11. Some echoes of the intertestamental literature may also be present. For example, Mounce notes that the Maccabees are referred to as horned lambs [rams?] in *1 Enoch* 90:9, and that in *T. Jos.* 19:8–11 a lamb destroys Israel's enemies. In *1 Enoch* 90:37 the military leader of Israel is said to be a bull with large horns.[4]

Now that we are informed that the Lion of Judah has conquered and is worthy to open the seals, it remains to consider the means by which he has conquered. The answer is consistent throughout Revelation. He has conquered by becoming the Lamb who bears the marks of slaughter (v. 6). He has conquered by absorbing the worst that evil humanity could do to him, and without retaliation. This sort of conquering is alien to all the instincts of human nature. The human tendency is to overcome by crushing the object of victory with superior power. No doubt the Lamb possesses that superior power, but he redefines for us the means of omnipotence.

When John turns to see the Lion of Judah he sees instead a Lamb. He is described as being "in the midst" of the throne, the living creatures and the elders. As I mentioned briefly earlier, quite a few commentators get waylaid by attempting to locate the Lamb in relation to the throne, the living creatures, and the elders.[5] I consider this inquiry to be futile. Once more the human inability to visualize without reference to time and place gets in the way of understanding. In the opening vision we see the resurrected Christ walking among the lampstands. We are left in no doubt that the lampstands are the churches, the people of God. As I have noted previously, the four living creatures are a symbol of the created order and the twenty-four elders represent the people of God. Where is the Lion or Lamb? He is everywhere and no*where*! No place can contain the resurrected and exalted Christ any more than a place can contain God or the Holy Spirit. The emphasis of the Seer at this point is the presence of Christ in the created order and, most especially, among the people of God.

As John sees the Lamb, that Lamb has taken his stand as one having been slain. Both verbs for "stand" and "slain" are in the Greek perfect tense, which cannot be fully captured in English. This tense represents an action as completed at some time in the past but with ongoing consequences.

---

4. Mounce, *Revelation*, 145.

5. Cf. Caird, *Commentary on Revelation*, 75–76; Mounce, *Revelation*, 146; Charles, *Critical and Exegetical Commentary*, 1:140.

Something like "he has stood and is still standing," as one who "was slain and still remains slain" would be about as close to a literal translation of these verbs as English speakers can get. The Greek verbs focus on the "once for all" dimension of the victory of Christ through his death and resurrection. Mounce appropriately speaks of these verbs as emphasizing "the lasting benefits of his sacrificial death and resurrection."[6]

The final elements of the description of the Lamb imply complete power and unlimited vision, among other things. His seven horns imply complete power, but again not the kind of power that humans are inclined to visualize. Caird notes that John is attributing deity to Christ at this point, but that he has also redefined omnipotence. "Omnipotence is not to be understood as the power of unlimited coercion, but as the power of infinite persuasion, the invincible power of self-negating, self-sacrificing love."[7]

After observing that the seven-horned Lamb is derived from Jewish apocalyptic, Beasley-Murray notes just how different John's conception of the Lion or Lamb is from the Jewish apocalyptic speculations: "The Messiah has been slain as a sacrifice . . . the warrior-Lamb then has conquered through accepting the role of the Passover-Lamb."[8]

The power of unlimited vision is attributed to the Lamb via the symbolism of the seven eyes. The eyes are further described as the seven spirits of God. As Charles notes, "Omniscience appears to be here attributed to the Lamb. The possession of the seven eyes has this import: for these belong to Yahweh in the Old Testament." He then cites Zech 4:10 as a probable source of the symbolism.[9] The reference in Zechariah to the eyes as ranging to and fro throughout the earth is too similar to the present passage to be a mere coincidence. Admittedly there is some ambiguity in the present passage as to whether the eyes or the spirits are sent out. Strong manuscript evidence exists for both the neuter and the masculine form of the participle translated as "sent out." The Greek word for "eye" (*ophthalmos*) is masculine in gender, and "spirit" (*pneuma*) is neuter. Since the Seer has identified the seven Spirits with the seven eyes, the way one reads this verbal form has little interpretive significance, in my judgment.

---

6. Mounce, *Revelation*, 146.
7. Caird, *Commentary on Revelation*, 75.
8. Beasley-Murray, *Revelation*, 125.
9. Charles, *Critical and Exegetical Commentary*, 1:141.

The key issue for the purposes of this study is whether we have anything like a trinitarian formulation in this passage. I have previously taken the position that the seven spirits of God should be understood in accordance with the symbolism of the number seven as the complete Spirit of God, the Holy Spirit. Commentators seem reluctant to take a stand on this issue regarding the present passage. When Mounce refers to the seven eyes as symbolizing the seven spirits of God he capitalizes the word "spirits" but does not use it in the singular.[10] Charles takes no position in his discussion of this passage.[11] Morris says, "This *may* represent the Holy Spirit [emphasis mine]." Two sentences later he says, "But there is little reason for an allusion to the Holy Spirit here, and it is possible that John is simply ascribing omniscience to the Lamb."[12] Beasley-Murray seems to accept Caird's interpretation that "the energies of the sevenfold Spirit are loosed into the world through the slain and risen Lamb."[13] Farrer, after discussing Zechariah's vision of the seven-branched lampstand (which he sees as expressing "the grace of the Spirit in some fashion"), goes on to say, "St. John is free to deduce from these texts (a) that seven lamps express the Spirit, (b) that they are God's seven eyes, ranging the earth, (c) that, as eyes, they are given to Jesus, (d) that Jesus, as the branch or shoot, is equipped with sevenfold spiritual power."[14] If Farrer be correct, we have here at least in embryonic form a doctrine of the Trinity.

If it should be objected that the seven eyes are the possession of the Lamb in this passage, I would point out that the sending of the Spirit by Jesus is not without New Testament precedent. In the Fourth Gospel Jesus speaks of asking the Father to send the *parakletos* (variously translated as "Comforter," "Helper," and "Advocate") [John 14:16], who is later identified as the Holy Spirit (John 14:26); but also says that *he* will send the *parakletos* (John 15:26). That the *parakletos* is nothing less than Jesus' own presence seems to be indicated by John 14:16–18. These passages should suggest caution in any interpretation of the Holy Spirit in relation to Jesus Christ.

As we begin to explore the "unholy trinity," I have chosen to begin with Rev 13:1–3. Verse 1 has been explored somewhat in the chapter on

---

10. Mounce, *Revelation*, 146.
11. Charles, *Critical and Exegetical Commentary*, 1:141–43.
12. Morris, *Revelation*, 95.
13. Beasley-Murray, *Revelation*, 124.
14. Farrer, *Revelation*, 95.

diadems, and verse 3 in the chapter titled "Who is like . . . ?" My focus at this point will be on the dragon as the head of the unholy trinity. In Rev 5:13–14 we are told that the elders and the four living creatures jointly worshiped the One sitting upon the throne and the Lamb. In the present passage we are told that they worshiped (*prosekynēsan*) the dragon because he gave his authority to the beast, and they worshiped (*prosekynēsan*) the beast. Hence we have the worship of the dragon and the beast set over against the worship of God and the Lamb. As we explore the matter further, we will find other reasons for suggesting that the beast is a parody of the Lamb. As we take in the first three verses of this chapter, we find the vision of the beast coming up out of the sea. His seven heads and ten horns have been discussed previously, as was his relationship to the four beasts of Dan 7. I will focus now on the much-discussed stricken head of the beast. To identify in a historical manner the referent of the wounded head is beyond the scope of this study even if an identification be possible. The head of the beast is said to have been smitten (*esphagmenēn*) unto death. In 5:6 we examined the vision of the Lamb standing as if slain (*esphagmenon*). The only reason there is any difference at all in the two words for "slain" is that "head" is a feminine noun in Greek whereas "lamb" is masculine. Aside from this difference in gender, the two participles are identical. That John has used this same expression for the Lamb and the beast from the sea can hardly be accidental. Lohmeyer says very explicitly that "The beast from the sea stands in clear contrast to the Lamb having been slain in 5:6f."[15] Swete makes and elaborates the same point in these words: "'*hos esphagmenen*' hints at a comparison between the Beast and the *arnion hos esphagmenon*. Like the Lamb, the Beast has sustained a mortal wound, a deathblow, which has fallen on one of his seven heads."[16] Morris both notes this point and suggests that the recovery of the beast may be the implication of death followed by resurrection, i.e. a parody of both the death and resurrection of Christ.[17] Caird uses the specific term *parody* in reference to the marks of slaughter borne by the Lamb and the beast and, like Morris, he also hints at a parody of the resurrection.[18]

---

15. "steht in deutlichem Gegensatz zu 5/6f.: arnion hos esphagmenon," Lohmeyer, *Offenbarung*, 108; cf. C. Scott, *Revelation*, 236–37.

16. Swete, *Apocalypse*, 163.

17. Morris, *Revelation*, 162; cf. Preston and Hanson, *Revelation*, 96.

18. Caird, *Commentary on Revelation*, 164.

This setting of the beast from the sea over against Jesus Christ has been noted by a number of commentators. Though Mounce does not refer to the language mentioned above, he quotes Preston and Hanson as remarking that man is made to worship some absolute power and will ultimately give allegiance either to the beast (whose power is that of inflicting suffering) or to the Lamb (whose power lies in accepting suffering).[19] Beasley-Murray does note that the same phrase is used in reference to the Lamb who arose from the dead, and he refers to "the satanic imitation of the Devil's 'Christ.'"[20] Caird also notes the parody but without referring to the verb "slain." He refers to the "little apocalypse" (Mark 13) as promising both false prophets and false messiahs, and remarks that "since John calls the second of his two monsters 'the false prophet' (16:13, 19:20, 20:10), it is a reasonable inference that he thought of the first as a false Christ."[21] Farrer notes the parody in even greater detail. He remarks that "the dragon is the God of heathens, and the beast is his anointed. . . . Men worship the dragon because he has conferred authority on the beast. This is the epitome of political religion; gods are worshiped as the support of established power. It is also a parody of Christianity; the divine Father is worshiped, that is, given praise and glory, for sending us a savior and king." He goes on to speak of the smitten head as "a more striking feature of the parody."[22] Charles also refers to the application of the verb "slain" to Christ, and notes that when referred to the beast it marks him as "the Satanic counterpart of Christ." Rowland makes the significant further comment that "The plausibility of the beast is seen, as it is like the Lamb and appears to deserve worship."[23]

Morris notes the curious detail that the beast has ten diadems on his seven horns. Diadems are a symbol of sovereignty, and the dragon wears them on his heads. Morris is probably correct in suggesting that John intended for us to see the beast's sovereignty as resting on brute force alone, and furthermore that the wearing of the diadems on the horns would leave the beast's heads free for the blasphemous name or names.[24]

19. Mounce, *Revelation*, 253.
20. Beasley-Murray, *Revelation*, 210.
21. Caird, *Commentary on Revelation*, 165.
22. Farrer, *Revelation*, 152; cf. Wilson, *Revelation*, 111; Barnett, "Polemical Parallelism," 112.
23. Rowland, *Revelation*, 113.
24. Morris, *Revelation*, 161. The manuscript evidence is divided between the singular

Thus far we have seen the dragon as the head of the unholy trinity set over against God, and the beast from the sea set over against Christ. Now we need only to look for a counterpart to the Holy Spirit to complete the unholy trinity. This we will find in the person of the beast from the earth, who first appears in Rev 13:11. He is described as having two horns (symbolizing strong power?) like a *lamb*, but speaking like a dragon. He also is said to exercise all the authority of the first beast and to cause all who dwell upon the earth to worship the first beast. As noted earlier, the phrase "those dwelling upon the earth" does not refer in the Apocalypse to all people, but only to those whose names are not in the book of life.

The language of this verse seems to suggest an imposter. This beast looks like a lamb but speaks like a dragon. Mounce aptly notes that this "impression of gentle harmlessness" is reminiscent of Jesus' warning against false prophets in sheep's clothing who inwardly are ferocious wolves. He notes Moffatt's position that the horns like a lamb refer to such things as loyalty, patriotism, self-interest, and the like held out to Christians by the beast.[25]

Interpreters frequently connect the two beasts with the sea monster Leviathan and the land-monster Behemoth.[26] Caird refers to these mythological creatures as they are reflected in *1 Enoch* 60:7-10 and in *4 Esd* 6:49-52. He also suggests that because the features of the beast from the sea rely so heavily on Daniel, it is possible that the second beast relies upon the two-horned ram of Dan 8:3-4; although he admits that the similarity ends with the two horns.[27] The appearance as having two horns like a lamb is contrasted with the beast's speaking like a dragon. This feature has been a puzzle to quite a few interpreters. Charles is perhaps correct in his suggestion to add the definite article and read "the dragon" instead of "a dragon." If this be done, and the dragon equated with the ancient serpent as at 12:9, "then the text becomes intelligible and would refer to the seductive and deceitful character of the serpent in the Garden of Eden."[28] Garrow has taken the idea of seduction and deceit in an entirely different direction and has made the interesting, though highly improbable,

---

and the plural.

25. Mounce, *Revelation*, 258-59; cf. Charles, *Critical and Exegetical Commentary*, 1:357-58.

26. E.g., ibid.

27. Caird, *Commentary on Revelation*, 215-16.

28. Charles, *Critical and Exegetical Commentary*, 1:358; cf. Michaels, *Revelation*, 162.

suggestion that the second beast is to be identified as John's opponents, Jezebel and Balaam.[29] I have noted earlier that though Jezebel "calls herself a prophet," (Rev 2:20) no prophet named Balaam is mentioned in the Revelation, but only people holding to the teachings of Balaam.

Probably a majority of interpreters today connect the second beast with the imperial cult. Beasley-Murray, says in discussing v. 12, "There can be no doubt that the second beast is thereby identified with the promoters of the cult of the emperor." He does not stop with this identification, but rightly argues that "this priesthood was set within a wider institutional life." He then quotes approvingly Cullmann's interpretation of the second beast as "the religio-ideological propaganda authority of the totalitarian state."[30] Finally we arrive at an interpretation broad enough to allow the text to speak to its first recipients, and also to people of any age who may be under the jurisdiction of a totalitarian, self-deifying government.

Caird has noted the parody in the account of the two beasts, but has mistakenly identified the beast from the earth as, like his master the beast from the land, a parody of Christ.[31] Morris has made the same mistake, saying "*like a lamb* (cf. Mt. 7:15) seems to be a parody of Christ which is further brought out when this beast is called 'the false prophet' (16:13, 19:20, 20:10)." In fairness to Morris, he does go on to say, "All in all this beast looks like a dreadful parody of the truth."[32] Mounce correctly notes that "in the parody which runs throughout this section it is the first, not the second, beast who corresponds to the Lamb."[33] Farrer notes that, with the addition of the beast from the land, "the trio is now complete, dragon from the sky, first beast from the sea, second beast from the land. We may call them a satanic triad." Thus far he is on the right track, but then he spoils everything by adding that "it is not, however, the Trinity of Father, Son and Spirit they traduce, but the triad of revelation: God, his Messiah, and his servant the prophet."[34] This interpretation not only overlooks the subtle hints connecting the dragon with God, the first beast with the slain Lamb, and the second beast with the Spirit, but also violates the chain of

---

29. Garrow, *Revelation*, 89.
30. Beasley-Murray, *Revelation*, 216.
31. Caird, *Commentary on Revelation*, 172; see also Kealy, *Apocalypse*, 173.
32. Morris, *Revelation*, 166.
33. Mounce, *Revelation*, 259.
34. Farrer, *Revelation*, 155; cf. Michaels, *Revelation*, 161.

revelation that John established in his opening sentence. That chain runs from God to Christ to an angel to John.

The most specific clue that the beast from the earth parodies the Holy Spirit comes at 13:15. This verse depicts a phenomenon widespread in the ancient world. As Farrer has noted, the false prophet is reflected in the Gospel tradition and at least as early as the Deuteronomic history.[35] Such ancient magicians as Simon Magus and Apollonius of Tyana were credited with the ability to make images speak and move. Ventriloquism, along with ropes and pulleys, was the stock-in-trade of the magical arts.[36] Certain magicians were even credited with calling down fire from heaven. According to Matt 7:22, Jesus warned that in the last days many would come who had preached in his name and had even cast out demons and done miracles, who would be told, "Depart from me, you who practice lawlessness." As Caird notes, several of the emperors even brought magicians to their courts. He mentions Tiberius as surrounding himself with astrologers; Caligula as welcoming Apelles of Ascalon; and Apollonius of Tyana's friendship with the emperors Nero, Vespasian, and Titus.[37]

Who pronounces the death sentence on those who refuse to worship the beast is not clear from the text. Wilson seems to understand the idol itself as pronouncing the sentence.[38] Others interpret this verse as meaning that the beast pronounces the sentence.[39] Whether the image itself is depicted as pronouncing the death sentence or whether this authority is given to the false prophet (cf. v. 12) makes little difference, however. More significant is the fact of the death penalty that the churches addressed by John would have to face. Charles took this verse to mean that John believed a universal martyrdom of Christians would occur.[40] Most recent interpreters have not followed Charles at this point.

For the purposes of this study the first phrase of v. 15 is the key. The word translated "breath" is *pneuma*. It can mean "wind," "breath," or "spirit." It is the same word for *spirit* as in the phrase "Holy Spirit" (*hagia*

---

35. Farrer, *Revelation*, 156.

36. Cf. Krodel, *Revelation*, 255; Caird, *Commentary on Revelation*, 172; McDowell, *Meaning and Message*, 143; Mounce, *Revelation*, 261.

37. Caird, *Commentary on Revelation*, 172; cf. Mounce, *Revelation*, 261.

38. Wilson, *Revelation*, 116.

39. E.g., Summers, *Worthy Is the Lamb*, 178; Michaels, *Revelation*, 162; Talbert, *Apocalypse*, 57.

40. Charles, *Critical and Exegetical Commentary*, 1:361.

pneuma). Just as the Seer used the word "slain" of the first beast to show that it is a parody of the Lamb that was slain, so here he has used the word *pneuma* to show that the false prophet is a parody of the Holy Spirit. Although Boesak has misunderstood the beast from the earth as a parody of Jesus Christ instead of the Holy Spirit, his remarks that "In its parody . . . this beast is doing precisely what Jesus in his life refused to do: tricks and wonders in order to deceive and, in deceiving, to persuade" are worth noting.[41] Morris also sees this second beast as a parody of Christ, though he notes that he "is seen by some as a parody of the Holy Spirit, with its miracles and its fire from heaven."[42]

With the appearance of the beast from the earth—hereafter always designated the false prophet—the unholy trinity is complete. The dragon, the beast, and the false prophet are depicted as a parody of the triune God. Bauckham has stated it well: "The introduction of the second beast (13:11) is at least partly intelligible through the theme of christological parody . . . . But the distinction also enables him to create a satanic trinity: the dragon from heaven, the beast from the sea and the beast from the earth. The dragon relates to the first beast as God the Father to Christ."[43] Hughes puts it this way: "In Satan (the dragon), antichrist (the first beast), and the false prophet (the second beast) there is the manifestation of the unholy trinity of the Anti-God, the trinity of evil."[44] In similar language Mounce says, "Together with the dragon the two beasts constitute an unholy trinity of malicious evil."[45] Farrer expands this appraisal, saying, "Satan aspires to be a false God, the Beast a false Christ, and the second Beast a false prophet. Satan bestows on Antichrist 'his power and his throne, and great authority': the False Prophet 'executes all the authority of the First Beast in his sight, and makes the earth . . . to worship the first beast.' In doing so they worship also the Dragon for having bestowed the power upon him."[46] Neil has taken the parody a couple of steps further in remarking that "one of the astonishing features of the book of Revelation is the way in which it sets forth evil as a parody of the good. Evil is a trinity: the dragon, the

---

41. Boesak, *Comfort and Protest*, 104; cf. Morris, *Revelation*, 166.
42. Ibid.
43. Bauckham, *Climax*, 435–36; cf. Beasley-Murray, *Revelation*, 207.
44. Hughes, *Revelation*, 151.
45. Mounce, *Revelation*, 248.
46. Farrer, *Revelation*, 285.

first beast, and the second beast. There is a death and resurrection in the common belief about Nero. The followers of the beast bear a mark even as do the followers of the Lamb. The mystery of iniquity is as much a mystery as the mystery of redemption."[47] In their turn all three members of the unholy trinity are cast into the lake of fire in the end (Rev 19:20 and 20:10) to convey the message that evil itself, not just some particular historical embodiment of it, would ultimately be destroyed.[48]

---

47. Niles, *Seeing the Invisible*, 165.
48. Cf. Robbins, *Revelation*, 220.

33

The Seal of God and the Mark of the Beast

And I saw another angel coming up from the east, having the seal of the living God. And he cried out with a loud voice to the four angels who were given (authority) to hurt the earth and the sea, saying, "Do not hurt the earth nor the sea nor the trees until we seal the servants of our God upon their foreheads."

(Rev 7:2–3)

And it was said to them that they were not to hurt the grass of the earth, nor any green (plant) nor any tree, but only the people who do not have the seal of God upon their foreheads.

(Rev 9:4)

And he makes all people, the small and the great, and the wealthy and the poor, and the free and the slaves, that they might give to them a mark upon their right hand or upon their forehead; and that no one might be able to buy or to sell except the one having the mark, the name of the beast, or the number of his name.

(Rev 13:16–17)

And the first (angel) went out and poured out his vial into the earth; and wicked and evil sores came upon the people who had the mark of the beast and were worshiping his image.

(Rev 16:2)

Exploring the concept of the seal of God takes us first to Rev 7:2–3. The context is the series of events following the breaking of the sixth seal. Among other things, this breaking results in a variety of people trying to hide themselves in the caves and rocks, and calling for the rocks and the mountains to fall on them and hide them from the presence of God and the wrath of the Lamb (6:15–16). Revelation 6 then ends with the question as to who will be able to stand, now that the wrath of God and of the Lamb has begun to be manifested. The next chapter, Rev 7, may be seen as answering that question. That chapter opens with a vision of four angels holding back the "four winds of the earth." Another angel coming up from the east gives orders that the earth, the sea, and the trees are not to be hurt until the sealing of the servants of God is completed.

The reason for the detail that the commanding angel comes from the east cannot be determined with any certainty. Charles lists three answers that various scholars have suggested: some base it on the fact that the light-giving sun rises from the east, and hence this is the appropriate direction for divine blessings to come from. Others associate this scenario with the vision of Ezek 43:2, in which the prophet sees the glory of God coming from the east. Still others have noted the expectation in the *Sibylline Oracles* that the Messiah would come from the east.[1] Mounce adds to these the suggestion that the presence of the wise men from the east at Jesus' nativity has influenced this passage. He concludes, however, "This reference to the east is probably no more than a picturesque detail."[2] Beasley-Murray adds the further note that Paradise was set in the east, and according to *1 Enoch* 32 still was so considered.[3]

The phrase "the seal of the living God" is of primary concern for this study. There is a widespread consensus that this seal should be thought of at least partially in terms of the signet ring used by ancient Eastern monarchs to validate and protect royal property.[4] In the passages just cited, both Mounce and Beasley-Murray express the conviction that Ezek 9 is the background of this scene. In that passage a mysterious man clothed in linen and holding a writing case is commanded to go through the city of Jerusalem and place a mark upon the forehead of all who are grieved because of the sinfulness of Jerusalem. The mark is usually interpreted as the Hebrew letter tau, written like an X or a plus sign (+).[5] All those in Jerusalem who do not have the mark are then ordered to be slain. Caird

---

1. Charles, *Critical and Exegetical Commentary*, 1:204.
2. Mounce, *Revelation*, 167; cf. Morris, *Revelation*, 110–11.
3. Beasley-Murray, *Revelation*, 142.
4. Cf. Mounce, *Revelation*, 167; Beasley-Murray, *Revelation*, 142.
5. Cf. Mounce, *Revelation*, 167; Beasley-Murray, *Revelation*, 143 n. 1.

has suggested as a second influence from the Jewish Scriptures the sprinkling of the blood on the door posts of the Israelites in Egypt at the first Passover. He goes on to say, "Now John undoubtedly envisaged the great martyrdom as a new Exodus, so that the sealing can properly be regarded as part of the new Passover."[6]

Farrer, on the other hand, has connected the sealing with baptism in a very explicit way: "Sealing with the name is surely the imparting of Christian status in baptism."[7] Both Beasley-Murray and Mounce explicitly reject this view.[8] Mounce correctly points out that nowhere in the New Testament is baptism referred to as a seal; it is the Holy Spirit himself who is the seal. In 2 Tim 2:19, God's seal is "The Lord knows them that are his." In the same passage Mounce also tersely remarks, "Ownership entails protection."[9] The obvious question is then, protection from what? To this question Caird gives the curious answer that the protection is from the damages to be inflicted by the four winds, which he equates with the four horsemen, "because God has another and more significant death in store for them."[10] This is a curious form of protection—God prevents those who are sealed from being killed by natural disasters or warfare so he can allow them to be killed by lions in the Coliseum at a later date! Charles has more plausibly argued that the protection is not against physical death or suffering but against a final struggle by the Satanic hosts for mastery of the world.[11] Rowland appropriately notes that the protection is also from the wrath of God, and does not guarantee either spiritual or physical well-being. "Those who stand up for the ways of God will find themselves at the receiving end of the anger and retribution of the rich and powerful, who will see their death as a reason for rejoicing because that which pricks their conscience has been removed from the scene" (11:10).[12] Sleeper in similar fashion argues that the primary purpose of this passage is to declare "the spiritual security of God's people throughout the final judgments."[13] Perhaps the best perspective on the sealing is to view it as

6. Caird, *Commentary on Revelation*, 97.
7. Farrer, *Revelation*, 105; see also Preston and Hanson, *Revelation*, 99.
8. Beasley-Murray, *Revelation*, 143; Mounce, *Revelation*, 167.
9. Ibid.
10. Caird, *Commentary on Revelation*, 97.
11. Charles, *Critical and Exegetical Commentary*, 1:205; cf. Mounce, *Revelation*, 167.
12. Rowland, *Revelation*, 89.
13. Sleeper, *Victorious Christ*, 21, 123.

protection *through* tribulation, suffering, and death, rather than protection *from* these experiences—although it is the latter form of protection that we as human beings would like to obtain.

The protective function of the seal is reflected in Rev 9:4. The demon locusts coming out of the shaft of the abyss are given temporary authority ("five months") to hurt those who do not have the seal of God. We have encountered these locusts in a previous chapter. That they are demonic in nature, and hence the damage they do is not physical, is generally acknowledged. As Charles puts it, "The sealing of the faithful secures them—not against physical evil, but—against the demonic world which is now coming into actual manifestation."[14] Morris's statement that the locusts have no power against God's people is a bit off target.[15] They have no spiritual power, but that is quite different from saying that they have no power at all.

Wilson is another who sees the protection as security against the spiritual torments arising from the abyss rather than from physical injury or death.[16] Farrer focuses on the judgmental nature of the locusts. "Their scorpion-like sting is a demonic and penal substitute for the stamp of God's seal, which their victims lack."[17] Beasley-Murray notes the supreme irony in that these creatures, which spring from the very abode of evil—the abyss—attack and torment those who follow the way of opposition to God.[18] Caird notes both the permissive function of these demonic forces and the self-destructive nature of evil in these words: "It is not God's gracious purpose that the denizens of the abyss be let loose to ravage the earth, but he allows evil to be evil's own destruction."[19]

That John has used the plagues of Egypt as his model here is so widely attested as not to require elaboration. Mounce sums it up well in these words: "As the children of Israel were protected from the plagues which fell upon the Egyptians, so also will the new Israel escape the torments which are to arise from the abyss."[20] In typical fashion the Seer has taken a

---

14. Charles, *Critical and Exegetical Commentary*, 1:243.
15. Morris, *Revelation*, 126.
16. Wilson, *Revelation*, 84–85.
17. Farrer, *Revelation*, 118.
18. Beasley-Murray, *Revelation*, 161.
19. Caird, *Commentary on Revelation*, 118.
20. Mounce, *Revelation*, 194.

model in which the Israelites were protected from physical harm and has applied it to spiritual protection.

The parody of the seal of God appears first in Rev 13:16–17. The context is the appearance of the beast from the land or the false prophet. Six classes of men receive a mark upon the right hand or the forehead, without which any form of commerce cannot be pursued. Wilson appropriately notes the parody of the sealing of the servants of God in 7:2–3.[21] Beasley-Murray in similar fashion says "This is clearly intended as a parody of the seal of God on the forehead of his servants" (7:3). He says later, "Clearly the idea is to provide a parallel to the 'seal of the living God' (7:2), stamped on the foreheads of God's servants. . . . The seal of God marks out people as belonging to God, and so for preservation for his kingdom. The mark of the beast similarly identifies men as his servants, and without this mark they cannot live."[22] Caird comments, "Satan, the 'deceiver of the whole world', [sic] has persuaded men to exchange the truth of God for a lie . . . , and they bear a mark which is a parody of the seal of God."[23] Lohmeyer writes, "The mark is further a contrast to the 'sealing' [7:3ff.] and has the same meaning; also there stands here an old view in the background from Psalms of Solomon 15:9ff.: 'The ones practicing lawlessness shall not escape the judgment of the Lord . . . for the sign of destruction [is] upon his [sic] forehead.'"[24]

The number six may be symbolic here. Although some would argue that six is not an apocalyptic number, I am inclined to disagree. How does one define what is or is not an apocalyptic number? I suggest that usage alone is the determining factor. Robbins, Rowland, and others have argued that because six falls short of the perfect number seven, it symbolizes incompleteness.[25] Boesak seems to echo this understanding of the number six when he says concerning the mark of the beast, "Look, his number

---

21. Wilson, *Revelation*, 116.

22. Beasley-Murray, *Revelation*, 208, 218.

23. Caird, *Commentary on Revelation*, 92.

24. "Die 'Zeichnung' ist wieder Gegenbild der 'Siegelung' (7.3ff.), und hat den gleichen Sinn wie diese; auch hier steht wohl eine alte Anschauung im Hintergrund, Ps Sal 15.9f.: ouk ekpheuxontai hoi poiountes anomian to krima kuriou . . . to gar semeion tes apoleias epi tou metopou autou," Lohmeyer, *Offenbarung*, 114.

25. Robbins, *Revelation*, 165; Rowland, *Revelation*; 114; cf. McDowell, *Meaning and Message*, 145.

is 666, three times it is almost perfect."[26] That symbolism fits well in the present context. Those who have the mark of the beast are characterized by incompleteness, among other things.

Mounce, on the other hand, suggests reading the classes of people in this passage as three pairs of opposites that he takes as a way of expressing the totality of human society.[27] I doubt that John intended to say that all human beings received the mark of the beast, so I will stand by the interpretation I have suggested above.

The much-disputed number of the beast should perhaps be read as a threefold repetition of the number of incompleteness, thus conveying the paradoxical idea of "complete incompleteness" or "perfect imperfection."[28] A complete discussion of the number of the beast is beyond the scope of this study. I refer the interested reader to the thorough discussions of this issue by Bauckham, Beasley-Murray, and Charles.[29]

The suggestions for a precedent to the mark of the beast are many and varied. Some have connected it with the practice of branding runaway slaves or soldiers defeated in battle. Others have connected it with tattoos signaling devotion to some particular deity. Since the word *charagma* ("mark") is also used for the impression of the emperor's image on coins, some have suggested numismatics as the background.[30] Sleeper notes that "Since the mark appeared on Roman coins, one plausible explanation is that John was telling Christians to resist using those coins. That would certainly put them at a disadvantage in the marketplace. It would be consistent with John's other warnings against the seductiveness of wealth."[31] Still others connect the mark with a certificate issued to those who completed the ceremonial obligations of the emperor cult. Since *charagma* also referred to the seals on commercial documents stamped with the name and date of the emperor, this practice is yet another possible precedent.[32] Mounce has appropriately remarked, "Whatever the background

---

26. Boesak, *Comfort and Protest*, 106.

27. Mounce, *Revelation*, 261; cf. Morris, *Revelation*, 167.

28. Cf. Boesak, *Comfort and Protest*, 106; Robbins, *Revelation*, 167; Pinn, *Revelation Today*, xvi.

29. Bauckham, *Climax*, 384–431; Beasley-Murray, *Revelation*, 218–20; Charles, *Critical and Exegetical Commentary*, 1:364–68.

30. E.g., Oman, *Revelation*, 121.

31. Sleeper, *Victorious Christ*, 120–21; cf. Caird, *Commentary on Revelation*, 173.

32. Mounce, *Revelation*, 261–62; cf. Beasley-Murray, *Revelation*, 218; Caird,

of the word, its significance in the present passage is to parody the sealing of the servants of God in chapter 7. As the elect are sealed upon their foreheads to escape the destruction about to fall upon the earth, so the followers of the beast are to escape his wrath against the church by bearing his mark."[33]

Ford makes yet another suggestion that the mark is "an obvious travesty of the practice of orthodox Judaism which required the faithful to wear phylacteries (small leather pouches containing written passages from the law, especially the *shema* of Deut 6:4–5) on the left hand and the head."[34] Preston and Hanson have made a further suggestion that comports well with the thesis of this study, suggesting that "the mark of the beast was a parody of making the sign of the cross on the forehead of the new Christian.[35] Morris follows Mounce (above) by suggesting that the mark was probably a parody of the seal of God.[36]

Was the mark of the beast a visible mark, or was it understood as a mark of spiritual character? Mounce answers dogmatically that "In the apocalyptic vision of John the mark is obviously visible."[37] Beasley-Murray is more cautious in saying, "We cannot be sure." He goes on to note that God's mark is invisible and hence its counterpart (parody?) could be "a sinister mark of satanic ways as well as worship."[38]

Admittedly the economic sanctions against those who did not have the mark of the beast would seem to indicate some sort of visible mark. Ramsay is among those who thought it referred to an official certificate of compliance with emperor worship.[39] Charles also seems to think of the mark as visible, and indicates that one of the primary purposes of the mark was to bring Christians to the notice of imperial authorities. He goes on to conclude, "He made everyone to wear the mark, and that none

---

Commentary on Revelation, 173.

33. Mounce, *Revelation*, 262.

34. Ford, *Revelation*, 225; cf. Charles, *Critical and Exegetical Commentary*, 1:362; Morris, *Revelation*, 168.

35. Cited in Mounce, *Revelation*, 262.

36. Morris, *Revelation*, 168.

37. Mounce, *Revelation*, 262; see also Oman, *Revelation*, 121.

38. Beasley-Murray, *Revelation*, 218–19.

39. Ramsay, *Letters*, 79.

should escape his scrutiny he forbade the means of life to such as had not the mark."⁴⁰

While I readily concede the force of these arguments, I am not convinced that they are insuperable. If the mark were an outward sign, what would have prevented John from being more specific and describing its appearance? Personally I can think of no good reason for him to have withheld such information. If on the other hand he intended his readers or hearers to think of an invisible mark of character, we have obvious grounds for not describing the mark. Goldsworthy is probably on the right track in identifying the mark of the beast as the unbelief that rejects Christ and his gospel.⁴¹

Perhaps it is worth noting at this point that neither the seal of God nor the mark of the beast is ever described in Revelation. Hence any argument for a visible mark in either case goes beyond the evidence in the text. Caird stays within the evidence by arguing that John "did not expect the mark to be visible to the eye, any more than the seal of the living God, of which it is a travesty."⁴²

There are exegetical grounds for equating the mark, the name, and the number of the name of the beast. While some uncertainties about the text are clearly evident,⁴³ if the Nestle-Aland text be followed, the mark and the name of the beast seem to be identified. And if Charles is correct in equating the name with the number of the beast, then all three elements, mark, name, and number refer to the same reality.⁴⁴ I am inclined to the view that the mark is a mark of the ownership and character of the beast. The root of the word *charagma* was at some point associated with character. Placing a different suffix on this root (*charagtēr* instead of *charagma*) yields the direct antecedent of the English word *character*. While I would not place any great argumentative weight on this point, it is at least interesting to consider. I would place more weight on the well-known Jewish notion of the inseparability of name from character. To have the name of the beast would therefore be equivalent to having its character as well. Wilson, like Mounce, argues that the mark of the beast

---

40. Charles, *Critical and Exegetical Commentary*, 1:363–64.
41. Goldsworthy, *Gospel in Revelation*, 157.
42. Caird, *Commentary on Revelation*, 173.
43. Cf. Mounce, *Revelation*, 263 n. 52–53.
44. Charles, *Critical and Exegetical Commentary*, 1:364.

is not a visible one and also supports the position that the mark signifies partaking of the character of the beast.[45] While, as noted above, economic sanctions would make an outward mark the most natural interpretation, the text does not in my judgment necessitate such a view. A simple verbal test could have been devised, such as the confession "Jesus is Lord" vs. "Caesar is Lord," which was known only a few years after John wrote, to prove which "mark" a person possessed.

Of the other references to the mark of the beast I have limited my focus to Rev 16:2. The context is the outpouring of the first of the seven vials of God's wrath by which "the wrath of God is completed" (15:1). The connection between this bowl and the sixth plague on Egypt described in Exod 9:8–12 has been widely recognized.[46] As Mounce has noted, Deut 28:27 may also be in view at this point.[47] Caird, after observing that this plague is one panel "in the one great sevenfold picture of the last days of Babylon," goes on to describe those having the mark of the beast as "those who are too deeply involved in Babylon's sins to be dissociated from her fall."[48] Morris's comment that "there are some evils that afflict those who give themselves over to wickedness but do not affect other people" adds another point worthy of consideration in assessing the nature of the beast's mark.

Charles has bracketed the phrase "the people who had the mark of the beast and were worshiping his image" as a gloss. Pointing to the universality of the second, third, and fourth plagues, he argues that we should see the first as likewise universal. Thus far I have no quarrel with his argument. He goes on to say, however, that unless his conclusion is accepted "we must assume that only the adherents of the Roman Empire, and not the rest of the heathen, are affected by the first Plague."[49] In this last claim Charles has slipped into the common pitfall of equating the beast solely with the Roman Empire. That this was its primary referent for John I would agree, but I would again argue that the beast must be

---

45. Wilson, *Revelation*, 116.

46. See for example Beasley-Murray, *Revelation*, 241; Charles, *Critical and Exegetical Commentary*, 2:43; Caird, *Commentary on Revelation*, 201; Farrer, *Revelation*, 175; Mounce, *Revelation*, 293–94; and others.

47. Mounce, *Revelation*, 294 n. 5.

48. Caird, *Commentary on Revelation*, 201–2.

49. Charles, *Critical and Exegetical Commentary*, 2:43.

interpreted in such a way that it is not limited to any particular historical self-deifying empire.

The mark of the beast is mentioned again in Rev 14:11 and 19:20. I have chosen not to deal with these passages because doing so would add nothing new to the mark of the beast as a parody of the seal of God in my judgment.

To summarize, we saw in 7:2–3 that God's judgments are withheld until the servants of God have been sealed. This seal is the mark of God's possession and protection from all the assaults of the powers of evil that are imminent, but is not a protection from physical suffering or death. Over against the seal of God is set the *charagma* ("mark") of the beast in 13:16–17. This parody of the seal of God has been widely recognized. After discussing the various views of the nature of the mark Beasley-Murray says, "In any case the chief point John wishes to make is that the mark of the beast represents the climax of that satanic imitation of Christ which is traced all through chapter 13."[50] Farrer is also very explicit in saying, "The stamping with the mark is a blasphemous parody of the divine sealing in vii [sic]."[51] Charles argues that the seal of God and the mark of the beast have a common origin and that the purpose of both is to show that the bearer has supernatural protection, "the former under the protection of God, the latter of Satan."[52] In my judgment Charles is very much on target at this point although, as noted above, I disagree with his interpretation of the mark as outwardly visible.

The parody is further elaborated by a passage describing the dire straits of those who do *not* have the seal of God (9:4), and of those who *do* have the mark of the beast (16:2). In the former case the protection of God proves steadfast and dependable, whereas in the latter, the "protection" of Satan is seen to be illusory and fleeting.

---

50. Beasley-Murray, *Revelation*, 262.
51. Farrer, *Revelation*, 157.
52. Charles, *Critical and Exegetical Commentary*, 1:363.

Conclusion

In the Introduction I claimed that the Seer has consciously and deliberately cloaked much of his theological thought in parody and counterimages. I also maintained that the difference between the two literary devices is only a matter of form; they function in precisely the same manner. Now it remains to see just how much of the theology of the Apocalypse is involved in the parodies and counterimages that I have presented. I will be using Bauckham's work on the theology of the book of Revelation as a measuring gauge.[1]

In the opening chapter I examined the phrase *"kings of the earth."* While this is predominantly a negative image designating unbelieving rulers, one neutral (1:5) and one positive usage (21:24) also occur in Revelation. In the former, the sovereignty of the exalted Christ appears in the designation "ruler of the kings of the earth," and in the latter God's purpose of salvation for all people is implied. The sovereignty of the exalted Christ basically identifies him with God, a theme that is interspersed throughout Revelation.[2] The salvation of people throughout the entire world, not just national or ethnic Israel, is also a prominent theme.[3]

My second chapter dealt with the counterimaging of the term *sword*. The sword as a weapon of murder and bloodshed was set over against the "sharp double-edged sword" coming out of the mouth of the exalted Christ. The latter was portrayed as the only offensive weapon in the arsenal of God by which God defeats all the forces of evil. Again the sovereignty of the exalted Christ and his identification with God are portrayed. The mimicry of God by the forces of evil is seen in the *ius gladii* ("right of the sword") as a pale imitation of the One possessing the true right of the sword. The sword as a battle weapon, an implement of murder, or even the instrument of imperial justice must yield in the final analysis to the sword

---

1. Bauckham, *Theology*.
2. Cf. Bauckham, *Theology*, 55–57.
3. Cf. ibid., 68.

that is the Word of God. In this holy war, the forces of evil are defeated by that Word alone, not by any human weapons or strategies of war. Despite all the atrocities and dangers of "harlot Babylon," Christians are told only to come out of the wicked city, not to conquer her.[4]

Another dimension of the sword as the Word of God is the prophetic word of rebuke and discipline to the churches (2:12, 16).[5] The same sword that defeats the forces of evil also disciplines wayward believers.

In Chapter 3 I examined the phrase "*out of the mouth.*" Two passages referred to the two-edged sword issuing from the mouth of the exalted Christ. In another, fire is depicted as issuing from the mouth of the two witnesses to destroy their enemies. Given Jer 5:14 as a precedent, it is likely that the reference was to the Word of God coming out of the mouth of the witnesses. And, although the witnesses are said to be killed by the "beast," they come to life and are caught up to God and God's throne (11:7–12). In this manner, to use Bauckham's words, "the witness became the judge."[6]

In yet another passage Christ is portrayed as about to vomit the lukewarm Christians at Laodicea out of his mouth (3:16). Salvation and judgment are two sides of the same coin.[7] The fact that Christ, not God, issues the word of judgment is another of the several ways in which Christ is identified with God in Revelation. The identification is not total but what might be designated a functional equivalency.

In the arena of evil, it is fire, smoke, and sulfur that come out of the mouths of the "demon locusts" (9:17–18); "water like a river" that comes out of the mouth of the dragon (12:15–16); and "unclean spirits like frogs" that come out of the mouth of the dragon, the beast, and the false prophet (16:13). The idea of evil mimicking the divine may be seen in the reference to fire, smoke, and sulfur, in that these manifestations are reminiscent of the divine action against Sodom and Gomorrah (Gen 19:24–28). Also, since the locusts could hurt only those not having the seal of God, the inherent self-destructiveness of evil is depicted.[8] In the reference to the river coming out of the mouth of the dragon, the ultimate impotence

---

4. Cf. ibid., 88–89.
5. Cf. ibid., 121–25.
6. Ibid., 73.
7. Cf. ibid., 67.
8. Cf. ibid., 21.

of evil and the sovereignty of God are implied.[9] In the "unclean spirits like frogs" coming out of the mouth of the dragon, the beast, and the false prophet, the reader may discern the Roman pretensions to sovereignty (or that of any other self-deifying human empire).[10] If, with Summers and others, we understand the "unclean spirits like frogs" as symbols of the lying propaganda by which the dragon, the beast, and the false prophet retain their hold upon people and recruit them for the eschatological battle,[11] we are again dealing with the mimicry of the divine and pretensions to sovereignty by the forces of evil.

In Chapter 4 I explored the counterimaging of the *keys*. In the arena of divine operations the exalted Christ is said to possess the keys of death and Hades (Rev 1:17c–18) and the key of David (3:7). An angel is depicted as possessing the key to the abyss (20:1). In the arena of evil, a star fallen from heaven has the key to the shaft of the abyss (9:1).

Christ as victor through his death and resurrection and his sovereignty over both death and the place of the dead are reflected in the passages describing Jesus' possession of the keys of death and Hades, and the key of David.[12] His sovereignty over the world is actualized through the human Jesus and the exalted Christ.

In the depiction of the angel holding the key to the abyss and a great chain, we find the sovereignty of God delegated to an unnamed angel who restrains the chief of the forces of evil. In the counterimage of the angel with the key to the abyss, we find a messenger among the forces of evil who acts to unleash disasters on the world. The fact that he *was given* the key again underscores the sovereignty of God and the truth that evil has no existence independent of God but merely operates with permission from God to a limited degree and for a limited time.

In Chapter 5 I discussed the term *mystery*. The initial mystery is the revelation that the seven stars in the hand of the exalted Christ are the messengers of the seven churches and the seven lampstands are those churches. Then the term *mystery* appears in the prelude to the seventh trumpet blast that was said to complete the mystery of God. I suggested earlier that we should regard the seventh seal as containing the seven trumpets and the

---

9. Cf. ibid., 31–35.

10. Cf. ibid., 39.

11. Cf. Summers, *Worthy Is the Lamb*, 187–89; Robbins, *Revelation*, 189; Mounce, *Revelation*, 299; Caird, *Commentary on Revelation*, 266 et al.

12. Cf. Bauckham, *Theology*, 64.

seventh trumpet as containing the seven vials. In Bauckham's words, "The three series are so connected that the seventh seal-opening includes the seven trumpets and the seventh trumpet includes the seven bowls."[13]

Included in the mystery are God's sovereignty in judgment, his transcendence, and the mystery of God's being.[14] Also, the exalted Christ holding in his hand of power (the right hand) the messengers of the churches depicts active concern for the welfare of the messengers and the churches as well as Christ's continuing presence among the churches.

The counterimage of the mystery of Babylon, the great prostitute, and the beast on which she rides depict the evil forces' pretensions to sovereignty.[15] Complete knowledge (seven heads) and humanly complete power (ten horns) link this beast to the beast from the sea (13:1) and the dragon (12:3). The mystery of the woman and the beast are the revelation that the apparent power and knowledge of the forces of evil are only a sham imitation of the knowledge and power belonging to God and the Lamb.

In Chapter 6 I explored the counterimaging of the term *crown*. Faithful witness to the point of death merits the crown of life (2:10, 3:11). The twenty-four elders, which I have interpreted as the complete people of God, are depicted as sitting upon thrones with crowns on their heads (4:4, 10). Another passage portrays the woman of 12:1 as wearing a crown of twelve stars. Then, Rev 14:14 describes the exalted Christ as wearing a golden crown.

The crown of life underscores the fact that, contrary to all appearances, God's people already share in God's sovereignty. These people are not just the citizens of national Israel, but those purchased from "every tribe and tongue and people and nation" (5:9).[16] Through their witness to the point of death they continue the witness of Christ, the ultimate faithful witness, and participate in a new exodus.[17]

The woman in 12:1 wearing a crown is a portrait of the true Israel, the messianic community out of which the Messiah was born, sharing in the sovereignty of God and the exalted Christ. The "one like a son of man" (14:14) depicts that sovereignty.

---

13. Ibid., 40.
14. Cf. ibid., 42–43, 45.
15. Cf. ibid., 35, 39.
16. Cf. ibid., 68.
17. Cf. ibid., 68, 78, 84–85.

When the crown appears in the arena of evil, we have an image of the counterfeit sovereignty of evil forces.[18] The rider on a white horse (6:2) *was given* a crown, a typical expression in Revelation for permission given to the forces of evil to operate on a temporary and limited basis. That rider's crown leads to warfare, bloodshed, famine, death, and Hades.

The only other usage of *crown* in the arena of evil comes with the demon locusts in Rev 9:3–11 who are described, among other things, as wearing something like golden crowns on their heads. Once more the prominent idea is the mimicking of the sovereignty of God by the forces of evil.

I discussed the counterimaging of *thrones* in Chapter 7. Four positive images of throne were depicted: the throne of God, the throne shared by God and the Lamb, the thrones of the twenty-four elders, and the unnamed occupants of thrones in Rev 20:4. Because the latter passage says that judgment has been given either to or for the occupants of these thrones and, as the larger context would indicate, these are the saints who come to life and reign with Christ during the millennium, the picture is again one of God's people sharing in his sovereignty in that the most obvious connotation of a throne is sovereignty.[19] That sovereignty ultimately belongs to God but is shared with the exalted Christ and with faithful witnesses. If I have correctly identified the twenty-four elders, their sitting upon thrones indicates their sharing in God's sovereignty.[20] If one opts for the reading in 20:4 that judgment was given *to* them, this reading also implies the principle that the witness has become the judge.[21]

Thrones in the arena of evil include the throne of Satan at Pergamum (2:13), the throne of the dragon (13:2), and the throne of the beast (16:10). Since the dragon and the beast are eventually consigned to the lake of fire (19:20 and 20:10), their sovereignty has no ultimate reality. Their thrones are a counterfeit of the true sovereignty that belongs to God and Christ, and in which the people of God are allowed to share.[22]

Chapter 8 dealt with the counterimaging of the term *star*. The "early morning star" that Christ promises to the faithful witnesses (2:28) appears in the divine arena. Since Christ later identifies himself as the early morn-

---

18. Cf. ibid., 35.
19. Cf. ibid., 106–8.
20. Cf. ibid., 31.
21. Ibid., 73.
22. Cf. ibid., 31, 35.

ing star (22:16), this text may be a promise of the gift of Christ himself to the believer. In Rev 8:10–11, a star out of heaven makes one-third of the waters bitter and causes the death of many.

The promised early morning star may, as indicated above, be a promise of Christ himself, or the idea may be the illumination and new opportunities promised to the believer. The star that falls at the blast of the third trumpet is another sober reminder that God's salvation and judgment are two sides of the same coin.[23]

Over against the uses of *star* in the divine arena the Seer has counterimaged the star that falls from heaven and opens the shaft of the abyss to unleash demonic forces (9:1). Whether the star should be seen as a fallen angel or as merely descending from heaven is a much disputed point. I concluded that the star represents either Satan himself or an evil angel. One significant piece of evidence in favor of this interpretation is that the key to the shaft of the abyss *was given* (*edothē*) to him. The motif of evil forces mimicking the forces of God is repeated here.

Chapter 9 treated the counterimaging of the phrase "*they are worthy*." On the positive side are the few believers at Sardis who have not soiled their garments and are therefore worthy to walk with Christ in white robes (3:4). I concluded that the soiling of the garments refers to actions opposed to those of a faithful witness of Christ; and that the white robes are symbolic of purity, victory, holiness, justification, and the like. While the white garments could not be earned, they could be forfeited by faithless actions. Worthiness is a gift grounded in the ultimate faithful witness, Christ himself.[24]

Over against the white-clad believers at Sardis, the Seer has juxtaposed the worthiness of those who shed the blood of saints and prophets to "drink blood." As the worthiness of those at Sardis to walk with Christ in white is conditioned by ethical conduct, so is the worthiness of the murderers of God's people to receive retributive punishment. An inescapable implication here is the justice of God manifest in judgment.

Chapter 10 discussed the phrase, "*They have no rest day and night*." In the divine arena the four living creatures are said to have no rest day and night from praising God (4:8). I interpreted this image as a picture of the

---

23. Cf. ibid.,42, 67.
24. Cf. ibid., 73, 78, 84–85.

entire creation offering constant praise and worship to God.[25] In contrast to this picture is a tableau of the worshippers of the beast and his image, and those who receive his mark. These are said to have no rest day and night from the torment they have brought on themselves by their choice to worship the beast and his counterfeit sovereignty, which are nothing more than the deification of merely human power.[26]

Chapter 11 dealt with the phrase *"having been slain."* This phrase is applied first and foremost to the Lamb (5:6, 12; 13:8), but also to the "souls under the altar" (6:9) who had been slain because of their faithful witness, and to the prophets and saints whose blood is found in "Babylon." In this fashion John portrays the solidarity of those slain because of their faithful witness with the ultimate faithful witness, the Lamb.[27]

Over against the slain Lamb and the martyrs is set the head of the beast from the sea (13:3). The counterimaging is accomplished by the use of the perfect passive participle *esphagmenonēn* ("having been slain") in each case. The slain head of the beast that was healed reflects the temporary defeat and the persistent ability of the beast to come back to life over and over again.[28]

Chapter 12 described the counterimaging of the term *lamb*. In the divine arena the slain Lamb is depicted in three passages. He is said to possess the fullness of the Spirit of God ("seven eyes which are the seven spirits of God").[29] He is also described as meriting a *sevenfold* ascription of praise and worship. The Lamb merits the same worship and praise as God the Father (4:11, 5:13).[30] In the scene of the one hundred forty-four thousand "virgins" on Mount Zion, they are prepared for the holy war in which all the forces of evil will be defeated,[31] although I have taken the position, along with several other interpreters, that the virgins do not actually play a part in the battle. The Seer moves from the preparations for the battle to the final victory without ever depicting an actual battle scene.

---

25. Cf. ibid., 33.
26. Cf. ibid., 35, 39, 59.
27. Cf. ibid., 78.
28. Cf. ibid., 152.
29. Cf. ibid., 110–15.
30. Cf. ibid., 33.
31. Cf. ibid., 88–89.

The victory has already been won through the death and resurrection of Christ, and only remains to be actualized.[32]

Over against the slain Lamb is set the beast from the sea, one of whose heads had been slain (*esphagmenēn*). He possesses the character of and functions as the dragon's lackey. Once again we encounter the theme of the forces of evil imitating the divine.

Chapter 13 dealt with the counterimaging of *white horses*. The triumphant Christ appears when heaven is opened, riding upon a white horse (19:11). The soldiers in heaven—whether martyrs, saints, angels, or some combination thereof cannot be determined with certainty—follow Christ upon white horses. While the color white may have connotations of purity, victory, justification, and perhaps other things, in the present context the dominant theme seems to be victory. Once again it is a victory won but still to be fully actualized.[33]

The rider on the white horse in 6:2 has been shown to be an imposter and a counterfeit. He bears the signs of sovereignty and victory—a crown and bow—but represents only the pretext of sovereignty and temporary victory, all that the forces of evil can ever claim.[34]

Chapter 14 counterimaged the phrase *"from the east."* In positive usage, an angel comes from the east to seal the servants of God on their foreheads. He commands the four angels who *were given* authority to hurt the earth not to do so until the sealing was completed (7:2–3). Such concepts as God's sovereignty over both creation and redemption, and his protection of the redeemed dominate this passage.[35]

Against the sealing angel from the east are juxtaposed the kings from the east. At the outpouring of the sixth vial the Euphrates dries up to prepare their way. For Jew and Roman alike, "kings from the east" would have been understood as the most fearsome enemies. The idea that God causes evil to accomplish his purposes may be seen in the fact that, while it is divine activity that dries up the Euphrates, the kings from the east represent evil forces and the temporary sovereignty that is only a pale imitation of the sovereignty of God and the Lamb.

32. Cf. ibid., 73.
33. Cf. ibid., 83, 88–89.
34. Cf. ibid., 35, 88–89.
35. Cf. ibid., 31, 43.

Chapter 15 dealt with the counterimaging of the phrase "*I heard the number*." In the number who received the seal of God (7:4) we are again reminded of God's sovereign ownership and protection of those who are God's. The number of the demonic cavalry (9:16) portrays both the strength and the limitation of the forces of evil. Though the demons' numbers are great, the sovereignty of God limits their work to a third of humanity.

Chapter 16 discussed the counterimaging of *smoke*. In the divine arena, smoke ascends with the prayers of the holy ones (8:4) to the presence of God. The smoke in this passage probably symbolizes divine assistance to the prayers of God's people (cf. Rom 8:26). Smoke also appears as a symbol of the presence of God in Rev 15:8. In light of the antecedents for this symbolism in the Jewish Scriptures (cf. Isa 6:4, Exod 40:34–38, and Ezek 10:4), several themes may be interwoven. The unapproachable nature of God by mere humans is mentioned in the passage from Exodus. In the passage from Isaiah the primary idea seems to be God's presence in the course of a revelation to the prophet. The presence and glory of God shine through the passage from Ezekiel. The Seer, by placing this scene in Rev 15 just before the outpouring of the seven vials, indicates that he would have us to understand the symbol of smoke as the presence of God in judgment.[36]

The appearance of smoke in the arena of evil confronts us first in Rev 9:2–3. The smoke pouring from the shaft of the abyss harbors the demonic locusts to whom it *was given* (*edothē*) to hurt those who do not have the seal of God (9:4). The idea that evil can operate only with the permission of God as well as having a self-destructive nature are again portrayed in this passage.[37]

Smoke as a symbol of the torment of the beast's worshippers confronts us in Rev 14:11. In a less direct but nevertheless realistic way, this passage again speaks to the self-destructive nature of evil. Those who choose to accept the mark of the beast and worship it bring on themselves eternal torment, whatever may be the precise nature of that torment.

In Rev 9:17b–18 the smoke is combined with fire and sulfur spewing from the mouths of the demonic cavalrymen. This is a picture of the forces of evil mimicking the actions of God. The language is clearly reminiscent of the destruction of Sodom and Gomorrah because of their wickedness

---

36. Cf. ibid., 42.
37. Cf. ibid., 21, 31.

(Gen 19:24–29). Here the forces of evil are portrayed as destroying a third of humanity by fire, smoke, and brimstone.

In Rev 14:11, smoke symbolizes the ceaseless torment suffered by the worshippers of the beast and those who receive his mark. The same ideas of the self-destructiveness of and limitations imposed on the forces of evil noted earlier apply to this passage as well.

In the final three passages the smoke arises from the burning of the "great prostitute," Babylon or Rome. This image fulfills the prophecy of Rev 17:16, which most explicitly portrays evil as turning in upon and destroying itself.[38] It also exposes the pretensions to divinity and counterfeit nature of Roman sovereignty; and especially her just recompense.[39] The false worship of merely human power leads to drinking from the cup of divine judgment. In Bauckham's words, "The polemical significance of worship is clear in the Revelation, which sees the root of evil of the Roman Empire to lie in the idolatrous worship of merely human power."[40]

Chapter 17 dealt with the counterimaging of the term *river*. Its positive usage is limited to the "river of the water of life" in the New Jerusalem. Bauckham makes the interesting comment that "in one sense the whole of the Revelation could be viewed as the fulfillment of the first three petitions of the Lord's Prayer:" 'Your kingdom come, Your will be done, on earth as it is in heaven' (Matt. 6:9–10)."[41] [sic] In the image of the river of the water of life flowing from the throne of God, the petition "Thy kingdom come" is vividly portrayed. We confront here God's eschatological new creation at the climax of its development.[42] Furthermore, it is God's faithfulness to his creation that is the foundation of this eschatological hope.[43]

Two of the three negative uses of the term *river* refer to the Euphrates. At the sounding of the sixth trumpet (9:13–14), four angels are released from this river to kill one-third of humanity (9:15). Then, at the outpouring of the sixth vial (16:12), the Euphrates is dried up to make way for the kings of the east to amass their armies for the battle of Armageddon. These passages reflect the repetitive theme of the progression of God's

---

38. Cf. ibid., 21.
39. Cf. ibid., 35, 39.
40. Ibid., 59.
41. Ibid, 40.
42. Cf. ibid., 49, 63, 140.
43. Cf. ibid., 51.

judgment[44] and God's compelling the forces of evil to serve God's own sovereign purpose. The third negative use of *river* is metaphorical. The dragon is said to have cast water like a river after the woman in Rev 12:1–2 in an attempt to destroy her (12:15). His inability to do so again reflects the limitations on the powers of evil and the sovereignty of God.

Chapter 18 dealt with the phrase "*to do battle and to conquer*." The triumph of Christ because he is "King of kings and Lord of lords" (17:14) is set over against the conquering of the two witnesses by the beast from the abyss (11:7); and the defeat of the holy ones by the beast from the sea (13:7). The latter is said to have a kind of universal sovereignty—"over every tribe and people and tongue and nation" (13:7). The concept of Jesus' functional equality with God[45] and the pretensions of the beast to sovereignty and divinity are also exposed here.[46]

Chapter 19 discussed the counterimaging of the term *city*. For the most part only two cities are involved—the New Jerusalem and the great prostitute, Babylon or Rome. In another sense historical Jerusalem is implied by the phrase "where also their Lord was crucified" (11:8). This identification is, however, only one of the three designations of the "great city," which, with only a few dissenting voices, is interpreted as either Babylon or Rome. Once more the ideas of Rome's pretensions to sovereignty and divinity are addressed. The twofold nature of Jerusalem[47] and of the New Jerusalem as a place, a people, and the divine presence[48] are among the more significant concepts in these passages.

Chapter 20 explored the usage of the term "*Rejoice!*" (*euphrainō*). Heaven and earth are exhorted to rejoice over the defeat of Satan (Rev 12:12) and the "great prostitute" (18:20). In the realm of evil, we encounter the rejoicing of the "earth-dwellers" over the death of the two witnesses. The self-destructive nature of evil[49] is reflected in the demise of the great prostitute. The witnessing church as continuing the witness of Christ[50]

---

44. Cf. ibid., 42.
45. Cf. ibid., 55.
46. Cf. ibid., 35, 39.
47. Cf. ibid., 126–28.
48. Cf. ibid., 132–43.
49. Cf. ibid., 21.
50. Cf. ibid., 78.

Conclusion

and experiencing the same fate[51] is another theme. The sovereignty of God is an additional motif in these passages.

In Chapter 21 the *"great sign"* of the woman who gives birth to the Messiah (12:1) and the seven angels holding the seven last plagues are set against the sign of the great fiery-red dragon. The woman implies God's redemptive purpose through Jesus.[52] God's progressive judgment[53] and its ultimate completion are portrayed in the seven vials of God's wrath. The chief of the forces of evil is depicted as having complete knowledge (seven heads) and humanly complete power (ten horns), as well as pretensions to sovereignty (seven diadems)[54] in imitation of God.

In Chapter 22 the *woman* giving birth to the Messiah (12:1) and the bride of Christ or the New Jerusalem are contrasted with the great prostitute. The New Jerusalem as place, person, and divine presence enter the picture once more. The great prostitute is again described in terms of her pretensions to sovereignty and divinity.[55]

In Chapter 23 the victorious Christ wearing many *diadems* (19:12) was set over against the dragon with his seven diadems (12:3) and the beast from the sea with his ten diadems (13:1). Christ's lordship and victory over the forces of evil and chaos unmask the pretended sovereignty of the dragon and the beast.[56] Though the dragon and the beast have apparently complete sovereignty, represented by their seven and ten diadems respectively, the many diadems of the conquering Christ set at naught their pretensions.

In Chapter 24 the name *Michael*, which means "*Who is like God?*" was contrasted with the adoration of the beast and the "great city," in which people ask, 'Who is like the beast?' and 'Who is like the great city?' The latter may also have been intended as a counterimage to the question, 'Who is like God?' which appears in several passages in the Jewish Scriptures, most notably Exod 15:11. The counterfeit worship of the dragon and the beast are contrasted with the true worship of God.[57]

---

51. Cf. ibid., 84–85.
52. Cf. ibid., 73.
53. Cf. ibid., 42.
54. Cf. ibid., 35.
55. Cf. ibid., 35, 39.
56. Cf. ibid., 53.
57. Cf. ibid., 37, 59, 100.

In Chapter 25 I explored the Seer's use of *thymos* ("wrath" or "passion") and discussed seven passages in which *thymos* was translated "wrath" and in which the wrath was attributed to God. Over against this usage of *thymos* was set the *thymos* of Satan because of his defeat and his being cast down to earth (12:12) and the *thymos* of the great prostitute (14:8, 18:3). In the latter passages *thymos* is usually translated "passion" or synonyms thereof. The concept of God's sovereignty in judgment dominates the passages referring to the wrath of God.[58] That, plus the idea of the victory won over Satan through Christ's death and resurrection are depicted in the passages where *thymos* is used in the arena of the forces of evil.[59]

In Chapter 26 I discussed the Seer's counterimaging of the term *mountain*. The holy city, Mount Zion, and the "great and high mountain" from which the Seer is invited to view the New Jerusalem or bride of Christ (14:1, 21:10) were contrasted with the mountain of Megiddo or Armageddon, the location of the climactic conflict between the Lamb and the forces of evil. The theological concepts of God's leadership and protection of his people—the one hundred forty-four thousand—and the notion that God's salvation and judgment are two sides of the same coin[60] appear again in these passages. The larger context of 16:16 also depicts the complete defeat of the forces of evil by the two-edged sword coming from the mouth of the Lamb.

In Chapter 27 we looked at two passages that spoke of a "*cup*" containing the wrath of God (14:9b–10, 16:19) and two passages that referred to the "cup" of the great prostitute containing the "abominations and unclean things of her fornication" (17:4, 18:6). The latter cup is the reason for the cup of God's wrath. The repeated theme of the beast's pretensions to sovereignty and divinity[61] is portrayed in 14:9b–10 and perhaps implied in the other passages that mention a cup. One may also see a contrast between the counterfeit wealth of the prostitute and the true wealth of God.[62]

In Chapter 28 the "*one hour*" in which the ten kings receive authority from the beast was contrasted with the "one hour" of the judgment of the

---

58. Cf. ibid., 31, 42–43.
59. Cf. ibid., 73.
60. Cf. ibid., 67.
61. Cf. ibid., 35.
62. Royalty, *Streets of Heaven*, presents a very thorough discussion of this subject.

great prostitute. The former depicts the limits set to the powers of the forces of evil. In the "one hour" of the judgment of the great prostitute, all those who profited from their illicit dealings with her stand at a distance lamenting her fate but make no attempt whatever to come to her aid. The suddenness of the overthrow of the forces of evil and the self-destructive nature of evil are again pictured here.[63]

Chapter 29 contrasted the "*one purpose*" of God with the "one purpose" of the ten kings to give their authority to the beast. The latter is made to serve the former. The sovereignty of God and the counterfeit sovereignty of the forces of evil are repeated in these passages.

In Chapter 30 the marriage *supper* of the Lamb was counterimaged with the "great supper of God" in which the vultures are invited to feast on the carcasses of those slain by the sword of the Lamb. In these vivid images one again detects the portrayal of God's salvation and judgment as inseparably bound together.[64] The almost ubiquitous idea of the sovereignty of God may also be noted.

Chapter 1 of Part II dealt with the counterimaging of *threefold designations*. Three passages (Rev 1:4, 8; and 4:8) describe God as the One who is, who was, and who is coming. In 4:8 the first two elements are reversed. Then in 16:5 the designation is changed to "the One who is and who was, the holy One." These were set over against the designation of the beast as the one who was, and is not and will come" (17:8), and the dragon's giving to the beast his power, throne, and great authority (13:2). In these passages the eternal rule of God is contrasted with the transitory nature of the beast and the dragon and their counterfeit sovereignty.[65]

In the next chapter the *Holy Trinity* of God, Christ, and the Holy Spirit were contrasted with the *unholy trinity* of the dragon, the beast from the sea, and the beast from the earth, later designated as the false prophet. The imitation of the divine by the forces of evil is one of the more obvious themes in these passages. Another is the false worship of the dragon and the two beasts[66] versus the true worship of the triune

---

63. Cf. Bauckham, *Theology*, 21.
64. Cf. ibid., 67.
65. Cf. ibid., 31, 35, 39.
66. Cf. ibid., 37, 59, 100.

God.[67] The sovereignty of God and the worship of Christ as God are also found in the immediate context.

In the final chapter *the seal of God* was set over against *the mark of the beast*. The former is the stamp of God's ownership, character, and ultimate protection of his people against the powers of evil. The latter is the mark of the beast's ownership, character, and inability to protect his people. God's sovereignty and the imitation of the divine by the forces of evil are once more depicted.

Readers who follow the references to Bauckham's work can readily see that by far the majority of theological ideas he mentions are to be found in the passages that have been the focus of this study, in addition to a few concepts Bauckham does not explicitly discuss. I believe I have successfully demonstrated that the heart of the theology of the book of Revelation is to be found in the passages that make use of the literary devices of counterimaging and parody.

---

67. Cf. ibid., 33.

Bibliography

Abbott-Smith, G. *A Manual Greek Lexicon of the New Testament*. 3rd ed. Edinburgh: T & T Clark, 1981.
Aland, Barbara, et al., eds. *The Greek New Testament*. 4th rev. ed. Stuttgart: Biblia-Druck, 1993.
Ashcraft, Morris. "Revelation." In *Broadman Bible Commentary* 12: 337. Nashville, TN: Broadman, 1972.
Aune, David E. "The Form and Function of the Proclamations to the Seven Churches (Revelation 2-3)." *NTS* 36 (1990): 182-204.
———. *Revelation 1-5*. Word Biblical Commentary, edited by David A. Hubbard et al., 52A. Waco, TX: Word, 1997.
———. *Revelation 6-16*. Word Biblical Commentary, edited by David A. Hubbard et al., 52B. Nashville, TN: Thomas Nelson, 1998.
———. *Revelation 17-22*. Word Biblical Commentary, edited by David A. Hubbard et al., 52C. Nashville, TN: Thomas Nelson, 1998.
Barclay, William. "Great Themes of the New Testament." *ExpTim* 70 (1959): 260-64.
———. *The Revelation of John*. 2 vols. Philadelphia: Westminster, 1959.
Barnard, L. W. "Clement of Rome and the Persecution of Domitian." *NTS* 10 (1963-64): 251-60.
Barnett, Paul. "Polemical Parallelism: Some Further Reflections on the Apocalypse." *JSNT* 35 (1989): 111-20.
Barr, David L. "The Apocalypse of John as Oral Enactment." *Int* 40 (1986): 243-56.
———. *New Testament Story*. 2nd ed. New York: Wadsworth, 1995.
Bauckham, Richard. *The Climax of Prophecy: Studies on the Book of Revelation*. Edinburgh: T & T Clark, 1993.
———. *The Theology of the Book of Revelation*. Cambridge: University, 1993.
Beagley, Alan James. *The "Sitz im Leben" of the Apocalypse with Particular Reference to the Role of the Church's Enemies*. Berlin and New York: Walter de Gruyter, 1987.
Beale, G. K. *The Book of Revelation: A Commentary on the Greek Text*. Grand Rapids, MI: Eerdmans, 1999.
Beasley-Murray, G. R. *The Book of Revelation: Based on the Revised Standard Version*. New Century Bible Commentary, edited by Ronald E. Clements and Matthew Black, 23. Grand Rapids, MI: Eerdmans, 1981.
Beasley-Murray, G. R., Herschel H. Hobbs, and Ray Frank Robbins. *Revelation: Three Viewpoints*. Nashville, TN: Broadman, 1977.
Bell, Albert A., Jr. "The Date of John's Apocalypse: The Evidence of Some Roman Historians Reconsidered." *Int* 25 (1979): 93-102.
Boesak, Allan A. *Comfort and Protest: Reflections on the Apocalypse of John of Patmos*. Edinburgh: Saint Andrew, 1987.

Boring, M. Eugene. *Revelation*. Louisville, KY: John Knox, 1989.
———. "The Theology of Revelation." *Int* 40 (1986): 257–69.
Brady, David. *The Contribution of British Writers between 1560 and 1830 to the Interpretation of Rev. 13.16–18: (The Number of the Beast): A Study in the History of Exegesis*. Tübingen: C. B. Mohr (Paul Siebeck), 1983.
Buchanan, George Wesley. *The Book of Revelation: Its Introduction and Prophecy*. Lewiston, NY: Edwin Mellen, 1993.
Burdon, Christopher. *The Apocalypse in England: Revelation Unraveling, 1700–1834*. New York: St. Martin's, 1997.
Burr, David. *Olivi's Peaceable Kingdom: A Reading of the Apocalypse Commentary*. Philadelphia: University of Pennsylvania, 1993.
Caird, G. B. *A Commentary on the Revelation of St. John the Divine*. London: Adam & Charles Black, 1966.
Carrell, Peter R. *Jesus and the Angels: Angelology and the Christology of the Apocalypse of John*. Cambridge and New York: Cambridge: University, 1997.
Chapman, Charles T., Jr. *The Message of the Book of Revelation*. Collegeville, MN: Liturgical, 1995.
Charles, R. H. *A Critical and Exegetical Commentary on the Revelation to St. John*. 2 vols. Edinburgh: T & T Clark, 1920.
Charlesworth, James H., ed. *The Old Testament Pseudepigrapha*. 2 vols. Garden City, NY: Doubleday, 1983
Cline, Eric M. *The Battles of Armageddon: Megiddo and the Jezreel Valley from the Bronze Age to the Nuclear Age*. Ann Arbor: University of Michigan, 2000.
Coggan, Donald. *Five Makers of the New Testament*. London: Hodder & Stoughton, 1962.
Collins, Adela Yarbro. *The Apocalypse*. Collegeville, MN: Liturgical, 1979.
———. *The Combat Myth in the Book of Revelation*. Missoula, MT: Scholars, 1976.
———. *Cosmology and Eschatology in Jewish and Christian Apocalypticism*. New York: E. J. Brill, 1996.
———. "Reading the Book of Revelation in the Twentieth Century." *Int* 40 (1986): 229–42.
Collins, John J. *Apocalypticism in the Dead Sea Scrolls*. New York: Routledge, 1997.
Conybeare, F. C., and St. George Stock. *Grammar of Septuagint Greek*. Exp. ed. Peabody, MA: Hendrickson, 1995.
Corsini, Eugenio. *The Apocalypse*. Edited and translated by Francis J. Moloney. Wilmington, DE: Michael Glazier, 1983.
Court, John M. *Myth and History in the Book of Revelation*. London: SPCK, 1979.
———. *Revelation*. Sheffield, UK: Sheffield Academic, 1994.
Denison, James C. *Life on the Brick Pile: Answers to Suffering from the Letters of Revelation*. Macon, GA: Mercer University, 1997.
Dumbrell, Bill. *The End of the Beginning*. Sydney: Lancer, 1985.
Efird, James M. *Revelation for Today*. Nashville, TN: Abingdon, 1989.
Emmerson, Richard K., and Bernard McGinn, eds. *The Apocalypse in the Middle Ages*. Ithaca, NY: Cornell University, 1992.
Enroth, Anne-Marit. "The Hearing Formula in the Book of Revelation." *NTS* 37 (1990): 598–608.
Ewing, Ward. *The Power of the Lamb: Revelation's Theology of Liberation for You*. Cambridge, MA: Cowley, 1990.
Farrer, Austin. *A Rebirth of Images: The Making of St. John's Apocalypse*. Westminster, UK: Dacre, 1949.

———. *The Revelation of St. John the Divine*. Oxford: Clarendon, 1964.
Fekkes, Jan III. "His Bride Has Prepared Herself: Revelation 19–21 and Isaian Nuptial Imagery." *JBL* 109 (1990): 269–87.
———. *Isaiah and Prophetic Traditions in the Book of Revelation: Visionary Antecedents and Their Development*, JSNTSS 93. Sheffield, UK: Sheffield Academic, 1994.
Feuillet, Andrew. *The Apocalypse*. Staten Island, NY: Alban House, 1964.
Ford, J. Massyngberde. *Revelation: Introduction, Translation, and Commentary*. The Anchor Bible, edited by William Foxwell Albright and David Noel Freedman, 38. Garden City, NY: Doubleday, 1975.
Franzmann, Martin H. *The Revelation to John: A Commentary*. St. Louis, MO: Concordia, 1968.
Garrow, A. J. P. *Revelation*. New York: Routledge, 1997.
Giblin, Charles Homer. *The Book of Revelation: The Open Book of Prophecy*. Collegeville, MN: Liturgical, 1991.
———. "Recapitulation and the Literary Coherence of John's Apocalypse." *CBQ* 56 (1994): 81–95.
———. "Revelation 11:1–13: Its Form, Function, and Contextual Integration." *NTS* 30 (1984): 433–59.
Goldsworthy, Graeme. *The Gospel in Revelation: Gospel and Apocalypse*. Carlisle, Cumbria: Paternoster, 1994.
Gonzalez, Justo L. *For the Healing of the Nations*. Maryknoll, NY: Orbis, 1999.
Hall, Robert G. "Living Creatures in the Midst of the Throne: Another Look at Revelation 4:6." *NTS* 36 (1990): 609–13.
Hanson, Anthony Tyrell. *The Wrath of the Lamb*. London: SPCK, 1957.
Hasper, Stephen. "An Exegetical Study of Revelation 1:1–8." PhD diss., Oxford University, 1995.
Howard-Brook, Wes, and Anthony Gwyther, *Unveiling Empire: Reading Revelation Then and Now*. Maryknoll, NY: Orbis, 1999.
Hughes, Philip Edgcumbe. *Revelation*. Grand Rapids, MI: Eerdmans, 1990.
Hurtgen, John E. *Anti-Language in the Apocalypse of John*. Lewiston, NY: Edwin Mellen, 1993.
Jeske, Richard L. *Revelation for Today*. Philadelphia: Fortress, 1983.
Kealy, Sean P. *The Apocalypse of John*. Collegeville, MN: Liturgical, 1987.
Kerkeslager, Allen. "Apollo, Greco-Roman Prophecy, and the Rider on the White Horse in Rev. 6:2." *JBL* 112 (1993): 116–21.
Kiddle, Martin. *The Revelation of St. John*. The Moffatt New Testament Commentary, edited by James Moffatt. London: Hodder & Stoughton, 1940.
Kraybill, J. Nelson. *Imperial Cult and Commerce in John's Apocalypse*. Sheffield, UK: Sheffield Academic, 1996.
Kreitzer, Larry J. *Striking New Images*, JSNTSS 134. Sheffield, UK: Sheffield Academic, 1996.
Krodel, Gerhard A. *Revelation: Augsburg Commentary on the New Testament*. Minneapolis, MN: Augsburg, 1989.
Laws, Sophie. *In the Light of the Lamb: Imagery, Parody, and Theology in the Apocalypse of John*. Wilmington, DE: Michael Glazier, 1988.
Lilje, Hanns. *The Last Book of the Bible: The Meaning of the Revelation of St. John*. Translated by Olive Wyon. Philadelphia: Muhlenberg, 1957.

Lohmeyer, Ernst. *Die Offenbarung des Johannes.* Tübingen: J. C. B. Mohr (Paul Siebeck), 1926.
Louw, Johannes P., and Eugene A. Nida, eds. *Greek-English Lexicon of the New Testament Based on Semantic Domains.* 2 vols. 2nd ed. New York: United Bible Societies, 1988, 1989.
Lund, Nils W. *Chiasmus in the New Testament.* Peabody, MA: Hendrickson, 1970.
Malina, Bruce J. *On the Genre and Message of Revelation: Star Visions and Sky Journeys.* Peabody, MA: Hendrickson, 1995.
Maurice, Frederick Denison. *Lectures on the Apocalypse.* London: Macmillan, 1861.
Maxwell, Marcus. *Revelation.* New York: Doubleday, 1998.
McDowell, Edward A. *The Meaning and Message of the Book of Revelation.* Nashville, TN: Broadman, 1951.
Mealy, J. Webb. *After the Thousand Years,* JSNT 70. Sheffield, UK: Sheffield Academic, 1992.
Metzger, Bruce M. *Breaking the Code: Understanding the Book of Revelation.* Nashville, TN: Abingdon, 1993.
Michaels, J. Ramsey. *Interpreting the Book of Revelation.* Grand Rapids, MI: Baker, 1992.
———. *Revelation.* IVP New Testament Commentary Series, edited by Grant R. Osborne. Downers Grove, IL: InterVarsity, 1997.
Moore, Stephen D. "The Beatific Vision as a Posing Exhibition: Revelation's Hypermasculine Deity." *JSNT* 60 (1995): 27–55.
Morris, Leon. *The Revelation of St. John: An Introduction and Commentary.* 2nd rev. ed. Grand Rapids, MI: Eerdmans, 1987.
Moule, C. F. D. *An Idiom-Book of New Testament Greek.* 2nd ed. Cambridge: Cambridge University, 1959.
Mounce, Robert H. *The Book of Revelation.* The New International Commentary on the New Testament, edited by Ned B. Stonehouse, F. F. Bruce, and Gordon D. Fee, 17. Grand Rapids, MI: Eerdmans, 1977.
———. *What Are We Waiting For? A Commentary on Revelation.* Grand Rapids, MI: Eerdmans, 1992.
Moyise, Steve. *The Old Testament in the Book of Revelation,* JSNTSS 115. Sheffield, UK: Sheffield Academic, 1995.
Mulholland, M. Robert Jr. *Revelation: Holy Living in an Unholy World.* Grand Rapids, MI: Francis Asbury Press of Zondervan, 1990.
Muse, Robert L. *The Book of Revelation: An Annotated Bibliography.* New York: Garland, 1996.
Niles, D. T. *As Seeing the Invisible.* London: SCM, 1962.
Oman, John. *The Book of Revelation.* Cambridge: Cambridge University, 1923.
Orr, James, general editor. *International Standard Bible Encyclopedia.* 4 vols. Grand Rapids, MI: Eerdmans, 1939.
Pate, C. Marvin, general editor. *Four Views on the Book of Revelation.* Grand Rapids, MI: Zondervan, 1998.
Pinn, James R. C. *Revelation Today.* New York: Vantage, 1957.
Pippin, Tina, *Death and Desire: The Rhetoric of Gender in the Apocalypse of John.* Louisville, KY: Westminster/John Knox, 1992.
Porter, Stanley E. "The Language of the Apocalypse in Recent Discussion." *NTS* 35 (1989): 582–603.

Preston, Ronald H., and A. T. Hanson. *The Revelation of Saint John the Divine: Introduction and Commentary.* London: SCM, 1949.

———. *The Revelation of St. John the Divine.* Reprint ed. London: SCM, 1968.

Ramsay, W. M. *The Letters to the Seven Churches.* Edited by Mark W. Wilson. Peabody, MA: Hendrickson, 1994.

Reader, William W. "The Twelve Jewels of Revelation 21:19-20: Tradition History and Modern Interpretation." *JBL* 100 (1981): 433-57.

Richard, Pablo. *A People's Commentary on the Book of Revelation.* Translated by Phillip Berryman. Maryknoll, NY: Orbis, 1995.

Robbins, Ray Frank. *The Life and Ministry of Our Lord.* Nashville, TN: Convention, 1970.

———. *The Revelation of Jesus Christ.* Nashville, TN: Broadman, 1975.

Roloff, Jürgen. *The Revelation of John: A Continental Commentary.* Translated by John E. Alsup. Minneapolis, MN: Fortress, 1993.

Rossing, Barbara R. *The Choice between Two Cities: Whore, Bride and Empire in the Apocalypse.* Harrisburg, PA: Trinity, 1999.

Rowland, Christopher. *Revelation.* London: Epworth, 1993.

Royalty, Robert M., Jr. *The Streets of Heaven: The Ideology of Wealth in the Apocalypse of John.* Macon, GA: Mercer University, 1998.

Ruiz, Jean-Pierre. *Ezekiel in the Apocalypse: The Transformation of Prophetic Language in Revelation 16,17—19,10.* Frankfurt am Main and New York: Peter Lang, 1989.

Russell, D. S. *Apocalyptic Ancient and Modern.* London: SCM, 1978.

Schmidt, Daryl D. "Semitisms and Septuagintalisms in the Book of Revelation." *NTS* 37 (1991): 592-603.

Schüssler Fiorenza, Elisabeth. *The Book of Revelation: Justice and Judgment.* Philadelphia: Fortress, 1985.

———. *Revelation: Vision of a Just World.* Minneapolis, MN: Fortress, 1991.

Scott, C. Anderson. *Revelation.* The Century Bible, edited by Walter F. Adeney, 34. Edinburgh: T.C. and E. C. Jack, 1925.

Scott, E. F. *The Book of Revelation.* London: SCM, 1939.

Sinclair, Scott Gambrill. *Revelation: A Book for the Rest of Us?* Berkeley, CA: Bibal, 1992.

Sleeper, C. Freeman. *The Victorious Christ: A Study of the Book of Revelation.* Louisville, KY: John Knox, 1996.

Smalley, Stephen S. "John's Revelation and John's Community." *BJRL* 69:2 (1987): 549-71.

Smith, Christopher R. "The Portrayal of the Church as the New Israel in the Names and Order of the Tribes in Revelation 7:5-8." *JSNT* 39 (1990): 111-18.

Spicq, Ceslas. *Theological Lexicon of the New Testament.* 3 vols. Peabody, MA: Hendrickson, 1994.

Stagg, Frank. "Interpreting the Book of Revelation." *RevExp* 72 (1975): 331-45.

Summers, Ray. *Worthy Is the Lamb: An Interpretation of Revelation.* Nashville, TN: Broadman, 1951.

Sweet, J. P. M. *Revelation.* Philadelphia: Westminster, 1979.

Swete, Henry Barclay. *The Apocalypse of St. John.* London: Macmillan and Co., 1909.

Talbert, Charles H. *The Apocalypse: A Reading of the Revelation of John.* Louisville, KY: Westminster/John Knox, 1994.

Thayer, Joseph Henry. *Thayer's Greek-English Lexicon of the New Testament.* Marshallton, DE: National Foundation for Christian Education, 1889.

Thiering, Barbara. *Jesus of the Apocalypse: The Life of Jesus after the Crucifixion.* London: Transworld Publishers, 1996.

Thompson, Leonard L. *The Book of Revelation: Apocalypse and Empire*. Oxford and New York: Oxford University, 1990.

Torrance, Thomas F. *The Apocalypse Today*. London: James Clarke & Co., 1960.

Wainwright, Arthur W. *Mysterious Apocalypse: Interpreting the Book of Revelation*. Nashville, TN: Abingdon, 1993.

Wall, Robert W. *Revelation*. Peabody, MA: Hendrickson, 1991.

Wengst, Klaus. "Babylon the Great and the New Jerusalem: The Visionary View of Political Reality in the Revelation of John." In *Politics and Theopolitics in the Bible and Postbiblical Literature*, 189–202. Sheffield: JSOT , 1994.

Wigram, George V., and Ralph D. Winter. *The Word Study Concordance*. Wheaton, IL: Tyndale House, 1972, 1978.

Williams, Michael. *The Power and the Kingdom*. Eastbourne, UK: Monarch Publications, 1989.

Wilson, Geoffrey B. *Revelation*. Durham, UK: Evangelical, 1985.

Index of Ancient Sources

JEWISH SCRIPTURES

Genesis

1	180
3	165
9:12–13	105
15:18	125
19:24–28	263
19:24–29	270–71
19:28	11
24:55	61
32:29	179
37:9	65, 161
49:9	242

Exodus

3:14–15	231
4:9	82
7:17–21	82
9:8–12	260
12:14	161
13:3	199
15:11	183, 187
15:25	79
19:4	161
19:6	65, 140
24:16	171
32:32	95
40:34–35	116
40:34–38	171, 270

Leviticus

11:10	37
18:25	31
18:28	31
20:22	31
21:9	11

Numbers

16:31–37	36

Deuteronomy

1:7	125
6:4–5	258
10:17	130
15:15	199
17:6	212n10
19:15	32, 212n10
28:27	260
32:8	49

Joshua

1:4	125

Judges

4:21–22	208
5:20	127, 208
13:18	179

1 Kings

6:20	140
6:20–35	138
8:10–12	171
17:18	199
18:10	207
18:17	159
22:21–23	37n34

2 Kings

1:10–12	32n6
19:28	10

1 Chronicles

16:31–33	86
24:9–19	63

Esther

8:7—9:5	24
9:19	158n31
9:22	158n31

Job

21:20	192
26:12–13	164
28:14	180
38:16	180
40:18	165
41:1	118
41:19–20	35
41:19–21	118

Psalms

2	204
2:9	19, 20, 21, 33
18:4	36
19:1	86
23	20
32:6	36
35:10	183
69:28	95
74:13–14	165
74:14	165
75:8	192
89:5	86
89:6	183
89:27 (LXX 88:28)	5
124:4–5	36
137	55
145:10	86
148:3–13	86

Isaiah

1:9–10	144
2:1–3	206
2:2	12
2:5	12
2:12–17	126
2:12–19	6
5:26–30	105
6	85
6:1–3	85
6:3	84
6:4	270
11	242
11:3–5	33
11:4	19
11:15	128
13:6–13	126
14:12	78, 79, 183
14:14	183
18:7	12n41
21:8–9	201
22:22	41
23:16–17	55
23:27b	10
24:22	43
25:6–8	222
26:16–27	162
26:17	65
27:1	24, 165

34:1–10	120	31:34	199
34:5	24	40:14	105
34:10	11, 148	51:7	8, 211
34:11–15	202	51:13 (LXX 28:13)	7, 8, 55
40:2	212	51:37	202
40:25	183	51:60–64	150
42:15	36		
43:2	36	**Lamentations**	
44:23	153		
49:2	18	1:15	20
49:13	153–54		
50:2	36	**Ezekiel**	
51:9	165		
51:17	192	1	71, 85
54	169	1:1	85
54:5	7n22	1:5–28	84
54:11–12	139	5:25	85
55:5	12n41	9	253
60:1	172	9:3–4	111
60:2	172	9:4	107
60:3	12	10:4	116, 270
60:3–11	12	10:20	85
60:5	12	14:21	26
60:11	12	16:46–49	144
60:19	140, 172	21:3–5	24
61:10	169	23	169
63:1–3	21	23:1–49	7n22
63:1–6	33, 200	23:10	146
66:6	198	23:18	146
66:7	162	23:25	146
66:7–8	65	23:27	146
		26–27	148, 217
Jeremiah		26:16–17	119
		26:19	217
1:38	128	27	217
3:17–18	12n41	27:32	149, 188
5:14	32, 34, 263	28:12–19	139
9:15	79	28:13–14	206
15:2	26, 27, 28	29:3	165
16:18	212	38:8	207
17:2	8	38:21	207
23:15	79	39:2	207
25:15–38	192	39:14	207
31:31–32	7n22	39:17	207

Ezekiel - Continued

39:17–18	223–24
40–43	137
40:1—44:3	93
40:2	170, 205
43:2	253
43:5	171
43:5–6	107
47:1–2	123

Daniel

1:8–15	61
2:47	130
4:17a	216
4:19	216
4:28–33	184
7	66, 131, 180, 236, 245
7:1–8	97
7:2–21	131
7:7	165
7:9–14	73
7:13	65
7:22	73
8:3–4	247
11:31	211
12:4–9	51
12:11	211
13	66

Hosea

2	169
2:16	7n22
3:1	7n22
10:8	6
13:7–8	236

Joel

2:10	43
2:11	126
2:52	204
3:13	20, 195

Amos

3:7	54
5:18–19	126

Micah

4:10	65
7:18	183

Nahum

3:4	55

Zechariah

2:5	138
4	48, 241
4:10	243
8:20–23	12n41
9–14	xiv
9:9	103
14:3–5	145, 146
14:4–8	199
14:14–19	12n41

Malachi

3:1–2	126

APOCRYPHAL/DEUTERO-CANONICAL SOURCES

2 Baruch

30:4	192
85:13–15	118

2 Esdras

7:35–38	192
7:36	118

10:25–27	169	24:31	156
13	204	24:36	156
13:10	18	25	22
		25:34	22
		25:41	22

4 Esdras

6:49–52	247

26:42	28n70
26:60–61	212n10

1 Maccabees

1:54	211

Mark

5:8–9	178
5:13	150
10:38–40	21
12:39	22
13	104, 246
13:14	211
13:27	156, 196
14:32	156
14:56	212n10

2 Maccabees

13:4	130

Sirach

17:17	49

Tobit

8:3	175
13:16–18	169

Luke

9:26	240
9:51–56	32
10:17	184
10:18	184
11:24	175
12:50	21
17:2	150
20:15	22

Wisdom of Solomon

18:15–16	18
18:22	19

CHRISTIAN TESTAMENT

Matthew

5:8	141
6:9–10	271
7:15	101, 248
7:22	249
8:11	143
13:39	196
13:49	196
24:15	211

John

1:1	162
4:35	196
5:22	20, 74
8:9	90
9:22	61
9:34	61
10:1	143
14:16	244
14:16–18	244
14:26	244
15:26	244

Acts

5:1–11	19n17
8:1–3	127
19:29	150
24:25	159

Romans

1:18–31	87
1:18–32	193
1:24	87
1:26	87
1:28	87
8:19–22	169
8:26	270
11:25	47
13:1–4	5

1 Corinthians

2:11	178
6:3	72
15:20	5
15:23	5
15:51	47

Ephesians

6:17	22

Philippians

2:15	172
3:15	234

Colossians

1:26–27	47

1 Timothy

5:19	212n10
5:21	241

2 Timothy

2:19	254

Hebrews

4:12	22
5:9	234
13:12	22

James

1:1	20

1 Peter

1:10–12	55n51
2:12	20
2:13–14	5
4:3	20
5:13	55

1 John

2:18	101
2:22	101
4:7	101

2 John

7	101

Revelation

1	41, 47, 66
1:1	52, 163
1:1—8:5	xiii
1:3	xiv, 141
1:4	227, 228, 231, 234, 235, 236, 238, 238n61, 240, 275
1:4–5a	239
1:5	3, 4, 9, 14, 262
1:8	57, 227, 232, 233, 235, 275
1:9—3:22	xii

1:10	205	4:6	69
1:11	50, 223, 228, 229	4:8	84, 87, 118, 227, 232, 233, 235, 236, 238, 267, 275
1:12–16	66	4:10	59, 63, 69, 72, 265
1:13	17, 194	4:11	268
1:14	176	4:12	91
1:16	16, 30, 31, 34, 78	5	100, 101
1:17a	39	5:2	150, 183
1:17c–18	39, 264	5:4–6	241
1:18	42, 236	5:4–7	239
1:19	223	5:5	23
1:20	17, 47, 55, 78	5:6	89, 90, 98, 101, 242, 245, 268
2	xiv	5:7	69, 72
2–3	xiii	5:8	72, 115, 197
2:3	189	5:9	82, 92, 97n51, 265
2:5	63, 103	5:9–10	14, 64
2:7	62, 142	5:10	64
2:8	236	5:12	89, 98, 268
2:9	60, 189	5:13	8, 96, 268
2:10	59, 60, 62, 68, 265	5:13–14	245
2:12	16, 18, 263	6	67
2:13	4, 70, 75, 76, 93, 266	6:1–8	26
2:14	18, 100	6:2	xii, 19n18, 44, 60, 66, 67, 68, 102, 104, 105, 266, 269
2:16	16, 18, 29, 63, 103, 263	6:2–17	xiii
2:20	168, 248	6:4	16, 23, 25, 44, 67, 97n51
2:25	103	6:6	85
2:26	77	6:8	16, 25, 40, 44, 67
2:28	77, 79, 266	6:8b	26
3	xiv	6:9	89, 93, 125n16, 268
3:1	81	6:9–11	115, 132
3:3	103	6:10	41, 154, 212
3:4	81, 82, 83, 178, 267	6:11	44, 67, 155, 200
3:7	39, 264	6:14	209
3:9	189	6:15	3, 6, 11, 15
3:11	59, 62, 68, 103, 265	6:15–16	209, 253
3:12	135, 152	6:16–17	106
3:14	102	7	99, 100, 109, 203, 253, 258, 261
3:16	30, 263	7:1	126
3:21	69, 71, 76, 177	7:1—9:21	xiii
4	71, 74, 84, 115	7:2	44, 67, 256
4:1—6:1	xiii	7:2–3	106, 252, 256, 261, 269
4:2	69, 71, 205	7:3	256
4:3	105, 138, 172	7:3ff.	256, 256n24
4:4	59, 63, 68, 69, 265		
4:5	91, 115		

Index of Ancient Sources

Revelation - Continued

Reference	Pages
7:4	109, 113, 270
7:9	92
7:9–17	99, 204
7:10	8, 69, 72
7:12	91, 92
7:14	142
7:15	56, 154
7:15–17	204
7:16	123
7:17	20
8:3	44, 67, 69, 72, 93
8:3–4	125n16
8:4	114, 115, 270
8:5	93
8:6—14:5	xiii
8:8	13, 209
8:10	128
8:10–11	77, 78, 267
8:13	51, 154, 155, 224
9	42
9:1	39, 42, 43, 44, 67, 77, 80, 112, 264, 267
9:1–2	131
9:1–12	68
9:2–3	114, 117, 270
9:2–5	43
9:3	44, 67
9:3–11	266
9:4	13, 252, 255, 261, 270
9:4–5	35
9:5	44, 67
9:7	60
9:8	168
9:13–14	122, 124, 271
9:14	8
9:15	271
9:16	109, 112, 270
9:17	117
9:17–18	30, 34, 38, 263
9:17b–18	114, 117, 270
9:18	35, 38, 125
10	53
10:1	105, 150
10:1—14:5	xii
10:5–6	51
10:6	53
10:7	47, 51, 52, 54, 58
10:10	xiii
10:11	8, 92
11	162, 163
11–13	130
11:1	44, 67, 137
11:2	44, 67, 152
11:3	4
11:5	30, 31
11:7	12, 129, 130, 132, 133, 180, 214, 272
11:7–10	34
11:7–12	263
11:8	134, 143, 145, 151, 188, 272
11:9	92
11:9b	143
11:10	153, 154, 158 254
11:13	152
11:14	155
11:14–19	xiii
11:17	232, 235
12	xi, 56, 64, 160, 161, 162, 163, 164, 168, 173, 174, 184
12:1	59, 64, 160, 162, 164, 165, 166, 167, 168, 174, 175, 184, 265, 273
12:1–2	272
12:3	12, 23, 57, 97, 129, 154, 160, 164, 166, 176, 179, 239, 265, 273
12:4	168
12:6	168, 184
12:7	43, 182
12:7–12	153
12:8–9	52
12:9	45, 183, 247
12:12	153, 155, 156, 157, 191, 200, 202, 272, 274
12:13–17	168
12:15	272
12:15–16	31, 35, 122, 126, 128, 263
12:17	8, 163
13	26, 53, 131, 205, 236, 261

Index of Ancient Sources 291

13:1	12, 57, 97, 129, 154, 173–74, 176, 180, 214, 236, 237, 244, 265, 273	14:15–17	195
13:1–3	244	14:16	xiii
13:1–4	239–40	14:17	66, 194
13:1–10	26	14:19	190, 194, 195, 202, 211
13:2	70, 76, 227, 236, 266, 275	14:19b–20	xiii
13:3	28, 89, 96, 238, 238n61, 245, 268	14:20	21, 152, 196
13:3a	186, 187	15	270
13:3c–4	182, 186	15:1	13, 152, 160, 163, 164, 165, 166, 190, 202, 260
13:4	182, 189	15:3	232, 235
13:5	44, 67, 76, 180	15:5	163
13:7	28, 44, 67, 76, 92, 129, 130, 133, 272	15:5—16:16	xiii
		15:5ff.	164
13:8	28, 89, 94, 98, 268	15:7	190, 197, 202
13:9	28	15:8	114, 116, 198, 270
13:10	17, 26, 237	15:11	273
13:11	28, 37, 98, 100, 180, 247, 250	16	198
13:11–12	240	16:1	190, 202
13:12	28, 248, 249	16:1–7	13
13:13–14	166	16:2	252, 260, 261
13:14	17, 28, 44, 186, 187	16:4	82, 128
13:14–15	67, 76	16:5	227, 233, 275
13:15	44, 240, 249	16:5–6	82–83
13:16	37	16:5b–7	83
13:16–17	252, 256, 261	16:6	81, 82, 83
13:17	191	16:7	232, 235
14	99, 194, 203	16:8	44, 67
14:1	98, 99, 203, 274	16:10	70, 76, 266
14:4	168	16:12	36, 37, 106, 107, 122, 124, 128, 271
14:6	92, 194	16:13	31, 36, 37, 38, 100, 107, 125, 206, 246, 248, 263
14:6–11	xiii		
14:8	191, 201, 274	16:13–16	36, 124
14:9a–10	190	16:14	107, 124, 166, 207, 232
14:9b–10	191, 202, 210, 211, 274	16:15	xiii, 103, 141
14:9b–20	xiii	16:16	203, 206, 274
14:10	201	16:17	13, 52, 152, 155n15, 163
14:11	84, 86, 87, 114, 118, 120, 261, 270, 271	16:17—19:9a	xiii
		16:19	135, 144, 145, 152, 190, 193, 198, 202, 210, 212, 274
14:12—15:4	xiii		
14:13	141, 177, 178, 223	16:20	209
14:14	59, 65, 195, 265	17	13, 58, 131
14:14–16	194	17:1	9, 152, 167, 173, 175
14:14–20	13	17:2	3, 7, 11, 15
14:15	195		

Revelation - Continued

17:3	151, 173, 175, 205, 213, 236, 237
17:3–4c	167
17:4	146, 149, 152, 210, 211, 217, 274
17:5	47, 55, 56, 58
17:5–7	58
17:6	4, 56, 57, 146, 188
17:6–7	168
17:7	47, 55, 57, 58, 188
17:8	57, 95, 186, 228, 236, 275
17:9	168, 209, 219
17:10	97, 219
17:11	187, 236, 237
17:12	57, 129, 213, 218, 219
17:12–14	148
17:13	219, 220
17:14	58, 129, 130, 133, 272
17:14b	129
17:15	92
17:16	58, 87, 146, 271
17:16–17	58
17:17	219, 220
17:18	3, 9, 11, 15, 57, 135, 146, 152, 168
18	13, 147, 216, 217
18:3	3, 9, 10, 11, 15, 191, 201, 274
18:4	189
18:6	157, 210, 212, 274
18:6a	157
18:7	10, 11, 152
18:8	148
18:9	4, 10, 11, 15, 115, 119
18:9–10	135, 147, 213, 216
18:9–19	152
18:9a	147
18:10	11, 148, 150, 217
18:11	11
18:12–13	149, 217
18:13	149
18:15–16	135, 148
18:15–17a	213, 216
18:17	10, 11, 150
18:17a	149
18:17b	149n95
18:18	115, 120, 182, 188
18:18–19	135
18:19	149, 150, 213, 218, 220
18:20	8, 153, 154, 156, 188, 272
18:21	135, 150, 152
18:21–23	156
18:24	89, 93, 96, 121
19	67, 102
19:1	121
19:2	120
19:3	115, 120, 121
19:4	8, 83, 234
19:5–9	223
19:6	232
19:7	135, 222
19:8	44, 67, 72, 82
19:9	141, 222, 223, 224
19:9b–10	xiii
19:11	67, 102, 176, 269
19:11–13	22
19:11–16	104
19:11–21	xiii, 67
19:12	176, 273
19:13	21
19:14	8, 20, 102, 130, 208
19:15	19, 30, 32, 34, 191, 193, 196, 199, 202, 232
19:17	209, 222, 223, 224
19:19	4, 12, 15, 22
19:19–21	13
19:20	23, 76, 100, 166, 220, 246, 248, 251, 261, 266
19:21	16, 29, 34
19:27	34
20	42
20:1	39, 42, 44, 45, 80, 264
20:2	76
20:3	155, 200
20:4	44, 67, 72, 73, 266
20:4a	70
20:6	141
20:9	152
20:10	76, 100, 246, 248, 251, 266
20:11–12a	70, 74
20:11—21:8	xiii

Index of Ancient Sources 293

21	135, 140, 169	22:5	152
21:1	127, 169	22:6	223
21:1–2	189, 205	22:6–8a	xii
21:1—22:5	23	22:6–9	xiii
21:2	134, 135, 137, 151, 167, 168, 171, 175	22:6–21	141n43
		22:7	xiv, 103, 141
21:2–3	12	22:9	xiv, 152
21:2–4	174	22:10	xiv
21:3	70, 74, 136, 154, 205	22:10–22	51
21:3—22:21	136	22:12	103
21:5	8, 74, 223	22:13	232
21:5–8	232	22:14	134, 141, 142
21:5a	70	22:16	8, 51, 77, 79, 267
21:6	123	22:17	123
21:9	175	22:18–19	xiv
21:9–10	12	22:19	152
21:9–11	135, 167	22:20	103
21:9—22:17	xiii		
21:10	134, 137, 151, 171, 203, 205, 274		
21:11	138, 172	**PSEUDEPIGRAPHA**	
21:12	8, 143		
21:13	106, 108	**1 Enoch**	
21:14	152		
21:15	151	1:3	41
21:15–16	134, 137	9:4	130
21:16–18	151	14:1	41
21:18	139	18:12–16	43
21:18–19	138	18:13	79
21:18–19a	134	21:3	79
21:19	152	24–25	206
21:19–20	151	27:3–4	192
21:21	134, 151	32	253
21:22	232, 235	37–71	66
21:23	123, 134, 140, 151, 172	48:9	192
21:24	4, 12, 13, 15, 262	60:7–10	247
21:24–26	141n40	62:2	19
21:26	13	66:2	234
21:27	14, 96	88:2	25
22	135	90:9	242
22:1	70, 75, 76, 128, 151	90:19	24
22:1–2	122	90:20–27	192
22:1–10	xiii	90:26–27	118
22:3	70, 75		

1 Enoch - Continued

90:34	24
90:37	242
91:12	24
108:3–6	79

Psalms of Solomon

15:9f.	256n24
15:9ff.	256
17:22–24	102
17:26–27	19
17:32	102
17:39	19

Sibylline Oracles

5:155–61	79

Testament of Joseph

19:8–11	242

Testament of Judah

13:5	211

Testament of Naphtali

5:3–4	161

www.ingramcontent.com/pod-product-compliance
Lightning Source LLC
Chambersburg PA
CBHW071233230426
43668CB00011B/1410